Impartiality, Neutrality and Justice

Impartiality, Neutrality and Justice

Re-reading Brian Barry's *Justice as Impartiality*

Edited by
Paul Kelly

Edinburgh University Press

© in this edition, Edinburgh University Press 1998, 2000.
Copyright in the individual contributions is retained
by the authors.

Published in paperback 2000

Transferred to digital print 2006

Edinburgh University Press
22 George Square, Edinburgh

Typeset by Norman Tilley Graphics, Northampton
Printed and bound by CPI Antony Rowe, Eastbourne

A CIP record for this book is available
from the British Library

ISBN-10 0 7486 1453 2
ISBN-13 978 0 7486 1453 0

Contents

Contents

Acknowledgements

The original idea for this book developed out of a conversation over a few glasses of whisky in a hotel room in Tokyo, between Fred Rosen, Roger Crisp and myself. I had already initiated a symposium and special issue of the journal *Utilitas*, on Brian Barry's *Justice as Impartiality*, and Fred and Roger encouraged the idea that this might be expanded into a book by adding additional chapters. I am grateful to Fred and Roger for that initial encouragement, whether they remember it or not.

At the time of initiating this project I was a lecturer in Swansea; I have since moved to LSE and become a colleague of Brian's. My return to LSE almost coincided with his premature departure as he suffered a major accident in the summer of my arrival. Despite this considerable inconvenience he managed to find the time to respond to the papers for the original symposium and has co-operated with this book since its inception. Without his co-operation this project could not have come to fruition. Editing a work of this kind can sometimes become a substitute for the real intellectual effort of writing a book of one's own. That the work on this book has been more than unusually demanding is to a great measure to the credit of Brian who forced me to think hard about the issues discussed and not merely about editorial consistency. It has been both a pleasure and a challenge to work with him, both on this book and teaching political theory at LSE and I have enjoyed that challenge and benefited immeasurably from it. I am also grateful to Annie Parker, for her hospitality and her work preparing the final essay. Her contribution to this book may be imperceptible, but it is considerable for all that.

I also owe a considerable debt of gratitude to all the contributors to this book and the original *Utilitas* symposium. I would especially like to thank John Horton and Andrew Mason. I would also like to thank John Charvet. Professor David Gauthier was unable to attend the original *Utilitas* symposium, but gave his paper at a special seminar at LSE with Professor Barry in March 1997. I would like to thank Dr Matt Mulford for hosting that seminar.

I would like to thank Edinburgh University Press for permission to reproduce four of the original *Utilitas* papers for this book. I would also like to thank Nicola Carr my editor, for her patience, support and encouragement from the beginning when I raised the possibility of expanding the *Utilitas* special issue. Susan Mendus's paper first appeared in *Political Studies*; I am grateful to the editor and to the publisher Basil Blackwell for permission to reproduce the essay. A version of Richard Arneson's paper will also appear in *Ethics*; I am grateful to the University of Chicago Press for permission to publish this version. Finally I would like to thank the Clarendon Press, for permission to quote extensively from *Justice as Impartiality*.

P. J. Kelly
LSE

Contributors

Richard Arneson is Professor of Philosophy at the University of California, San Diego. He has been a visiting Professor at the University of California at Davis, California Institute of Technology and Yale University. He has been an associate editor of *Ethics* since 1986. He has published numerous articles on issues of justice and is currently working on individual responsibility and social justice. Among his most recent publications are 'Against Rawlsian Equality of Opportunity', *Philosophical Studies* (forthcoming), 'Egalitarianism and the Undeserving Poor', *Journal of Political Philosophy* (forthcoming) and 'Feminism and Family Justice', *Public Affairs Quarterly* (forthcoming).

Brian Barry is a Fellow of the British Academy and Professor of Political Science at the London School of Economics and Political Science. He has taught at universities in Britain, Canada and the United States. His many publications include *Political Argument*, 2nd edn, Hemel Hempstead, 1990; *The Liberal Theory of Justice*, Oxford, 1973; *Sociologists, Economists and Democracy*, Chicago, 1978; *Democracy, Power and Justice*, Oxford, 1989. His most recent major work is the multi-volume *A Treatise on Social Justice*, the first two volumes of which have been published as *Theories of Justice*, Hemel Hempstead, 1989, and *Justice as Impartiality*, Oxford, 1995. He is currently working on the third volume to be entitled *Principles of Justice*.

Diemut Bubeck is Lecturer in Political Theory at the London School of Economics. Her work on women's unpaid work and the ethic of care debate is published in *Care, Gender and Justice*, Oxford, 1995. More recently, she has written papers on citizenship, impartiality, Condorcet and Nietzsche.

Simon Caney is Lecturer in Politics at the University of Newcastle. He has published articles on political perfectionism, liberalism and issues of international political theory. He is co-editor (with David George and Peter Jones) of *National Rights, International Obligations*,

Oxford, 1996. He is currently working on international distributive justice.

David Gauthier is Distinguished Service Professor of Philosophy at the University of Pittsburgh. His major publications are *The Logic of Leviathan*, Oxford, 1969; *Morals By Agreement*, Oxford, 1986; and a collection of essays, *Moral Dealing: Contract, Ethics and Reason*, Ithaca, 1992. His current research interests include contractarian moral and political theory, deliberative rationality and the thought of Thomas Hobbes and Jean-Jacques Rousseau.

Russell Hardin is Professor and Chair of Politics at New York University. He is author of *Collective Action*, Baltimore,1982; *Rational Man, Irrational Society*, ed. with Brian Barry, Beverly Hills, CA, 1982; *Morality Within the Limits of Reason*, Chicago, 1988; *One For All: The Logic of Group Conflict*, Princeton, 1995; and *Liberalism, Constitutionalism and Democracy*, Oxford, forthcoming. His current research interests include, trust, ordinary knowledge and Hume's moral and political philosophy.

Paul Kelly is Lecturer in Political Theory at the London School of Economics. His research interests cover the history of political thought and modern political philosophy. He is author of *Utilitarianism and Distributive Justice: Jeremy Bentham and the Civil Law*, Oxford, 1990, and co-edited (with David Boucher) *The Social Contract: From Hobbes to Rawls*, London, 1994. He is currently completing a monograph on the political philosophy and legal theory of Ronald Dworkin.

Matt Matravers is Lecturer in Political Theory at the University of York. He is co-author, with Brian Barry, of the entries on 'Justice' and 'International Justice' in the *Routledge Encyclopaedia of Philosophy* (forthcoming). He is currently writing a book on theories of distributive justice and the problem of punishment.

Susan Mendus is Professor of Politics and Director of the Morrell Studies in Toleration programme at the University of York. Her research interests lie mainly in contemporary political philosophy and feminist theory. She has published extensively on problems of toleration in modern political philosophy and is currently working on a book on Kantianism and feminism.

Albert Weale is Professor of Government at the University of Essex and co-editor of the *British Journal of Political Science*. He was Professor of Politics at the University of East Anglia (1985–92) and

Director of the Institute for Research in the Social Sciences (1982–5). His research interests cover political theory and public policy, especially the theory of justice and the theory of democracy. His principal publications include *Political Theory and Social Policy*, Basingstoke, 1983; ed. *Cost and Choice in Health Care*, King's Fund, 1988; *The Theory of Choice* (with others), Oxford, 1992; and *Democracy*, Basingstoke, forthcoming.

Jonathan Wolff is Reader in Philosophy at University College London and editor of the proceedings of the Aristotelian Society. He is author of *Robert Nozick*, Oxford 1991, and *An Introduction to Political Philosophy*, Oxford 1996, and has published a series of papers on the problem of political obligation. He is currently working on equality, competition and exploitation.

1

Introduction: Impartiality, Neutrality and Justice

PAUL KELLY

Over the last three decades the resurgence of normative political theory in the English-speaking world has been most closely associated with the issue of distributive justice. No other issue has had quite the same significance. In assuming this position of authority justice has been transformed from merely one among a list of important political values to the primary value, or as Rawls described it 'the first virtue of social institutions'.[1] Theories of justice provide an account of those principles which ought to regulate the distribution of the benefits and burdens of social co-operation. They also provide an account of the method and point of political theory. Democracy, civil rights and economic justice constitute the policy agenda of theories of distributive justice and a contractual agreement between the potential beneficiaries or subjects of such rules and policies forms the method of justification. A concern to justify the distribution of the benefits and burdens of social co-operation has become almost the sole object of normative political theory.

The contractarian justification associated with theories of distributive justice has contributed to the development of a vast literature focusing largely on the issue of method as opposed to the substantive content of such theories. Communitarian critics such as Michael Sandel have argued that the contractarian method cannot provide a reason for recognizing the bindingness of principles of justice, unless one already has an independent moral reason for adopting the perspective of impartiality.[2] Alasdair MacIntyre has criticized the claim of liberal (i.e. contractarian) theories of justice to be neutral between rival conceptions of the good life or fundamental values.[3] According to MacIntyre, liberal theories of justice are a fraud in claiming to offer neutral principles for regulating the affairs of those who disagree on fundamental values. This fact of disagreement over fundamental

---

[1] John Rawls, *A Theory of Justice*, Oxford, 1972, p. 3.

[2] M. Sandel, *Liberalism and the Limits of Justice*, Cambridge, 1982.

[3] A. MacIntyre, *After Virtue*, London, 1981; *Whose Justice? Which Rationality?*, London, 1988.

values is taken to be the prime reason why we need neutral reasons that do not advantage the standing of any social group or set of values. Other critics of justice theory, such as Michael Walzer, have attacked the conception of political theory that underpins the so-called distributive paradigm.

For Rawls, and theorists of justice following him, the main task of political theory has been to construct an abstract defence of impartial principles which should regulate the distribution of the benefits and burdens of social co-operation. Walzer rejects this whole conception of the point of political theory. Instead he argues that theorizing about issues of distribution should begin with history and anthropology, rather than economics and jurisprudence. The political theorist should try to describe and clarify the socially constituted meaning of the particular goods to be distributed and the distributive principles associated with such social meanings. There is no overall single theory of distributive justice, and there cannot be principles that extend beyond the shared social meanings of particular communities. He does modify this position slightly, but the main aim is to challenge the universal validity of theories of distributive justice.[4]

This communitarian critique has come to exercise a stranglehold over discussions of justice and the agenda of political theory. Many students are now first introduced to the subject through a survey of the 'liberal-communitarian' debate. The high-profile assault on liberal theories of justice mounted by Sandel, MacIntyre and Walzer, as well as that more recently initiated by liberal perfectionists such as Joseph Raz,[5] has come to dominate much contemporary normative political theory. Contractarian defences of justice appear to have fallen out of favour, with even John Rawls recasting his theory of justice as fairness as a *political* theory depending on an overlapping consensus between reasonable comprehensive conceptions of the good.[6]

It is in this context of the apparent retreat of contractarian theories that Brian Barry's recent *Justice as Impartiality*[7] has come to attract such attention. Although this book is only one volume of a multi-volume *Treatise on Social Justice*, it is particularly significant as it sets out to defend two main theses. First Barry defends the possibility

---

[4] M. Walzer, *Spheres of Justice*, Oxford, 1983; *Interpretation and Social Criticism*, Cambridge, Mass., 1993. It should, however, be pointed out that Walzer is only able to point to the variety of putative distributive principles to support his claim that all such principles are local. Walzer does not provide any philosophical defence of his anti-universalist position.

[5] J. Raz, *The Morality of Freedom*, Oxford, 1986.

[6] J. Rawls, *Political Liberalism*, New York, 1993.

[7] Brian Barry, *Justice as Impartiality*, Oxford, 1995. All references to this book in subsequent chapters will be given as page numbers in parentheses in the text rather than as footnote citations.

and value of a contractarian defence of distributive justice. And second, he explains just what impartiality does and does not entail. *Justice as Impartiality* can be read as a defence of a contractarian method, a modified version of that advanced by T. M. Scanlon, showing just what the use of this device is supposed to achieve. It is also a robust defence of an impartiality theory against many of the standard charges raised by critics of the priority of justice: by feminist care theorists, ethical particularists and communitarians. The analytical rigour, moral purpose and robust good sense of Barry's counter-attack on both critics and criticisms makes *Justice as Impartiality* a significant contribution to political theory in its own right, as well as an addition to Barry's own *Treatise*. Barry's arguments show, if they are correct, that many of the criticisms can either be accommodated into a carefully worked out second-order impartialist theory of justice, or else they can be ignored. Far from having the worst of the argument, Barry argues that there is not only life in the corpse of liberal theories of justice, but that his version – justice as impartiality – is superior to any of the rival positions adopted by critics and sympathizers alike.

Barry's overriding concern in a *Treatise on Social Justice* is with the substantive principles of distributive justice and their philosophical defence. Indeed, *Justice as Impartiality* can be seen as forming an interlude between the first volume in which Barry first identifies justice as impartiality as his preferred theory, and what will now be the third volume *The Principles of Justice*, which sets out his substantive contribution to political and economic justice.[8] These substantive issues of justice have been the dominant themes of his work since the publication of *Political Argument* in 1965.[9] This latter book, until the publication of John Rawls's *A Theory of Justice* seven years later, did more than any other to resurrect the possibility of normative political theory from the trough of crude utilitarian policy analysis into which it had fallen for much of the twentieth century. Following the publication of Rawls's book, and Barry's subsequent book-length critique – *The Liberal Theory of Justice*[10] – Barry became identified as a severe but sympathetic critic of post-Rawlsian political theory. Indeed since Rawls has subsequently reinterpreted his own earlier theory of justice as fairness in *Political Liberalism*, Barry has become the main defender not only of a broadly liberal conception of distributive justice, but also of the method of analytical normative political argument. The arguments of *Justice as Impartiality* continue the robust defence of a

---

[8] The third volume of a *Treatise on Social Justice*, *The Principles of Justice* is currently being completed as I write this introduction.

[9] Brian Barry, *Political Argument*, London, 1965 (reissued with a new introduction, Hemel Hempstead, 1990.

[10] Brian Barry, *The Liberal Theory of Justice*, Oxford, 1973.

theory of justice and of rational argument about political principles, by challenging many of the standard criticisms that are raised against the stance of impartiality and theories of justice based on it.

The essays in this collection, contributed by major British and American political philosophers, provide not only a detailed critical commentary on Barry's own writings, but a contribution to wider debates about the character of an adequate theory of justice and the possibility of rational argument about fundamental political principles. Although much of the text inevitably consists of close commentary on the text of *Justice as Impartiality*, the intention of the authors and of Barry himself has been to *do* political theory and not merely provide second-order philosophical criticism. This book is therefore intended to serve both as a critical commentary on Barry's *Justice as Impartiality* which will be of use to students and political theorists alike, and as a contribution to contemporary political theory by addressing some of its most important questions.

The main questions discussed in the various contributions to this book are: the nature and point of contractarian theories; justice as impartiality versus rival contractarian conceptions of morality and justice (i.e. justice as mutual advantage and justice as reciprocity); first- and second-order impartiality; impartiality and neutrality; and the priority of justice over other moral standpoints.

The first three essays by Albert Weale, Jonathan Wolff and myself all address aspects of Barry's contractarian methodology. In his chapter 'From Contracts to Pluralism?' Albert Weale is sympathetic to Barry's overriding commitment to a broadly liberal theory of social justice. He is also keen to locate Barry's arguments within a tradition of British political theory running back through H. L. A. Hart, Henry Sidgwick, the Mills and Bentham to David Hume. But Weale argues that Barry also departs from this British tradition by introducing an 'unnecessary epicycle' into his argument by using a contractarian justification. In a complex and detailed argument Weale assesses what the contract method adds to Barry's argument and concludes that it contributes nothing that cannot be achieved by the kind of normative theorizing found in Barry's earlier book *Political Argument*. Weale's broader point is to redirect normative political theory away from this preoccupation with method and to concentrate instead on substantive arguments for political principles.

Jonathan Wolff's chapter 'Rational, Fair and Reasonable' is also concerned to challenge Barry's contractarianism, but Wolff's concern is not the broadly Humean point of Weale; rather he pursues two different strands of argument. He criticizes the accuracy of Barry's account of the rival contractarian theories of justice as reciprocity and justice as mutual advantage. Then Wolff contests the idea that there must be one unified theory of justice. Instead, he argues for a pluralistic approach to distributive justice which can deploy the perspectives of justice as impartiality, justice as mutual advantage and justice as reciprocity or fairness on different occasions and for different reasons. Wolff concedes that as a single principle theory justice as impartiality has advantages over its rivals, but concludes that a pluralistic theory would prove more satisfactory still.

My own paper 'Taking Utilitarianism Seriously' challenges the claim that a Scanlonian contract provides a better account of public deliberation than a 'informed-preference' utilitarianism, because what it is reasonable to accept or reject can itself only be given some content in relation to a norm. I argue that a suitably sophisticated utilitarian theory is at least as good a candidate as any other rival decision principle for justifying the distribution of the benefits and burdens of social co-operation. A similar point about the concept of 'reasonableness' is taken up in Russell Hardin's paper 'Reasonable Agreement: Political not Normative'. Hardin's point is that the criterion of reasonableness is either itself the outcome of an agreement in which case the agreement is a form of mutual advantage bargain, or else it is an independent criterion such as utility maximization, in which case the criterion of reasonableness can be applied without recourse to the idea of an agreement or contract.

In replying to these arguments Barry clarifies what the contractarian method is supposed to achieve. Instead of providing a magic formula for deducing conclusions that were not already implicit in the premises, the contractarian method is merely – though importantly – a useful device for ordering substantive commitments to fundamental equality, the justification of inequalities to those who do least well under them, and a commitment to the separateness of persons. It is these ideas which are doing the real work. The Scanlonian device is simply a way of ordering and clarifying those fundamental commitments, without getting into the question-begging complexities of Rawls's original position.

An important feature of justice as impartiality is that it dispenses with the idea of bargaining and inequality of bargaining power, instead emphasizing the reasonable rejectability test of a Scanlonian contract as a way of securing fundamental equality. Wolff and Matravers address the issue of bargaining and Barry's treatment of justice as mutual advantage. However, the matter is treated most significantly in David Gauthier's defence of his theory of justice as mutual advantage expounded in great detail in *Morals by Agreement*.[11] Gauthier's subtle and robust defence of his own theory against Barry's

---

[11] David Gauthier, *Morals by Agreement*, Oxford, 1986.

criticisms is a significant restatement of the theory of justice as mutual advantage.

As a liberal theory of justice, Barry's theory of justice as impartiality is assumed to be neutral between different conceptions of the good. Although Barry avoids where possible the claim to neutrality, preferring to emphasize that his theory is an impartialist rather than a neutralist one, the issue of neutrality is taken up in different ways by Richard Arneson, Simon Caney and Matt Matravers.

In his chapter 'The Priority of the Right Over the Good Rides Again', Richard Arneson claims that Barry fails to provide neutral reasons which can serve as the basis of public policies for people who disagree about the good. This failure to provide neutral reasons is not a surprise because there are no such neutral reasons. What is wrong with Barry's theory is that the idea of reasonable agreement purports to offer reasons which can only come from a substantive theory such as utilitarianism. Furthermore, Arneson also criticizes Barry for devoting too much attention to the procedural level and insufficient attention to providing specific answers to policy questions. Barry's response to some of Arneson's arguments is instructive in that it further clarifies how a theory of justice is supposed to work, and just what sort of questions it can provide answers to. Arneson draws an interesting parallel between Barry's distinction between first- and second-order impartiality and the familiar distinction between act and rule utilitarianism. He suggests that just as the utilitarian distinction proved to be unstable so it appears is the case with Barry's distinction between two levels of impartiality.

Simon Caney's chapter 'Impartiality and Liberal Neutrality' challenges the idea that disagreement about the good is as endemic and uncontroversial as neutralist theories of justice maintain. Caney sets out a number of examples which he claims show incontrovertibly superior life choices. Public policies which set out to limit drug abuse and boring and repetitive work are hardly neutral but are far from controversial in the way in which imposing religious observance would be. The apparent liberal bias in favour of neutrality draws much of its force from a rather narrow focus on issues such as religious toleration. But if we extend the remit of justice beyond such concerns as all substantive theories do in the end, then the case against liberal perfectionism, according to Caney, is far from obvious. As well as arguing that there can be conceptions of the good which might well satisfy the Scanlonian test thus allowing for the pursuit of perfectionist policies, Caney also points out that Scanlonian argument provides an inadequate account of concepts such as moral wrongness. This issue is taken up and developed in Matt Matravers' chapter 'What's "Wrong" in Contractualism?'

Matravers argues that contractualism cannot draw a distinction between wrongs of unfairness – injustices – and wrongs in themselves without abandoning its claims to neutrality. If justice as impartiality cannot sustain this distinction then it must explain wrongness simply in terms of some action being reasonably rejected. But the reason why an action or principle can be reasonably rejected must often make appeal to its being wrong.

If Barry's theory cannot avoid appealing to a thick ethical commitment or a conception of the good, then his method is in danger of becoming, according to Matravers, little more than a more sophisticated version of Walzer's conception of political theory as the articulation of shared understandings within particular communities. Barry begins *Justice as Impartiality* with a rejection of Walzerian engaged social criticism on the grounds that such shared communal understandings are more deeply contested than Walzer allows – and thus a dubious resource for political theory. For his own theory to be in danger of collapsing back into this form of social criticism is a serious charge. Needless to say it is a charge that Barry rejects.

The last two chapters take up issues arising from Barry's appeal to second-order impartiality. Diemut Bubeck's essay 'Care, Justice and the Good', addresses a number of themes concerning neutrality and the priority of the right over the good. More importantly, however, it challenges the claim of justice as impartiality to arbitrate in case of conflict with other political and moral stances. Bubeck's main concern is with feminist care theory, which she offers as a rival candidate for a distributive theory to the more imperialistic (i.e. universalist) claims of justice as impartiality. She is particularly concerned with Barry's claim that justice as impartiality can incorporate much of the aspirations of care theory. This she claims can only be achieved by subordinating care theory to justice and therefore rendering it barren as a distinct moral and political standpoint.

In the penultimate essay Susan Mendus pursues a complex theme, building on arguments of Bernard Williams about the limits of any theory's ability to adequately capture real moral and political dilemmas and provide 'right' answers to them. Mendus does not go as far as Williams in her scepticism about the value of 'theory' in moral and political reflection, but she does emphasize that any theory, even a second-order impartialist theory, can distort our understanding of moral conflict or the true nature of personal projects and relationships. The aspiration of any theory to provide 'right' answers can, she argues, leave a sense of loss – that is a sense in which some crucial aspect of human experience has been left out of account. Mendus's concern accords with a commonplace criticism of the dangers and distortions of abstraction and rationalism in moral and political theory. This stance is particularly commonplace among some feminist care theorists. Barry claims in the final section of his reply that his argument is compatible with valuing personal relationships and care, but it is clear that he remains sceptical about how much weight such particularistic feelings should have when they come into conflict with the requirements of justice.

Barry's concluding essay provides a systematic clarification of the aims of his original argument in *Justice as Impartiality* and a detailed response to the criticisms advanced by all the contributors to this book. The five sections of the essay correspond to five broad themes that have emerged across all the contributions and which are of more interest than a line-by-line rebuttal of each critic. The concluding essay also serves as an independent overview of his argument and prelude to the next volume *The Principles of Justice*. As a statement of why a contractarian method is useful and what a theory of second-order impartiality involves, the closing essay is a significant contribution to the debate over social justice. It clarifies the issues between liberal theories of justice and their critics, but it also provides a considerable armoury of argument that can be deployed against particularists, care theorists and communitarians of various kinds, as well as mutual advantage theorists and libertarians. A further response to his critics will be the next volume of *A Treatise on Social Justice*, where we will get an account of those principles of justice which Barry thinks cannot be reasonably rejected. He has gone some way to outlining what the content of a theory of justice can be in *Justice as Impartiality* and in his concluding essay in this book. But in both cases, as Albert Weale points out in his essay, the focus of attention is directed towards civil and political rights. In the next volume we can expect to hear more about distributive economic justice. *Justice as Impartiality* and the concluding essay to this collection answer the question what is a theory of justice supposed to do? Answering this question is essential for defending the substantive principles of justice, and in so doing Barry has revitalized the method and content of contemporary normative political theory as this collection testifies. But for an account of the content of justice as impartiality we must await the next volume *The Principles of Justice*.

2

From Contracts to Pluralism?

ALBERT WEALE

Brian Barry's work stands in the line of what may be called, borrowing from F. R. Leavis, 'the great tradition' of British political thought. Leavis defines his own great tradition by saying that it refers to 'the tradition to which what is great in English fiction belongs'.[1] By analogy we may say that the great tradition of British political thought is composed of what is great in British political thought: a line that stretches from Hobbes through Locke, Hume, Bentham, the Mills to Sidgwick and Hart.

In this tradition there is both conceptual abstraction and an engagement with concrete problems. One important aspect of this tradition is that it takes the evaluation of institutions to be the subject-matter for the theory of political morality. To adapt the opening words of Barry's first book, *Political Argument*, published in 1965, this tradition studies 'the relation between principles and institutions', looking both at the practical implications of principles and at the theoretical justification of certain institutions.[2] Barry's work, both in *A Treatise on Social Justice* and in other publications, takes up the dominant concerns of this tradition and, drawing upon analytical philosophy and contemporary economics and political science, seeks to offer a theory of justice with an account of its institutional implications.

A second important feature of this tradition is that its method is analytic, resting upon an understanding of the logic of political argument, rather than metaphysical, resting upon any appeal to a putative philosophy of history. Historical teleology is not entirely absent from the concerns of those writing in the great tradition, as J. S. Mill's concern with the idea of progress goes to show. However, it is difficult to see how any crucial argument of authors within the tradition depends upon the correctness of a particular thesis about historical development, in the way that the claims of Marxism, for example, depended upon its historical analysis. Nothing in *A Treatise on Social Justice*, as

[1] F. R. Leavis, *The Great Tradition*, London, 1955, p. 7.
[2] Brian Barry, *Political Argument*, London, 1965, p. xvii.

far as I can see, rests upon any particular thesis about patterns of historical development, and, indeed, the idea that it is up to societies to choose justice seems inconsistent at a deep level with any historical teleology.

Despite these ways in which Barry's work is part of the great tradition, there is one important respect in which it diverges from that tradition, at least as it has evolved in the last two centuries. Since Hume's successful critique of the idea of the social contract, it has not been common in the great tradition to use a contractual device to derive principles of justice or political morality.[3] From the Humean conclusions that the appeal to a contractual situation adds nothing to what we know already (the obligation to keep our word in the promise cannot be accounted for 'without any circuit') and that contractual arguments can only be relished by those 'trained in a philosophical system', the post-Humean line of reasoning has been forward-looking and, initially at least, broadly utilitarian. Thus, the great tradition has always insisted on the need for the justification of institutional arrangements in terms of the broad social and political ends that they serve. Barry of course shares this insistence on the need to offer broadly based justifications for institutions, contrasting his own position with that of Burkean prescriptivism (p. 6). But it is an open question whether this insistence on the need for justification, with the requirement that social and political institutions be subject to approval by each person's reason, does have to proceed along the con-tractarian lines that Barry proposes in *Justice as Impartiality*.

I have said that the mode of justification in the great tradition was broadly utilitarian, but this simple judgement needs to be modified in various ways. In particular, as it developed, thought in the great tradition inclined to a form of value pluralism, so that institutions were to be justified not simply in terms of the advantages they produced, as measured in terms of the general welfare or happiness, but also in terms of their conformity to certain principles of fairness and equality. In part, this value pluralism arose because of the evident lack of success of purely consequentialist reasoning. Mill's failure in Chapter 5 of *Utilitarianism*[4] to show how utility underlay justice might easily lead to the thought that there was not one principle, that of the general social advantage, implicit in the evaluation of institutions but two: social advantage and a just distribution of the burdens and benefits of social co-operation. By this early stage, therefore, there is already a value pluralism implicit in the great tradition. This plural-

---

[3] David Hume, 'Of the Original Contract', *Essays, Moral, Political and Literary*, ed. T. H. Green and T. H. Grose, London, 1889, pp. 443–60.

[4] J. S. Mill, *Utilitarianism*, in *On Liberty and Other Essays*, ed. J. Gray, Oxford, 1991.

ism had become quite explicit by the time of Sidgwick, who, as Richard Braithwaite once famously remarked, had to sweeten the pure milk of the utilitarian gospel with a theory of equality.[5] Similarly, in Hart's work, the principle of fairness stands as an independent principle, distinct from that of utility.[6] Plural intuitions had thus failed to yield to the regimentation of a purely consequentialist, forward-looking system or method of ethics.

In his early work, Barry recapitulated this line of development, and the distinction in *Political Argument* between want-regarding and ideal-regarding principles runs along the same lines as Sidgwick's distinction between intuitional and utilitarian morality.[7] One way of reading *Political Argument* was to see it as consistent with, and in some ways supportive of, a version of intuitionism. Those values, like social integration, that could not be accounted for in want-regarding terms were to be seen as non-reducible ideal-regarding features of a society, even if they were only relatively weak values.[8] Political action and public policies were, on this account, to be judged by their conduciveness to certain states of affairs sometimes to be judged in ideal terms, although it would be impossible ever to measure the value of these states of affairs by reference to a single metric of 'happiness', and various, logically independent value-conferring properties provided the basis for evaluation instead. In so far as ideal-regarding principles are acceptable, it was clear that there was an ultimate plurality of such principles, and there was no 'method of ethics' that would provide an overarching framework.

The major modern competitor to both utilitarianism and intuitionism has of course been social contract theory. Thus, Rawls made it quite clear in *A Theory of Justice* that contractual reasoning was to be contrasted with both utilitarianism and intuitionism.[9] (Indeed, I would go further and say that in *A Theory of Justice* Rawls thinks he has shown utilitarianism to be wrong but holds that it is only a matter of conjecture as to whether he has shown intuitionism to be wrong.) Yet, in *The Liberal Theory of Justice*,[10] Barry's sharp critique of Rawls indicated some scepticism as to whether the contractarian method could provide the logical foundations for the principle of justice. By the time of *A Treatise on Social Justice*, however, the methodological wheel

---

[5] R. B. Braithwaite, *Theory of Games as a Tool for the Moral Philosopher*, Cambridge, 1955, p. 6.

[6] H. L. A. Hart, 'Are There Any Natural Rights?', *Philosophical Review*, 64 (1955), 175-91.

[7] I say 'runs along the same lines as' rather than anything stronger, because there were clearly differences. See Barry, *Political Argument*, p. 41.

[8] Barry, *Political Argument*, ch. 7.

[9] John Rawls, *A Theory of Justice*, Oxford, 1972, pp. 22–45.

[10] Brian Barry, *The Liberal Theory of Justice*, Oxford, 1973.

has taken a full turn. The device of the hypothetical contract becomes the means by which it is possible to argue for a particular interpretation of the potentially competing principles of justice.

What lies behind the development of Barry's thought in this contractarian direction? At one level the change can be seen as an expression of Barry's continual engagement with the work of John Rawls, at least since *The Liberal Theory of Justice*. In *Theories of Social Justice* Hume and Rawls are taken as the sparring partners, and the reader sees a process of refinement, rejection and modification of the work of the latter in particular. However, although the exposition and critique of the latter is the means by which Barry seeks to develop his own theory, I do not think it can be cited as the sole rationale for the contractarian turn in his thinking. Instead, I conjecture, the rationale is to be found in something deeper, namely a dilemma implicit in the utilitarianism that has been so dominant in the great tradition of British political thought. That dilemma can be stated as follows. If, as J. S. Mill asserted, the notion of utility has to include the 'permanent interests' of persons viewed as progressive beings, then there has to be some acknowledgement within our account of human interests of the fact that human beings are self-defining creatures, whose interests reflect the conceptions they have of themselves. Since the theory of justice has to provide us with principles for adjudicating among competing interests, any theory has to take into account this self-defining property of persons and the contractarian approach is one natural way of doing this. From this point of view, the task of political theory is not to formulate some principles that promote the general good, subject to some side-constraints of fairness, but instead to formulate principles of political organization that will enable citizens with competing conceptions of the good to live together in justice. The contractarian approach looks attractive, at least prima facie, in this context, since it abstracts from the partial attachments of citizens and asks what they could collectively agree to.

In this essay I wish to suggest that this turn to contractarian reasoning does not accomplish the defence of an egalitarian theory of justice in the way that Barry supposes. Rather than solve the theoretical problem of how to produce a method of political ethics, the contractarian device introduces an unnecessary theoretical epicycle into what is otherwise a coherent account of social justice in particular and political morality in general. Barry's earlier doctrine on the plurality of political principles was the right theory of political morality.

The essence of my argument will be to claim that the only way of construing the processes of reasoning within the original position of the sort that Barry envisages in *Justice as Impartiality* is through first-order political arguments available to anyone whether they occupy an original position or not. Thus, even if we use the device of the social contract, we cannot give 'without circuit', to use Hume's felicitous phrase, the reasons for favouring one conception of justice over another. This conclusion may not be uncongenial to Barry himself. At various points in his writings, as well as in sundry *obiter dicta*, he has said that he does not attach a great deal of importance to the contractarian device. Thus, in the *Utilitas* symposium on his work, Barry wrote that he did not see himself as a fundamentalist contractarian.[11] Similarly, he writes in *Justice as Impartiality*, that someone might object that the contractarian construction 'is little more than a device for talking about what is fair, on a fundamentally egalitarian conception of fairness' (p. 113). So it is, I shall argue, but, lacking some of the virtues claimed for it, it might as well be dispensed with.

To say this, of course, is not to dissent from other features of Barry's theory of justice. For example, I shall take it that Barry has adequately developed a two-level theory of justice, such that impartiality applies to the basic structure of institutions and not the routine dealings that individuals have with one another except outside of particular roles or institutional relations. This not only seems to me to be consistent with the emphasis in the great tradition on institutions as the subject of choice, but also to be a way of disposing of a number of misleading claims about the pernicious effects of impartiality on moral and political sensibilities. Similarly, there are a whole number of other substantive and methodological points in *Justice as Impartiality* with which I would agree, including the stress upon commensurability across different conceptions of the good, the rejection of interpretativism in political theory, the insistence that the ascription of rights should be the conclusion, not the premise, of an argument, and the compatibility of an ethic of care with an ethic of justice. My dissent is thus focused entirely on the methodological question about the utility of the contract device of the sort that Barry proposes.

TWO FORMS OF CONTRACT THEORY

What does it mean to construct a theory of justice? Here Barry adopts an approach which is currently widespread but which, so far as I am

---

[11] Brian Barry, 'Contractual Justice: A Modest Defence', *Utilitas*, 8 (1996), 357–80, at p. 357. Incidentally, the statement at this point that Barry was an anti-contractarian until reading Scanlon's 'Contractualism and Utilitarianism' must be wrong, at least as far as the published version of Scanlon's paper is concerned, since Barry had already used a contractual form of reasoning in an article published in 1979: see Barry, 'Is Democracy Special?' *Philosophy, Politics and Society*, Fifth Series, ed. P. Laslett and J. Fishkin, Oxford, 1979, pp. 155–96, especially at pp. 173–9.

aware, was first formalized by Henry Sidgwick in *The Methods of Ethics*.[12] According to this approach, the task is to take certain 'common sense' principles and opinions and build around them a logical structure which provides their rationale. The identification and systematizing of common sense principles is by no means a straightforward task in its own right, since everyday convictions typically have a formlessness and incoherence to them that means that some analysis and selection is necessary even to supply the data for the moral theory. You only have to think of the wide variety of uses of terms like 'desert' or 'equality' in order to understand what is involved. However, this is only the beginning of the story. Once the catalogue of principles and considerations is constructed, the theorist then has to propose a logical structure that will provide a rationalization of the principles so identified.

This logical structure provides the constructivist element of the theory. Constructivist theories are those which seek to characterize justice by reference to the features of some choice situation for putatively rational agents.[13] Barry defines constructivism by reference to two conditions: firstly, that what comes out of a certain situation is to be counted just and, secondly, that the construction is by the theorist and not by the people in the situation themselves.[14] Perhaps the best known constructivist theory on this definition is that of Rawls which seeks to give an account of justice by reference to the hypothetical choices of a set of individuals deprived of knowledge of their own identities.[15] Rawls calls this situation of choice the original position, and Barry takes this idea and generalizes it to cover all those approaches to the theory of justice that seek to account for justice in terms of the choices that free and rational individuals would make in some specified situation of choice.[16]

The major themes of *Theories of Justice* was that leading theories fall into one of two camps. Either they propose to understand justice as a form of mutual advantage, as did David Hume and as does John Rawls in some moods, in which the task is to find terms of generally acceptable co-operation, or they understand justice as a form of impartiality, in which the principles of justice are those that could not be reasonably rejected by persons in an initial situation of equality. The trouble with justice as mutual advantage, according to Barry, is that the baseline state from which mutual gains are sought may well

[12] H. Sidgwick, The *Methods of Ethics*, London, 1874.

[13] For a more general discussion of constructivism in ethics, see Onora O'Neill, *Constructions of Reason*, Cambridge, 1989, ch. 11.

[14] Brian Barry, *Theories of Justice*, Hemel Hempstead, 1989, p. 266.

[15] Rawls, *A Theory of Justice*.

[16] See *Theories of Justice*, p. 269.

contain significant inequalities of bargaining advantage, the effects of which would render the results of the negotiation inappropriate as theory of justice. Thus, a theory of justice must respect the constraint that any agreement on its terms must not be forced through the exercise of power or the exploitation of naturally or socially determined advantages. According to Barry, the best way of respecting this constraint is to construct the device of the contract, such that it generates principles that could not be reasonably rejected by persons who were seeking agreement on the terms of their association but who could not resort to power and exploitation to secure that agreement. This is the theory of justice as impartiality. *Theories of Justice* was thus built around the distinction between justice as mutual advantage and justice as impartiality. The two theories are distinguished by the different ways in which they conceptualize the relationship between the power and interests of social agents on the one hand and the rightful claims upon resources that those agents can exercise on the other.

In the theory of justice as mutual advantage, principles of justice are conceived as rules by which all individuals can promote their interests. This connection is definitional. Rules securing general interests are principles of justice, and only principles whose implementation will secure general advantage are admissible as candidates for principles of justice. As Barry points out, a paradigm for justice in this sense is Hume's theory of property.[17] Hume held that a generally respected rule of property gives members of a society secure possession of resources that would otherwise be subject to predation by others. Thus, the rule that settled possession gives title can be interpreted as a rule of justice, since it will be to everyone's advantage to acknowledge it. Another paradigm of justice as mutual advantage, Barry suggests, is games of fair division provided by the case of the non-zero-sum bargaining situations in game theory. These games include the so called 'bargaining problem' of Nash, an example of which is the case of two people having to agree upon a principle for dividing a legacy they have been left which will be lost unless they come to mutual agreement on the division, and Braithwaite's story of Matthew the trumpeter and Luke the pianist who live next door to one another and who can only avoid the disadvantages of silence or cacophony if they can agree to divide between them the number of evenings in the month on which each is allowed to practise.[18]

The central claim of the theory of justice as mutual advantage,

---

[17] Ibid., p. 152, citing David Hume, *Enquiries Concerning Human Understanding and Concerning Principles of Morals*, ed. L. A. Selby-Bigge, 3rd ed., Oxford, 1975, p. 495.

[18] J. F. Nash, 'The Bargaining Problem', *Econometrica*, 18 (1950), 155–62; R. B. Braithwaite, *Theory of Games*.

according to Barry, is that principles for solving such problems must advance the interests of all of the parties involved. From this central claim there flow a number of corollaries. One of these is that for there to be the possibility of mutual advantage, there must first be a non-agreement point as the status quo, providing the baseline from which individuals can judge the acceptability of potential gains. So, for example, in the Nash problem the non-agreement point is that neither party has any share in the legacy, and it is by reference to this situation that each individual is to assess potential gains. Moreover, relative advantages at this non-agreement point will typically be maintained in the final solution. For example, if one of the parties eligible for the legacy is rich and the other poor, then a solution to the bargaining problem will normally give the rich person more than the poor person because the rich person has a greater ability to hazard the risks of non-agreement. Over one-third of *Theories of Justice* is taken up with showing that any adequate solution to the problems of non-zero-sum bargaining games will have this feature.

With gains over a non-agreement status quo preserving relative advantage, it can be clearly seen why the account of justice as mutual advantage solves one major problem in the theory of justice, namely to explain how there is a motive to behave justly. If agreement can be reached on sharing out our joint gains, each individual can see that he or she is doing as well as possible, in circumstances in which other individuals are doing as well as they can. The conditions for a Pareto optimal equilibrium are thus satisfied: no one can be made better off without making someone else worse off and no one has an incentive to depart from the allocation that is specified in the agreement. If the rules of justice are equivalent to the solution to such bargaining situations, then there is a natural sense in which each individual involved has an incentive to behave justly. Justice is enlightened self-interest in a situation characterized by a mixture of co-operation and competition.

In *Theories of Justice* Barry contrasts justice as mutual advantage with the idea of justice as impartiality. Justice as impartiality is based upon the idea 'that justice should be the content of an agreement that would be reached by rational people under conditions that do not allow for bargaining power to be translated into advantage'.[19] This way of constructing the content prevents bargaining advantage from determining outcomes by refusing to identify a non-agreement point and treat it as a baseline from which only Pareto-superior departures can be justified. Moreover, the motive for acting justly on this conception is not self-interest. Instead, it is represented by a formula that Barry

---

[19] *Theories of Justice*, p. 7.

Table 2.1 Comparing theories of justice

Justice as mutual advantage	Justice as impartiality
1. Rules of justice enable joint interests to be advanced.	1. Rules of justice derive from the impartial point of view.
2. A baseline non-agreement point has to be defined from which only Pareto improvements are allowed.	2. There is no need to define a baseline point of non-agreement, and non-Pareto moves are allowed.
3. Hume's 'circumstances of justice' obtain, with moderate scarcity, moderate egoism and approximate equality of power.	3. The 'circumstances of impartiality' apply in the original position, with equal representation of all points of view.
4. Interests are aggregated.	4. Arguments are weighed.

borrows from Scanlon, namely that of acting on 'the desire to be able to justify one's actions to others on grounds they could not reasonably reject'.[20] Barry regards the desire to be able to justify one's conduct as an original principle of human behaviour, and affirms that 'the equation of rationality with the efficient pursuit of self-interest is … pure assertion'.[21] The key idea in this formulation, therefore, is that free and equal persons, placed in a situation in which they will have to defend the justice of their material and other possessions by argument, can be thought of as constrained by the notion of a reasonable agreement, in such a way that determinate principles of social justice will emerge from the process of discussion and debate. His own original position, then, is to be defined in terms of the circumstances that make for impartial discussion.

For Barry the theory of justice as impartiality implies a 'ground-floor egalitarianism',[22] so that proponents of unequal social arrangements will not be able to claim that their preferred patterns of society are consistent with principles that would be freely accepted by the disadvantaged. In short, justice as impartiality rests upon the requirement that a just arrangement is one which results from an equal consideration of interests. The logical differences, on Barry's exposition, between justice as mutual advantage and justice as impartiality can be conveniently summarized as in Table 2.1.

[20] Ibid., p. 284.
[21] Ibid., p. 285.
[22] Ibid., p. 348.

The distinction between the two types of theory is worked out by means of a reinterpretation of the works of Hume and Rawls. The link between these two theorists is found in the fact that Rawls accepts Hume's characterization of the 'circumstances of justice', that is the social conditions under which justice is an operative principle. According to Hume the circumstances of justice are ones in which there is moderate scarcity, moderate selfishness and an approximate equality of power. Acceptance of these conditions leads both Hume and Rawls to think of justice as a system of mutual advantage in which social co-operation makes it possible to reduce the extent of scarcity to which members of society are subject. But both theorists, according to Barry, also wish to characterize justice in terms of the impartial consideration of interests. It is this systematic ambiguity between the two approaches that Barry wishes to unpack. He argues that both theorists have elements of justice as mutual advantage and justice as impartiality in their accounts, and that in so far as they are wedded to the first conception they are unable to deal with key questions in the theory of justice. The most important of these questions is raised by the difficulty each of them has in providing an adequate theoretical account of convictions about intergenerational and international justice.

Whatever one may think of his expository claims (and my suspicion is that the centre of intellectual gravity in Hume is closer to the mutual advantage conception, whereas in Rawls the centre of gravity is closer to the impartial conception than Barry's exposition suggests), the main substantive point to emerge from the contrast seems unassailable. If we wish to give adequate weight to our reflective considerations about intergenerational and international justice, then the theory of justice as mutual advantage cannot be the whole of the story, and it cannot be taken as the foundation for a more general account. In other words, our construction of justice, whatever else it may do, must take a form other than that represented by a bargain to mutual advantage.

The reasoning behind this conclusion can be seen most clearly in the case of intergenerational justice. As a matter of logical necessity later generations do not enjoy even approximate equality of bargaining advantage with the present generation. (As Groucho Marx put it: why should we do anything for posterity, since posterity's never done anything for us?) If justice equals mutual advantage then there can be no justice between generations,[23] and Barry does a good job of showing that Rawls's attempt to finesse this difficulty by postulating a motive of concern by one generation for its immediate successor generations

---

[23] Ibid., p. 189.

will not overcome this problem. Hence, if we have well-founded concerns about intergenerational justice, the notion of mutual advantage is not going to be of much help. Since both environmentalists concerned about the long-term depletion of the earth's resources and market-orientated economists concerned about the future burden of present pension schemes have appealed to notions of intergenerational justice to support their preferred policy positions, it seems that Barry is on strong ground in using intuitions about intergenerational justice to cast doubt upon the adequacy of justice as a system of mutual advantage. An idea that so cuts across political divides represents a potent testing point for competing theories of justice.

If we cannot take the notion of mutual advantage as the starting-point for our theory of justice, what are we to make of Barry's suggested alternative, the notion of impartiality? Is the notion of impartiality sufficiently strong, when combined with assumptions about freedom and rationality, to generate the conclusions that Barry supposes? And if it is, does it need the contractarian device?

THE IMPARTIAL CONTRACT

A clear statement of the form of contract that Barry favours is to be found towards the beginning of *Justice as Impartiality*:

A theory of justice which makes it turn on the terms of reasonable agreement I call a theory of justice as impartiality. Principles of justice that satisfy its conditions are impartial because they capture a certain kind of equality: all those affected have to be able to feel that they have done as well as they could reasonably hope to (p. 7).

Later in the book, this idea is spelt out more fully by reference to Scanlon's test of morality, according to which an 'act is wrong under the circumstances if its performance would be disallowed by a set of rules for the general regulation of behaviour which no one could reasonably reject as a basis for informed, unforced general agreement' (p. 67). Barry makes it clear that he wishes this formula to be taken as defining justice, rather than morality in general, and that it could equally be as well rendered by a criterion of reasonable acceptance as by a test of reasonable non-rejection (pp. 68–70). It should also be clear that phrasing the requirement for agreement in terms of reasonableness rather than rationality is a way of distinguishing justice as impartiality from justice as mutual advantage.

Although Barry's appeal to the Scanlonian formulation of contract theory is continuous between *Theories of Justice* and *Justice as Impartiality*, there is one subtle, but important, shift of focus between the two works. *Theories of Justice* is typically concerned with questions of property and economic distribution, using as key examples problems of fair division and the dispossession from their lands of native peoples in North America. *Justice as Impartiality*, by contrast, is more focused on issues to do with civil and political liberties, most notably freedom of religion and freedom of sexual expression. The impartial rules that are supposed to emerge from the Scanlonian contract are therefore intended to provide a way in which citizens with competing conceptions of the good can nevertheless live together in society. It therefore marks an attempt to deal with a problem that I earlier suggested was implicit in the utilitarian tradition, namely how to make social decisions when there are divergent ways in which people could define their own conception of the good.

A clear statement of this ambition is provided in the following passage:

Justice as impartiality does not have any system for turning conceptions of the good into something else in order to bring them in relation to one another. Nor does it have a calculus for estimating the value of outcomes according to some common measure. How then does it put different conceptions of the good on an equal footing while leaving their status as conceptions of the good intact? It does so by insisting that, at the point where the basic principles and rules are being drawn up, no conception of the good should be given a privileged position. Putting the same idea less abstractly, we may say that nobody is allowed to assert the superiority of his own conception of the good over those of other people as a reason for building into the framework for social co-operation special advantages for it. This will not prevent people from pursuing their own conception of the good, in public life as well as private, but it will mean that they can do so only by means – casting votes, spending money, and exercising rights, for example – that are available to others on the same terms within a neutral constitutional framework. (pp. 160–1)

In this passage we see some of the characteristic features of Barry's conception of justice as it appears in *Justice as Impartiality*. The basic problem is that of how to sustain social co-operation in the face of competing conceptions of the good. The solution to this dilemma is to ensure that constitutional arrangements are such that they give no privileged status to any particular conception of the good, though adherents of any particular conception are free to seek to pursue their own views both in the public and the private realm.

Since the theory is intended to be constructivist, these requirements are supposed to follow from an analysis of what would be reasonable in the Scanlonian original position. Are social and political arrangements such that they could not be reasonably rejected by individuals in a situation of informed and unenforced agreement and under circumstances in which partisans of different conceptions of the good are desirous of reaching an agreement with one another? For Barry, this desire for agreement provides the motive for persons wishing to justify their preferred set of institutions to one another. Clearly, every-thing turns on how we are to gloss the term 'reasonable' here, and in particular on the question of whether we can offer a criterion for reasonableness that is neither circular nor tautological. However, rather than confront this problem of defining reasonableness directly, I think it will be more useful to look at the ways in which the supposed claims of reasonableness are actually worked out in the presentation of the theory.

If we look at the various examples that Barry offers of how this agreement might be worked out, then, there seem to be three main conjectures about the sorts of arguments that are available in the original position. The first sort of argument appeals to the principle that social institutions should avoid imposing unnecessary harms on individuals, where the harms are widely recognized according to a variety of conceptions of the good. For example, Barry argues that the parties to the hypothetical contract would reject a libertarian set of economic institutions on the grounds that these would not provide any safety net in the event of economic destitution (p. 203). From a variety of points of view, destitution is a harm, and almost everyone would have reason to fear the prospect of being reduced to destitution as a result of economic contingencies. Conversely, the reason why some paternalistic legislation – like the compulsory wearing of motorbike crash helmets – would *not* in itself be rejected in the hypothetical contract is that nobody can reasonably say that their lives are going to be blighted if they are forced to wear a crash helmet (p. 87). Finally, to take Barry's own running examples, religious and sexual freedom are to be built into constitutional arrangements, because, given the role that religious and sexual expression play in the way that people give meaning to their lives, parties to a hypothetical contract could reason-ably assert that their lives will be blighted if freedom is not allowed (p. 84).

If we ask what binds these rather diverse examples together, the answer is that they are all supposed to be cases in which vital interests are affected. They can thus be regarded as cases where absolute deprivation would result if certain rules were not rejected. Giving individuals a veto over the institution of social arrangements that work against their vital interests is thus a way of ensuring justice in social arrangements, whatever aggregate social advantages there might be in allowing absolute deprivation to occur. Justice for indi-viduals and minorities protects them from the consequences of aggre-gative reasoning.

The second form of argument that Barry envisages being used in the formulation of the hypothetical contract is one that points to un-fairness arising from relative disadvantages. For example, if one religion is established and others are not, then the adherents of those other religions may justifiably claim that they are placed at a disadvantage relative to adherents of the established religion, and they can reasonably reject such an arrangement. Note that this is logically a quite distinct argument from the previous one based on absolute deprivation. Relative deprivations may be unfair even when the disadvantage is suffered by those well above the level of absolute deprivation. Thus, adherents of a non-established religion suffer an unfairness if their religion does not receive the same protection as the established religion, even if they are free to practise their religion. For example, an established denomination may have privileged access to tax-based sources of finance or receive state support for its educational institutions which is denied to other denominations or religions. This will in itself be an injustice, even if the other denominations suffer no absolute deprivation because they are still free to worship and conduct their business. Injustice may exist, although departures from strict impartiality, like the existence of established churches in Great Britain or Scandinavia, make the injustice relatively unimportant, or, to use Barry's term, venial (p. 165, note c). In other words, relative and absolute deprivations are clearly distinct grounds for evaluating the justice of institutions.

The existence of either absolute or relative deprivation therefore indicates two possible sources of injustice that would enable contracting parties to veto certain social arrangements. Barry also suggests that a third reason for exercising the veto would be concern about the provision of public goods or collective benefits that could not be secured in the absence of government compulsion. According to Barry, contracting parties would veto any constitutional arrangements which prohibited the government from levying taxation for the purposes of providing public goods (p. 203). Such compulsory powers are needed to ensure that some citizens do not free ride on others by not making a voluntary contribution. The justificatory reasoning under this heading is double-barrelled therefore: society is better off with than without these public goods and fairness requires that all who benefit from the existence of such goods should make a contribution to their upkeep.

Putting these examples together it is easy to see how Barry's version of the contract argument is supposed to work. For any proposal to establish a set of social institutions, we ask first whether there is a set of people who would have grounds for objecting to the arrangement. If their objections are reasonable, in the sense that they can cite any of the three heads that I have identified, then the proposed institutions will be rejected. Only those institutions, if there are any, that cannot be rejected in this way are to be counted as just.

All of this still leaves the notion of reasonableness in the original position undefined, and Barry himself offers us no single criterion for reasonableness in the sense in which he intends it. In order to work towards what I take to be his notion, I shall consider some contrast cases in terms of possible methods of reasoning that might be available to the parties in the original position.

Clearly, the 'reasonable' cannot mean the 'rational' in the game-theoretic sense in which an agent's choice is rational if it maximizes a utility function. This sense cannot be meant since, if this is all that is involved, the contract would emerge logically as a Nash equilibrium, and justice as impartiality would reduce to justice as mutual advantage. To take just one example, there is no sense, within this notion of rationality, in which guestworkers are being irrational if they accept less than equal terms with domestic workers as a condition for their right to work in a labour market, although such an arrangement might well be considered unjust from the point of view of a reasonable contract negotiated under circumstances of impartiality.

A possible second sense of reasonable might be the sense in which it is used in English law in the notion of the 'reasonable man'. This legal notion gets away from the purely instrumental notion of rationality that we find in game theory, and so avoids the reduction of justice as impartiality to justice as mutual advantage. But of course the meaning of 'reasonable' in this sense is given by reference to prevailing norms of belief and behaviour, and so is not easily used as part of an intellectual device to establish such norms. For example, the law of contract has developed rules for dealing with cases of contractual failure due to circumstances beyond the control of the contracting parties, but what is allowed to count as a reasonable breach of contract will depend heavily upon the social context within which the contract was originally made, and what inferences people might be entitled to draw about performance given that context. When reasonableness is thus defined by reference to a prevailing set of institutions, it is difficult to use the notion to evaluate that set of institutions.

A third sense of reasonable turns on the idea that the agreement that is negotiated will only involve modest compromises of their interests by the parties from within their conception of the good. This sense of reasonable is certainly compatible with the stress upon the need within a just society to avoid imposing absolute deprivations on particular sets of individuals. However, it seems to work less well given the way in which the principle of avoiding relative deprivations also seems central. If no one is allowed to assert the superiority of their own conception of the good in defining the basic structure of political and social organization, it may well be that this involves quite large compromises on the part of some of the contracting parties. For example, adherents of conceptions of the good that have been given

historically privileged status may have to give up much in order
to implement principles of justice, and fundamentalist members of
certain religions, to whom it may seem very important that their
religion receives special privileges, will be disallowed from claiming
any special privileges by virtue of the Scanlonian formulation, perhaps
taking them a long way from the ideal point. In both sorts of case there
is a sense in which a large concession is made, but it is required by the
principles of impartial justice.

So the reasonableness of the parties in Barry's original position
cannot be defined in any of the above ways. A more interesting contrast emerges, however, if we take the notion of reasonableness and
put it alongside Hare's notion of universalizability. Hare's test of universalizability says that in making a proposal you must be prepared to
see it applied to you, even if it works to your own advantage. Hare
notes that on occasions the 'fanatic' will accept just these implications.[24] The Nazi will say that he would be prepared to see anti-
Jewish legislation, even if it should turn out that he is a Jew. Of course,
the role-reversal test may be *psychologically* destabilizing for such
a person, but Hare is right, I think, to claim that it is not *logically*
destabilizing. The Nazi, strictly speaking, is committing no logical
inconsistency in asserting his fanaticism.

By contrast, there is no room for the fanatic's principles on the test
of the Barry contract. To see this consider the previous example again.
Suppose that one religious group is putting forward a rule for general
acceptance which privileges its own position. Any other group that is
similarly situated can veto the adoption of such a rule, since they can
argue that it is their disadvantage in an unreasonable way. If the veto
works in the relatively simple case of religious disadvantage, it will
also surely work in the case of persecution or extermination. Thus, by
comparison with Hare's universalizability criterion, no hypothetical
test of role-reversal is called for in the Barry original position. Instead,
within the assumed construction, we simply posit groups who can veto
such a proposal.

It is built into Barry's original position that one important motive in
the contractual negotiation is the desire to put forward principles that
everyone can accept. In other words, the approach goes beyond Harean
universalizability in another way. On the Hare test each person is
supposed to ask in making a claim of moral principle: how would I like
it if this were done to me? On the Barry original position test, each

<hr />

[24] R. M. Hare, *Freedom and Reason*, Oxford, 1963, ch. 9. It is interesting to note that
Hare subsequently claimed that an impartialist version of the universalizability test
would avoid this problem. See R. M. Hare, 'Ethical Theory and Utilitarianism', in
Utilitarianism and Beyond, ed. Amartya Sen and Bernard Williams, Cambridge, 1982,
pp. 23–38, p. 29.

person or group proposing a principle is supposed to say: is this something that is acceptable to others on reasonable terms? Barry discusses this under the heading of the 'agreement motive', which is said to arise from the desire to live in a society whose members all freely accept its rules of justice and its major institutions (p. 164). Barry holds that this agreement motive, combined with a sense of scepticism about the extent to which adherents to a particular conception of the good can vindicate their beliefs to others, is sufficient to lead to impartialist conclusions of the sort he endorses.

It is possible to render the agreement motive in another idiom as the principle of equal respect. This is clear from Barry's discussion of Larmore on the principle of equal respect, where it is made clear that Larmore's attempt to derive a principle of toleration from the principle of equal respect provides 'a backing for the agreement motive' (p. 177). Barry is right to hold, I think, that the principle of equal respect alone is insufficient to yield a principle of toleration, since those convinced of the rightness of their beliefs may think that they are showing respect to those who disagree by bringing non-believers to the truth, even if this entails using forcible means. But it is equally true that acceptance of scepticism alone will not yield a principle of toleration either, since this would be compatible with an attitude that, since we cannot know the truth of any conception of the good, we might as well impose any conception of the good that was likely to succeed in securing adherence.

Impartialist tolerance can therefore be seen to follow from the conjunction of two principles: equal respect and scepticism. Reasonableness in the original position is simply a way of representing the conjunction of these two principles. Reasonableness therefore means that parties in the original position do not think of themselves as infallible, and in making proposals for the basic structure of social and political organization they seek to act in a way in which they accept the burden of justifying their own point of view to others.

But if we accept this construal of the notion of reasonableness, it brings us to the central question of method. How far does the contractual device advance the argument over the first-order assertion of the importance of equal respect and scepticism combined? In other words, how far are we dealing with a genuinely constructivist account of justice? In his article on 'Contractualism and Utilitarianism' Scanlon says that we have the subject of moral philosophy for much the same reasons that we have the subject of the philosophy of mathematics.[25] If this analogy is taken seriously, it suggests that the criterion of justice need only satisfy formal conditions, provided that it

[25] T. M. Scanlon, 'Contractualism and Utilitarianism', in *Utilitarianism and Beyond*, eds Amartya Sen and Bernard Williams, Cambridge, 1982, p. 104.

yielded results in conformity with the test of 'reflective equilibrium', just as the axiomatic structures of mathematics need to satisfy formal conditions if they are to do their job of generating theorems. The heart of contractualism as a method is that it is supposed to provide us with a formal device that, though it represents certain moral principles, provides us with a pattern of deduction in moral reasoning that can be identified separately from our first-order moral reasoning. It is the adequacy of the model in Barry's formulation to perform this function that I contest. To see this, we need to examine the role of the principle of equal respect in the theory of justice and the extent to which it is adequately represented by symmetry in the original position.

DECONSTRUCTING THE ORIGINAL POSITION

I have argued that for Barry reasonableness in the original position means accepting that one must advance arguments that abide by the twin constraints of accepting the principle of equal respect and avoiding the assumption of infallibility. I have already noted (pp. 19–20) that one of the shifts between *Theories of Justice* and *Justice as Impartiality* is a greater focus in the latter on problems of toleration by comparison with problems of economic justice in the former. This contrast suggests an interesting test for constructivism. We might ask: what is gained by recasting the argument from equal respect and scepticism in terms of the agreement motive combined with an assumption of no infallibility? One answer might be that we move towards a unified theory of justice, that is a theory that shows how intuitions about civil and political liberties can be linked with intuitions about the importance of redistribution. If the contractarian construction of justice could show that a free society had the same intellectual rationale as an economically fair society, that would certainly be a construction worth having. Unfortunately, it seems to me that the constructivist device is simply too indeterminate when it comes to matters of economic justice to accomplish this unification, and this is so for a number of reasons.

The first point to make about the Barry original position is that it will not of itself rule out an appeal to principles of mutual advantage of the sort that justice as impartiality is supposed to be contrasted with. To see why this is so, consider what Barry himself says about the relationship between bargaining and arbitration in the type of problem that Nash established. Barry says that resort to arbitration in the bargaining problem would just be another way of arriving at the same result as bargaining itself, including results in which relative advantage was preserved in the move from the non-agreement point to a negotiated principle.[26] This is surely correct. No arbitrator could realistically expect to depart from the allocation that would result from a process of rational bargaining, since no arbitrator would have reason to believe that any recommended outcome that departed from the putative negotiation would stick. The person who expected to do relatively well from negotiation would simply rule out resort to arbitration if arbitration threatened those gains. Does this mean that an arbitrator who followed the putative negotiated solution would be behaving less than impartially? In any common acceptance of the term it is difficult to see that she would be. The arbitrator is not showing favouritism to either of the parties; she is merely trying to ensure that the proposed allocation is feasible and will stick.

Moreover, there are some common ways of preserving initial advantages in agreements that seem fair to many people. For example, members of a partnership might adopt the principle of making returns proportionate to contributions in determining their relative shares from their collective efforts, making income depend upon the proportion of equity capital that each partner has invested. Acting in accordance with such a principle is not *ipso facto* acting with partiality. Indeed, a wide range of principles of distribution, including many forms of allocation according to marginal contributions, appear to be compatible with impartial consideration in this sense.

Barry's concept of impartiality is intended to be stronger than that of avoiding personal favouritism within an established system of rules. An impartial process of allocation, he seems to want to argue, ought simply to exclude certain grounds on which persons could lay claim to resources as being irrelevant. Impartiality would thus mean that certain advantages, for example the advantage of being born earlier in a sequence of generations, will not be an acceptable reason for allocating resources more favourably to one person than to another. Impartiality of consideration ought to yield an equality of allocation once irrelevant considerations, like natural endowments of bargaining advantages, are abstracted away.

Quite a lot at this point, however, will turn on how we evaluate the initial pattern of advantages, and in particular whether we think of them as arising from good fortune or injustice. To say that some people simply enjoy the good fortune of certain advantages provides no argument in itself for the redistribution of resources to those who are less favoured. Even if we say that those who suffer misfortune have a claim in justice to some compensation, the precise import of this claim is not easy to determine. I suspect that when this question arose in any original position, the contracting parties would soon fall to discussing

---

[26] Barry, *Theories of Justice*, pp. 24–8.

the extent to which maintaining one's sense of self-respect in a society depended upon a certain sense of economic security. In other words, they would have exactly the same conversation that we can have outside the original position in our own societies, and once we can predict the conclusion of our own conversation, we have no need to resort to the device of a hypothetical original position.

Moreover, Barry's construction of the original position is less amenable than Rawls's original position to representing the abstraction from considerations of natural endowment that can underlie arguments about redistribution. Barry neatly shows that it is possible to derive the difference principle, the principle that inequalities are just provided they work to the benefit of the least advantaged, without the Rawlsian devices of the original position and the veil of ignorance by appealing to the Rawlsian idea that certain grounds for the allocation of scarce goods are 'arbitrary from the moral point of view'.[27] It is certainly true that, once we allow the idea of grounds for claims being arbitrary from the moral point of view, we thereby have a powerful critical principle, but the force of the principle depends, as David Lyons[28] has pointed out, upon the assumption that every ground of desert must itself be deserved, and this is far from being a self-evident principle of justice.

Within the framework of Rawls's veil of ignorance the irrelevance of social circumstances and personal qualities had an obvious rationale in terms of the unpredictability of the process that projects contracting parties from the original position into the real world. In the absence of these Rawlsian contraptions, however, it is not clear why a hard-headed desert theorist should feel obliged to accept the infinite regress of the principle that every ground of desert must itself be deserved. It is by no means obvious that the designation of certain human characteristics as deserving of reward, even though the characteristics were not themselves deserved, is self-contradictory or absurd, although such an attitude raises difficult and controversial questions about the role of moral perfectionism in moral theory. It is, of course, possible to undercut the position of the desert theorist by holding to some substantive principle of equal respect that would *ipso facto* make certain grounds for desert, for example highly marketable abilities, irrelevant to the allocation of scarce goods, but then one is engaging in a different sort of argument from simply invoking the notion of personal characteristics being arbitrary from the moral point of view. Only with a first-order principle of equality, ascribing equal moral worth to persons who

---

[27] Ibid., pp. 217–34.
[28] David Lyons, 'Nature and Soundness of the Contract and Coherence Arguments', *Reading Rawls*, ed. N. Daniels, Oxford, 1975, p. 158.

are thereby entitled to dignity in terms of the basic circumstances of their lives, can one rule out certain contingencies and advantages as relevant to the allocation of scarce goods and commodities.

The original position with knowledge of personal circumstances will support a weak sort of egalitarianism, one in which arguments have to be uniformly applied across different types of interests, but it will not support some of the stronger egalitarian conclusions that Barry wishes to derive. In saying this, I am suggesting that Barry has not succeeded in one of his central methodological ambitions, namely to produce a theory that is constructivist in character, a theory in which people choose principles in appropriate circumstances of impartiality, and the objects of their choice are to be counted *ipso facto* as principles of justice. Any constructivist theory is attractive to the extent that it contains an element of surprise, rather as though you were getting a colour signal from a black and white broadcast. In other words, what comes out at the end should not have been deliberately put in at the beginning. By insisting that justice as impartiality needs a substantive principle of equality, I am undermining this ambition. After all, it does not seem very difficult to see how a concern for equality would lead one to favour the redistribution of economic and political power on grounds of justice. Indeed, it might be argued that if a concern for equality did not lead one to a concern for redistribution then there was something wrong with the theory.

One way of seeing the divergence between methodological ambition and substantive conclusion is to note the way in which the principle of equality is introduced into the putative reasoning of the parties in the original position via the notion of 'human decency', a concern that was clearly articulated in a passage in *Theories of Justice*:

> There must ... be some shared understanding of what counts as a convincing case, and everyone must be prepared to concede that his position is untenable if a sound argument is made against it ... We are thus, if you like, presupposing that it is possible to define a basic attitude of what you might call human decency, which can be imputed to the people in our original position. They do not have to be completely detached from their own interests – we should, indeed, do better not to attribute that kind of impartiality to the 'agents of construction' – but they do have to be prepared to view themselves as one among others, to borrow Adam Smith's formulation.[29]

Yet unless we are given an independent test of what reasoning is consistent with the requirement of thinking of ourselves as 'one among others', this view simply reduces to the requirement that any principles of justice should preserve a requirement of common human dignity. Substantively this is surely unexceptional, but it is misleading to say that it is modelled unambiguously with the construction of an

---

[29] Barry, *Theories of Justice*, pp. 352–3.

original position. It is clear that the demands of justice go beyond the bounds of formal symmetry in the treatment of competing claims. But the device of construction does not seem to have a feature that formally captures this notion of some minimum respect due to all persons as such.

The formal situation of the parties in the original position might be able to capture this moral sense of equality if we could appeal to a certain presumption of equality as built into patterns of distributive reasoning. There is an old idea that inequality without a reason is somehow irrational. As Sir Isaiah Berlin once put it:

> If I have a cake and there are ten persons among whom I wish to divide it, then if I give exactly one tenth to each, this will not, at any rate automatically, call for justification; whereas if I depart from this principle of equal division I am expected to produce a special reason.[30]

But I have argued elsewhere that this sort of procedural equality cannot form the basis for any strong egalitarian conception of justice, and may even be inconsistent with it, since the reason that may justify the departure from equal treatment may well consist of an attempt to bring about equality of condition from an initial situation of inequality.[31] The problem is that impartiality is a procedural concept, whereas any principle of allocation is substantive.

In fact, I doubt that Barry really thinks about his original position as having a constructivist role independently of first-order moral considerations in the typical case. Consider what he says about Scanlon's distinction between acceptance and non-rejection for example (p. 70). Scanlon had argued that his test of wrongness was to be phrased in terms of a system of rules that could not reasonably be rejected under informed and uncoerced conditions. The reason for Scanlon's formulation was to exclude agreement through what we may term 'false consciousness' or a willingness to allow one's good nature to be exploited by others. It may be reasonable for the good natured to allow themselves to be exploited, in the sense that we could not reject the reasonableness of a position that did not allow itself to be exploited in this way.

Barry wishes to argue that what is really going on here is the imposition of a substantive requirement of fairness to the effect that it is unfair for the generous to be exploited by the hard-hearted at the point at which general rules are being laid down. Here, I think, he is right. It surely is unfair, at a first-order level, to allow this to happen. But Scanlon is surely also right to insist that the only way to represent

---

[30] I. Berlin, 'Equality', *Proceedings of the Aristotelian Society*, New Series, lvi (1956), 305.

[31] A. Weale, *Equality and Social Policy*, London, 1978, ch. 2.

this within the device of construction that the original position is supposed to be is in terms of the distinction between agreement and non-agreement. Otherwise we are not giving an independent status to the original position, but simply using it to stand as a metaphor for moral requirements of a substantive sort that we believe to be justified in their own terms.

THE EMPIRICAL METHOD

However, we are not quite out of the woods yet in terms of under-mining the constructivist ambitions of *Justice as Impartiality*. Barry suggests one important way in which we might secure the force of the principle of equality without invoking it as an explicit assumption, via the idea of open representation within a democratic process. Towards the end of *Theories of Justice* Barry has some interesting speculations on the relationship between political argument, moral motivation and the institutional structure of a political system. Posing the question of how we could know what types of agreement could not be reasonably rejected, Barry suggests that we can use one of two methods, the a priori and the empirical.

The a priori method consists of asking whether there are things that nobody could reasonably accept in the original position in the absence of coercion or misinformation, but he accepts that, though not tooth-less, the a priori method may not always get us very far. Hence, the alternative, empirical, method is called for, which Barry describes in a passage worth quoting at length:

The empirical method starts from observation rather than pure thought. It is animated by the consideration that actual societies approximate more or less closely the conditions ... that I shall refer to for convenience as 'the circum-stances of impartiality'. Thus, a society in which each section of the population has its own organizations and organs of communication to articulate its interests and aspirations is closer to the circumstances of impartiality than one in which, say, business is well organized but labour is not, and in which almost all the organs of mass communication are owned and controlled by the rich. Similarly, a political system in which parties represent the distinctive interests and aspirations of different groups is closer to the circumstances of impartiality than one in which all successful candidates have either to have money or to be acceptable to those who have it. Again, a society in which there is a good deal of fellow feeling for other citizens will be closer to the cir-cumstances of impartiality than one in which many people are unmoved by the lot of sections of the population with which they do not identify. And, finally, a culture in which politics is widely regarded as a matter of debate rather than as a game – where arguments are thought of as more than the window-dressing for self-interest – will obviously be closer to the circumstances of impartiality.[32]

---

[32] Barry, *Theories of Justice*, pp. 347–8.

The passage goes on to make it clear that the best existing approximation to the circumstances of impartiality in this sense is to be found in the Scandinavian countries. The same idea is picked up in *Justice as Impartiality*, where it is said that it is possible to set out procedures of a kind familiar within many liberal democratic systems that will produce an empirical approximation of a Scanlonian original position by making it harder for rules that can be reasonably rejected to be adopted (p. 104).

The use made of the notion of the circumstances of impartiality is, in my opinion, one of the most interesting and potentially fruitful parts of the theory. Roughly speaking, if it can be made to work, it means that, whereas Rawls was able to make use of the economic conception of rationality to characterize with some plausibility what would happen in an abstract situation of choice, Barry would be able to make use of empirical evidence from political science to characterize, again with some plausibility, what would happen in his less abstract original position.

There are two ways of interpreting the relationship between democratic equality of the type that Barry here describes and the theory of social justice. On one interpretation the outcomes from decision processes characterized in terms of democratic equality are an analogue of just arrangements defined on other grounds. This would be an epistemic interpretation, since the function of the analogue would be to help us to know what constituted justice as defined by other independent procedures. On the second interpretation the outcomes from these decision processes are constitutive of just arrangements, and democratic processes provide another route to the establishment of what just arrangements are. This then would be a criterial interpretation, since the presumed outcome of open democratic processes would be one allowable test for establishing what justice was.

Barry makes clear that he wants his account to be taken in the epistemic sense, but that on either interpretation we should note that the outcomes arising from open democratic processes cannot be taken as being identical with the notion of reasonable agreement in the original position (pp. 195–9). This is surely right. Democratic processes are compatible with continuing disagreement on the merits of the alternatives confronting the members of a society, the participants to democratic processes agreeing only that the issue has to be settled for practical purposes and being willing to accept a certain range of procedures as appropriate for settling their disputes. The notion of reasonable agreement, however, implies the notion of consensus on some point of view, so that in a sense no more issues remain to be resolved.

Another difference between the ideas of reasonable agreement in the original position and the outcome of the democratic processes is that the former dispenses with any notion of power apart from the power of argument, whereas the latter requires a positive conception of what rough equality of political power might involve, especially in regard to its organizational and institutional bases. There is a danger of circularity in using some idea of approximate equality of political power to define a construction in which decisions were taken to be indicative or definitive of justice. Since not every legitimate interest will necessarily be organized, the only way that we can know whereto all interests are properly represented is to have some independent idea of the range of legitimate interests, and then observe whether they are articulated within the political process.

However, I think the most intractable difficulty for Barry at this point is that the examples of democratic practice to which he refers may well be incompatible with the assumption about neutrality and conceptions of the good that it is such a central part of *Justice as Impartiality*. The relevant point has been well made here by Fritz Scharpf in a discussion of policy decision rules.[33] In a contrast between bargaining and problem-solving styles of policy-making that is remarkably parallel to Barry's distinction between justice as mutual advantage and justice as impartiality, Scharpf points out that the emergence of problem-solving modes of policy making involves certain institutional and cultural preconditions. Although the common orientations needed for a problem-solving style may be rooted in a generalized altruism, they are more likely to stem from the perception of a common identity 'defined in terms of an ethnic or cultural homogeneity or a "community of fate" derived from shared perceptions of a common history, or of a common "manifest destiny" (or common ideological goals), or of a common vulnerability'[34] and it is clear that it is these factors that have underlain the decision-making practices of the smaller European democracies, including those in Scandinavia. What this may suggest, therefore, is that preconditions for economic justice may preclude the sort of neutrality about conceptions of the good that it is such a large part of *Justice as Impartiality* to justify.

CONCLUSION

I have argued that the constructivist character of Barry's theory is an attempt to overcome a problem of pluralistic intuitions as that

---

[33] Fritz W. Scharpf, 'The Joint-Decision Trap: Lessons from German Federalism and European Integration', *Public Administration*, 66 (1988), 239–78.

[34] Ibid., p. 261.

developed in the great tradition of British political thought. Contract theory, conceived as a constructivist device, is to be thought of as a second-order way of representing the justification and rationalization of principles that at the first-order level appear plural, complex and conflicting. I have also argued that the constructivist ambitions of the theory are not achieved. There is no way of using the social contract device to resolve the problems that putative first-order principles of justice give rise to. What conclusions follow from this claim?

One possible conclusion is that some theorist should have a go at reconstructing yet another version of contract theory that will overcome these difficulties. Personally, I do not see much future in this. A *Treatise on Social Justice* runs over pretty much most of the ground of recent attempts, and if its own construction does not do the job, I cannot see that someone else's will. If minds as good as Rawls, Gauthier and Barry have not by now come up with a plausible version of contract theory – one that really does yield implications from the device of construction in line with our considered judgements while also providing some ethical systematization – I do not see anyone else doing it. I cite as evidence for this view the fact that in *Political Liberalism* Rawls has in effect abandoned the contract argument and made his own theory rest on a particular conception of society as a scheme of fair co-operation among free and equal citizens.[35]

The second conclusion I draw is that we ought to distinguish far more clearly than has been the case in recent political theory between claims about the origin of a political principle and claims about its weight. One of the problems with social contract theory is that its very formulation – the attempt to state ground rules for forms of social organization in an a priori formulation – inclines people towards unsustainable statements, for example that justice is the first virtue of social institutions. Justice is important, but do we really want to say that small anomalies giving rise to injustice, like the existence of historically established religions, are more important to rectify than the civilizing of public discourse or the protection of cultural and natural heritages? Greater pluralism about principles might lead to a better balance in the discussion of public policies and public institutions more generally.

Thirdly, in intellectual terms, I think we are back to the doctrine of *Political Argument*. One of the considerable virtues of that book was the mapping of the first-order arguments that pervade political and public choice. Moreover, the intuitionist intellectual tradition that it reflected needs more development than it has received in recent years. Why not begin again where Hume left off?

[35] John Rawls, *Political Liberalism*, New York, 1993, esp. at pp. 15–22 and *passim*.

3

Rational, Fair and Reasonable

JONATHAN WOLFF

There can be no doubt that Brian Barry has made an enormous contribution to the clarification of the ideas of justice current in contemporary political thought. In Barry's *Justice as Impartiality* he explicitly distinguishes and sets in competition three models of justice: justice as mutual advantage; justice as reciprocity; and justice as impartiality (the 'rational', 'fair' and 'reasonable' of my title), and he argues that we should prefer the last of these. What I want to do here is to consider four questions. First, what is this competition a competition about? Second, has Barry adequately characterized the contenders? Third, can the competition be won on the grounds Barry suggests? Fourth, is it a competition that we should want to be won by a single theory? By contrast I want to argue that there are advantages in retaining a pluralist perspective in which all three approaches remain in play.

Barry's competition, clearly, is over the question of which of the approaches provides the best theory of justice. But what is a theory of justice, as Barry understands the term? It is clear that it is not meant to be a mere reconstruction of our ordinary ideas of justice, but at the same time it cannot be completely divorced from our intuitions. The closest Barry seems to come to an explicit statement occurs in the following passage:

Once we ask for some justification of social and political institutions that can be presented for the approval of each person's reason, we are launched on a journey that must, I contend, proceed along the lines of the argument of this book. (p. 6)

Barry's claim, then, is that of the three approaches he distinguishes, only justice as impartiality can present a justification of social and political institutions that will find approval with each (reasonable) person's reason.

What seems to me the structural crux of Barry's argument in favour of justice as impartiality, and against the other two approaches, is provided in a passage which is presented as a summary of some earlier arguments:

Let me suggest, then, that a theory of justice may be characterized by its answers to three questions. First, what is the motive (are the motives) for behaving justly? Secondly, what is the criterion (are the criteria) for a just set of rules? And thirdly, how are the answers to the first two questions connected? We want to know exactly how somebody with the stipulated motive(s) for behaving justly would be led to comply with rules that are just according to the stipulated criterion or criteria. A theory of justice that cannot answer the third question satisfactorily fails on the ground of internal inconsistency. (p. 46)

Immediately one might ask whether a theory of justice should do any more than answer the second question, but I shall leave that until later. My reason for introducing this passage is to show how it enables us both to set out the distinctions Barry wants to make between the three approaches to justice, and also to understand his arguments against the two unfavoured options, both of which are claimed to be internally inconsistent.

Justice as mutual advantage, suggests Barry,

answers the first question by saying that the motive for complying with the constraints imposed by rules of justice is that this is, taking a long view, a more effective way of advancing one's conception of the good than in not complying with these rules. The answer to the second question is that a set of rules is just if general compliance with the rules would be more advantageous to everybody (in terms of each person's conception of the good) than the alternative of a 'state of nature' in which everybody pursued their conceptions of the good without any constraints. (p. 46)

The third question, Barry argues, does not have an adequate answer. However one twists and turns, there will be circumstances in which the long-term advancement of one's conception of the good – for some people at least – is better pursued by acting unjustly. Thus, by the test Barry has set up, justice as mutual advantage is internally inconsistent.

Barry presents justice as reciprocity as an attempt to improve upon this difficulty. It retains the same answer to the second question: justice is mutual advantage. Its innovation is to provide a distinct motivation for acting justly: people are motivated by the idea of 'fair dealing'. Barry presents this theory by means of Gibbard's version of it,[1] and the problem he finds stems from the fact that Gibbard (so says Barry) does not provide a substantive theory of fairness. What strikes parties as fair will depend on local practices, 'salient' outcomes, and arbitrary appearances of symmetry. Thus, Barry claims that ultimately anything actually agreed will count, on this theory, as 'fair', so no real advance is made over the previous theory. In particular the theory is again claimed to be internally inconsistent, failing to show

[1] Allan Gibbard, *Wise Choices, Apt Feelings*, Oxford, 1990.

why everyone motivated by fair dealing will be motivated to accept as just whatever deal is actuated, whatever its conditions.

This argument is, perhaps, less clear than the previous one, and I am not completely confident that I have understood it. But before commenting further, I want to set out how Barry's favoured theory answers the three questions. First, the motive is to act fairly. Second, justice requires fairness: what can be agreed on by equally well-placed parties. Third, motive and rules of justice 'fit together perfectly': people motivated to act fairly will seek to act on rules that are fair – provided, at least that enough others do so too.

Before assessing Barry's arguments I want to take issue with some of the things Barry says to characterize the three types of theory in play. To do so might seem rather odd: why cannot Barry characterize the theories however he wishes? But I do not think that Barry sees himself as having invented the theories under discussion. The three approaches – in outline at least – are broadly familiar, and so there is a question of whether Barry has provided the most accurate account of them. Now, I have no quibble with his characterization of justice as mutual advantage, but I think that there are difficulties in the other two cases.

Barry formulates his version of justice as impartiality in terms initially borrowed from Scanlon,[2] representing Scanlon as proposing an alternative 'original position' to Rawls: 'One in which well-informed people in a situation of equal power (guaranteed by each having a veto) seek to reach agreement with others who are similarly motivated on terms that cannot be reasonably rejected' (p. 10).

My feeling is that talk of a veto and equal power here is inappropriate (and an unfortunate departure from Scanlon's own position). The background thought behind justice as impartiality is that a just outcome is one that could be agreed to by people who seek, and value the idea of being able, to justify their behaviour to others, provided that those others are reasonable. One can reject a proposal only if it is unreasonable. That is, I can exercise any veto I might have only with the agreement of others, if they accept that I am being treated unreasonably. But this is a way of saying that I do not have a veto. If others do not feel I am being treated unreasonably, then I am stuck. We might even say that the collective holds a veto which it can exercise on behalf of individuals who lack the right to do so themselves. Furthermore, power differentials seem irrelevant.

Now it might be that if we ever wish to implement the idea of justice as impartiality, then we will have to provide institutional safeguards

---

[2] T. Scanlon, 'Contractualism and Utilitarianism', in *Utilitarianism and Beyond*, ed. Amartya Sen and Bernard Williams, Cambridge, 1982, pp. 103–28.

to make sure that those who have the *wrong motivation* cannot prosper by exploiting others' good will. At this point we might want to insist that everyone has a veto, or, perhaps, only those with a weak bargaining position. But in other cases majority rule will drain everyone of bargaining strength and be more likely to produce an impartial outcome. My main point, though, is that Barry's insistence that the idea of a veto should be part of the foundational characterization of justice as impartiality is seriously misleading.

And I think there is something more misleading still about the representation of justice as reciprocity. As Barry presents the theory, it is a view in which justice is relative to bargaining strength (as with justice as mutual advantage) but dignified by the fact that parties so bargaining believe any resulting agreement to be 'fair'. As so presented, the proposal seems devoid of interest. However, Gibbard has suggested that Rawls's theory should be thought of as a theory of justice as reciprocity,[3] and Rawls has endorsed this description.[4] Yet the account of justice as reciprocity given is unrecognizable as Rawls's theory, or, indeed, any theory anyone would wish to hold. What has gone wrong?

There are, I think, two things to say. First, Rawls is almost certainly mistaken about how to describe his theory in Barry's terms (and Barry's distinction between first-order and second-order impartiality should prevent such misunderstandings in the future). But second, Barry is equally at fault. It is important to note that justice as mutual advantage and justice as impartiality are presented as *types* of theories, of which there can be many importantly different variants. Justice as reciprocity is considered in one – highly eccentric – version and as presented hardly can be said to exhaust the idea of reciprocity.

What can we do to do better? If, on the one hand, justice as mutual advantage makes justice relative to bargaining strength, and justice as impartiality takes justice to be the outcome of a hypothetical reasonable agreement, what is the natural mid-point between these theories? I suggest that we should consider the idea of justice as relative to contribution as the real core of justice as reciprocity.[5] This provides a basic notion of fair return, distinct from the two other theories.

---

[3] Allan Gibbard, 'Constructing Justice', *Philosophy and Public Affairs*, xx (1991), 264–79.

[4] John Rawls, *Political Liberalism*, New York, 1993, p. 17n.

[5] On arriving in the United States on a Fellowship in 1985 I was treated to a lecture by a political journalist who claimed that a new mood of 'reciprocity' was blowing through America. I expected to be given examples – as were under discussion in the UK at the time – involving new schemes for awarding ordinary employees shares in the companies in which they worked. Instead I was told about the idea of requiring beneficiaries of welfare benefits to perform community service. Both proposals, though, appeal to the idea of making benefits conform to burdens.

It differs from justice as mutual advantage as long as we are careful to distinguish bargaining strength from contribution. Some will think that this distinction cannot be made: what you can contribute determines bargaining strength. But that view is in error. One need only think of Hume's examples of farm animals. They make a large contribution to our welfare (we eat them, and in Hume's day they pulled our ploughs), but have no bargaining strength because they have no threat.[6] We can get what we want from them whether or not they agree. Now I do not want to consider the question of whether we owe animals a duty of justice; all I wish to say is that we can distinguish threat advantage from contribution, even if, in many cases, they are strongly related. Thus justice as reciprocity – understood as justice as fair return – is distinct from justice as mutual advantage.

And again, while it might often be co-extensive in its results with justice as impartiality, justice as reciprocity, so understood, is quite distinct. The main distinction is that, while reciprocity distributes according to contribution, impartiality investigates the question of what enables individuals to make a contribution. Justice as reciprocity, in contrast to justice as impartiality, shares with justice as mutual advantage the (quite unattractive) feature that those with nothing to contribute, such as the handicapped, are excluded from the concerns of justice. This is one reason why I would not want to say that it represents the highest idea of justice. But it does represent one idea of justice with important applications. (For example, I think it is on such a basis that we must argue for the 'principle of fairness'.) So Barry's failure to consider such a theory, and to consider what he presents as Gibbard's version of justice as reciprocity instead, seems odd indeed.

If Barry had discussed this theory, what could he have said against it? Could it be represented as internally inconsistent? I do not immediately see how. But then, I do not agree that such a criticism, at least in the style presented by Barry, is as damaging as he suggests.

This may seem a surprising claim. Surely, it will be said, there can be nothing worse than an inconsistent theory. Not only is it false in the actual world; it is false in all possible worlds. Now this is correct – if a theory really is internally inconsistent. But I doubt very much that Barry has shown any such thing.

Let us concentrate on Barry's clearest example: justice as mutual advantage. The argument has the following stages:

1. Any theory of justice has three parts: an account of the motivation to act justly; a criterion of justice; and an account of how

---

[6] David Hume, *Enquiries*, ed. L. A. Selby-Bigge, 3rd ed., Oxford, 1975, pp. 190–1.

anyone with the assumed motivation would be motivated to act justly, so defined.
2. Any theory that cannot provide an account to satisfy the third part is internally inconsistent.
3. Justice as mutual advantage cannot provide such an account.
4. Therefore justice as mutual advantage is internally inconsistent.

Now 4 is validly deduced from the earlier premises, and I am prepared to grant 3. But 1 and 2 seem problematic. I am not sure exactly where best to locate the weakness, but the first thing to say is that it is far from obvious that a theorist of justice need say anything at all about motivation. Why not claim that the definition of justice is a political question, but the issue of motivation is a psychological one? We would hope to be able to link the two, but it might be no more than that: a mere hope. So I would deny that Barry has shown that any theory of justice is internally inconsistent. Or, if he has, he has provided a motivation for a theorist of justice to moderate his or her ambitions, and make a strict distinction between questions of justice and questions of motivation.

So Barry's argument does not show that justice as mutual advantage is internally inconsistent. What does it show? I think he has shown that it is unstable. It cannot be relied upon in the long term. Sooner or later someone will have a powerful motive to act unjustly, and if this happens often enough, the system will unravel. Now the question is whether this is enough to refute the theory of justice as mutual advantage.

One prior question, though, is what advantages does Barry think justice as impartiality has in this respect? His answer is that the motivations of the just person naturally fit with the criterion of justice, and so the just person, on this theory, will automatically be motivated to act justly. Hence no such problems of instability threaten.

However, it seems to me that Barry's opponent could reply that this merely pushes the question one step backwards. Perhaps on the theory of justice as impartiality the just person has strong motivation to act as the criterion of justice demands, but, then, what motivation does anyone have to be a just person? After all, we have the greatest difficulty getting people to act justly, and the more rigorous the demands of justice, the more difficult it will be to motivate people the right way. Accordingly, outside of 'full compliance theory' we may find ourselves with stability problems that are equally acute.

But even waiving that *ad hominem* reply, how seriously should we take such a threat of instability? The question is whether a potentially unstable theory of justice could serve the task Barry has set for a theory of justice. That task, we saw, is to provide 'some justification of social and political institutions that can be presented for the approval of each person's reason'. Well, it is far from obvious that the answer 'these institutions are to everyone's advantage' will never do as a justification. Even if, on this basis, someone, sometimes, finds that the institutions lack justification (i.e. they do not further their long-term interest, all things considered), this is only threatening if the failure is widespread and accumulating. And this depends on contingent matters of fact. Accordingly, I do not accept that justice as mutual advantage is doomed to fail the test Barry sets for it, even if it is internally inconsistent in Barry's terms, for this is simply an artefact of Barry's presentation. This is not to say that I think it is the right or best theory, because I do not. But neither do I think that it can be refuted in the way that Barry attempts.

And in some respects I think it is a good thing that it cannot be refuted. For it seems to me to have an important role within a general theory of justice. What makes justice as mutual advantage at least superficially plausible is the idea that considerations of justice only emerge under conditions of co-operation. Ultimately this view might be false, but it has some plausibility. Do rich societies have a duty of *justice* to transfer resources to poorer ones, even if they have no trade or other co-operation or contact? In the film 'The Man Who Fell to Earth' David Bowie plays a creature in human form from an alien planet which is desperately short of water. It is hard to sustain the thought that we have a duty of justice to part with some of our water to help them. Of course we might think we have some moral duties to help, but justice is not the whole of morality.

So let us suppose that the applicability of norms of justice presupposes some sort of co-operative relations or interaction: not necessarily mutually advantageous economic exchange, but some level of shared fate and entangled lives. But co-operation comes in degrees. Nations who begin to trade with each other will also begin to develop norms of justice. In the case of relations between nations we might expect to see a development; first reflecting mutual advantage; at a second stage norms of reciprocity or fair return; and finally, if we are very lucky, norms of impartiality. To argue that the only acceptable type of norm comes from the idea of justice as impartiality takes us much too far, much too soon. We can be ready to co-operate under normative conditions, but not yet ready for justice as impartiality. In conclusion, then, we should not feel forced to have to choose between the three models. Each can have its place at various levels of integration and development.

Furthermore there is at least one further example where it is better not to feel forced to choose between the alternatives of justice as mutual advantage and justice as impartiality. Consider the following minimal principle of justice – call it a 'weak equity axiom' – which I believe to be one of our most widely shared ideas of justice, even if it is rarely, if ever, articulated: 'If a change generates a surplus or profit, then those who are already badly off should not be made worse off still as a result of the change.'[7] It is worth comparing the weak equity axiom with both the Pareto Principle, and the Maximin Principle. In effect it is a less demanding compromise between the two – entailed by them both – and thus should be widely accepted as a necessary (*not* sufficient) condition for the justice of a change.

The Pareto Principle tells us that no one should be made worse off by a change. The weak equity axiom attends only to those towards the bottom of the distribution. Unlike the Pareto Principle it does not rule out the possibility that those already rich should lose out from the change.

Maximin tells us that the worse off should be made as well off as possible. The weak equity axiom tells us only that we should not make the badly off any worse off, but not that we should improve their position.

I should repeat that this is not intended as a complete theory of justice: it is simply a necessary condition. But how should we argue for it? I think we can give an account which both provides a firm base, and explains its wide appeal, although here I can only be brief. If we adopt the justice as mutual advantage bargaining model, and take the *status quo* as the breakpoint in case of bargaining disagreement, then justice as mutual advantage entails the Pareto Principle as a necessary condition of justice. No one would rationally accept a bargain which made them worse off than they would be without it. As we saw, the Pareto Principle entails the weak equity axiom as a necessary condition of justice. Consequently anyone who adopts justice as mutual advantage – and accepts the *status quo* as the state-of-nature breakpoint – logically must accept the weak equity axiom.

Perhaps it hardly needs to be added that those who reject justice as mutual advantage in favour of justice as impartiality should also accept the weak equity axiom, as a necessary condition, too. Impartial justice surely requires us to treat the position of the worst off with great seriousness.

The fact that the weak equity axiom has foundations in both, competing, camps explains its robustness and appeal. Nevertheless, there are several possible objections to consider. First, the principle is stated loosely, and perhaps the most significant looseness is in the idea of those 'already badly off' or those 'already towards the bottom of the

---

[7] I have discussed this principle, with application to the European Union, in 'Integration, Justice, and Exclusion', *Principles of Justice and the European Union*, ed. U. Bernitz and Par Hallstrom, Stockholm, 1996.

distribution'. How can we give a precise specification of the group or groups affected?

It is unlikely, though, that anything very satisfying can be said here. The principle is of too general application for anything precise to be universally applicable. Cases will differ. Some will be very clear; others will fall into a grey area. Political argument on a case-by-case basis seems the only solution.

Secondly, there are cases where the norm, as stated, intuitively fails to apply. Suppose the disadvantaged knowingly take unnecessary and foolish risks, which fail to pay off, and thereby become even worse off. Should they be compensated? Their case, as a matter of justice, seems very poor. In a full treatment this issue requires serious attention. Perhaps such cases motivate the project of reformulating the principle in 'opportunity' terms. However, I cannot go into these complications here.

Finally, a counter-example to the principle could possibly be derived from the thought that, at least sometimes, benefits should be proportioned to contributions: from the theory of justice as reciprocity. Suppose that a beneficial change to a co-operative scheme is carried out, but, as a consequence, those who contribute little and receive little come to contribute even less. Would it be unjust for them to receive less, even if they are already towards the bottom of the distribution?

Note though, that even if this is accepted, it does not so much refute the principle, but call for further clarification concerning the ideas of co-operation, costs, and benefits. Is increased leisure, for example, itself a benefit? Or only so if it is sought out? If increased leisure is not the result of choice, is it a further harm: a blow to one's self-respect? Once again, I cannot pursue these issues here, but they do require examination.

So in brief conclusion, while I accept that justice as impartiality represents a 'higher' and more attractive idea of justice than the alternatives, I doubt very much that Barry's arguments against the other views are as strong as he maintains. Furthermore, I think we have good reason not to want to choose between the models.[8]

---

[8] For another reason for keeping a pluralistic perspective, see my 'Pluralistic Models of Political Obligation', *Philosophica*, lvi (1996), 7–28.

4

Taking Utilitarianism Seriously

PAUL KELLY

With a book as wide-ranging and insightful as Barry's *Justice as Impartiality*, it is perhaps a little churlish to criticize it for giving insufficient attention to one's own particular interests. That said, in what follows I am going to do just that and claim that in an important sense Barry does not take utilitarianism[1] seriously. Utilitarianism does receive some discussion in Barry's book, and in an important section which I will discuss he even appears to concede that utilitarianism provides a rival though ultimately inadequate theory of justice. Nevertheless, utilitarianism is not considered a rival to justice as impartiality in the way that justice as mutual advantage and justice as reciprocity are. One response, and perhaps the only adequate response, would be to construct a rival utilitarian theory. I cannot provide such a fully articulated defence of a utilitarian theory in this paper, and I certainly would be very cautious about claiming that I could provide such a theory elsewhere either. What I want to suggest is that utilitarianism *is* a genuine third theory to contrast with justice as mutual advantage and justice as impartiality – justice as reciprocity being merely a hybrid of 'justice as mutual advantage', at least as Barry presents it (pp. 46–51). I also want to argue that it poses a more significant challenge to a contractualist theory such as Barry's than his discussion of utilitarianism reveals.

In levelling this charge I am aware that there is a very real sense in which most of Barry's work in normative political theory since *Political Argument*[2] has involved an engagement with and critique of utilitarianism. In the revised introduction to that work Barry points out that it was precisely a dissatisfaction with the hegemony of utilitarianism that underlies his argument. That same dissatisfaction was

---

[1] As I do not intend to offer a fully articulated utilitarian theory here, I use the term simply to identify a family resemblance between a variety of distinct theories which promote good consequences defined in terms of some conception of welfare, individual well-being or utility, however each of these is conceived.

[2] Brian Barry, *Political Argument*, reissued with new introduction, Hemel Hempstead, 1990.

44

also responsible for the resurgence of a new kind of normative political theory since the nineteen sixties, something that Barry has played a large part in initiating. By contrast the construction and defence of a political theory which takes account of the fact of the pluralism of ultimate ends is arguably the overriding concern of all Barry's work, consequently, *Justice as Impartiality* is as much an engagement with utilitarianism as any of the other works. That said, in this paper I want to claim that his failure to discuss utilitarianism directly as a genuine third theory, results in a failure to appreciate both how close his own position is to a version of utilitarianism, and how his own attempt to distinguish justice as impartiality from utilitarianism begs the question in favour of contractualism. This I believe follows from the fact that Barry's arguments reflect an understanding of utilitarian theory as primarily an answer to questions about the nature of the good rather than about what ought to be done. I don't quite want to make the claim that utilitarianism is not a theory of the good – though it might be made – but I am concerned to suggest that much contemporary utilitarian theory has been concerned to contest the territory dominated by contractualisms, most notably the issue of fairness and equality of concern and respect.[3] My point in this paper will be the rather modest one, that contractualist theories are not obviously less problematic than utilitarian theories and that what ultimately favours one theory over the other is the substantive content of the theory rather than some intrinsic superiority of the method of justification.

The paper begins with a review of the Barry's attempt to show the superiority of justice as impartiality for its ability to avoid the counter intuitive consequences of a want-satisfaction theory as a justification of a democratic decision procedure. I will then turn to the substantive issue of contractualism and utilitarianism as rival theories of fairness. My argument will attempt to show that utilitarianism is not prima facie less plausible than Barry's contractualism. The paper will conclude with some reflections on justification in political theory and on remaining difficulties facing an adequate utilitarianism.

I

Although, as I have already said, Barry's implicit rejection of utilitarianism casts a long shadow over much of the book, the main

---

[3] A good case can be made for seeing the work of Hare, Griffin, Harsanyi, and Singer as concerned with giving content to the core idea of fairness and equality of concern and respect underlying fairness. See R. M. Hare, *Moral Thinking*, Oxford, 1984; J. Griffin, *Well-Being*, Oxford, 1986; J. Harsanyi, *Essays on Ethics, Social Behaviour and Scientific Explanation*, Dordrecht, 1976; and P. Singer, *Practical Ethics*, Cambridge, 1979.

discussion of utilitarian argument occurs in chapters 5, 6 and 9. I will concentrate on the arguments in chapters 5 and 6 as I am in agreement with much of chapter 9, and I think Barry would agree he mounts arguments there which are sound and with which utilitarians concur. The argument of chapters 5 and 6 is addressed to a charge levelled by Alasdair MacIntyre in his book *Whose Justice? Which Rationality?*[4] to the effect that justice as impartiality is a fraud in that it depends upon a distinctive conception of the good as liberal individualism. In a careful dissection of precisely what MacIntyre meant by this charge, Barry distinguishes two 'liberal' conceptions of the good: the good as autonomy and the good as want-satisfaction. Both conceptions are, according to Barry, second-order conceptions of the good because they do not specify the content of the good, that is those particular actions or forms of life which are valuable (p. 133). However, as Barry correctly points, out MacIntyre's concern is primarily with the good as want-satisfaction as this underlies his critique of the individualist character of liberal culture with its emphasis on reducing everything to the expression of preferences, and morality and substantive political argument to consumer choice and public opinion surveys. Want-satisfaction theories appear to give rise to neutral political outcomes, but only because they reduce issues to the weighing of preferences. MacIntyre's charge is that both utilitarianism and justice as impartiality collapse into the same broad conception of the good as want-satisfaction. Barry is right point out that even if we grant MacIntyre's argument, it is not clear what follows. MacIntyre is of the belief that linking impartialist theories of justice with utilitarianism in this way is an incontestable refutation of both theories – all forms of utilitarianism are obviously corrupt, any theory that shares common features of utilitarianism must be equally tainted.

Barry's response to MacIntyre's charge, is however, my main concern here. It has two strands. Firstly, that want-satisfaction theories do not necessarily result in liberal or neutral political institutions. And secondly, want-satisfaction theories do not adequately reflect shared understandings of what it is for something to be valuable, and consequently they give rise to counter-intuitive understandings of democratic decision procedures. I will deal with each in turn.

It is a commonplace criticism of utilitarianism that it can countenance severely illiberal policies and practices. This is because it is possible to imagine the aggregation of preferences, wants, or desires, including those or bigots and bullies, giving rise to principles and policies which maximize overall welfare but through illiberal segregation or persecution. Thus utilitarianism, it is claimed, can only too

---

[4] A. MacIntyre, *Whose Justice? Which Rationality?*, London, 1988.

easily countenance the criminalization of private sexual behaviour because of the sensitivities of prudes and busybodies. Defenders of utilitarianism as a source of liberal policies and institutions have been equally quick to appeal to what Barry calls 'stylized facts' (p. 135) in order to avoid such problems of the distribution of aggregate want-satisfaction. As Barry kindly points out, I argued elsewhere that Bentham was also happy to appeal to such 'stylized facts' in order to ground a distribution sensitive utilitarian theory of civil rights.[5] But what precisely is wrong with this strategy, if it works? Barry's point seems to be twofold. First, it is only with a considerable struggle that such want-satisfaction theories can be made to yield liberal neutrality, and second the issue of theoretical economy: justice as impartiality is a more efficient method of yielding liberal institutions and rules.

The force of this criticism depends ultimately on the possibility of deriving principles from a modified Scanlonian agreement,[6] and thus Barry seems to be loading the argument in favour of his own theory, which is hardly fair. Furthermore its force is derived from the ambiguity of what is meant by 'stylized facts' and their appeal in moral and political argument. Admittedly, there does seem something peculiar about the strategy of such utilitarian arguments, as it looks as though the evidence is being sifted to *suit* the conclusion rather than support it. But again, this depends upon what is meant by 'stylized facts'. Are, for example, the claims about the limits of knowledge that Russell Hardin[7] appeals to to show the compatibility of utilitarianism with some broadly liberal institutions and systems of rules, merely 'stylized facts'? If so they appear pretty uncontroversial. Barry himself concedes in his discussion of constitutional design that even justice as impartiality cannot avoid appealing to consequences, outcomes, and conceptions of harm. 'We cannot, in other words, hope to be able to specify the characteristics of a just constitution in purely procedural terms' (p. 93). Thus having claimed that utilitarian theories are 'bottom-up', starting from a conception of desired outcomes and moving to the appropriate rules, whereas justice as impartiality is 'top down' justifying rules independently of outcomes, Barry has had to conclude that the situation with justice as impartiality is not so simple. Outcomes have to be appealed to in order to determine to content and detail of a system of rules. Thus concepts such as harm have to be brought in. Whilst I certainly don't want to

[5] See P. J. Kelly, *Utilitarianism and Distributive Justice: Jeremy Bentham and the Civil Law*, Oxford, 1990.

[6] Barry's contractualist defence of 'justice as impartiality' is based on T. M. Scanlon, 'Contractualism and Utilitarianism', *Utilitarianism and Beyond*, ed. Amartya Sen and Bernard Williams, Cambridge, 1982, pp. 103–28.

[7] R. Hardin, *Morality Within the Limits of Reason*, Chicago, 1988.

claim that one can only use the concept of harm in the context of a substantive theory of the good, what constitutes a harm and what hierarchies of harm one might use, are going to involve making claims of fact, no less stylized than those made by many utilitarians to avoid the absurdities of some unsympathetic account of their theories.

It is not, therefore, obvious that contractualist theories are any more efficient than utilitarian theories at delivering the rules or institutions of a liberal political order, as they too require the factoring in of a considerable amount of information about human behaviour and capabilities. Indeed giving an account of the *reasonable* itself involves appeal to 'stylized facts' of some sort or other, for example, what it is or is not reasonable to accept, why the agreement motive can be assumed to have priority, and the psychological ability to adopt scepticism about certainty whilst also holding a particular conception of the good as true and a reason for action. It is not simply at the level of constitution building that 'stylized facts' must operate but also at the level of theory construction and justification.

However, even if one can show that a version of utilitarianism might give rise to a form of liberal neutrality, Barry has a further set of arguments which are designed to distinguish justice as impartiality from utilitarian neutrality. He turns his attention to an argument made by Richard Arneson to the effect that a version of considered preference utilitarianism, which Arneson calls 'subjectivism', can provide a weak neutral procedure for making public decisions given the fact of pluralism about ultimate ends.[8] A weak neutral procedure is one that requires that

state policy be justifiable without appeal to the presumed intrinsic superiority of any substantive conception of the good, so long as a substantive conceptions interpreted to be one that determines some aim that a person should seek regardless of her own evaluation of this matter.[9]

Arneson's argument, according to Barry, is a classic statement of the case for utilitarian neutrality. It proceeds by locating the second-order good in considered preference satisfaction, which is a version of want-satisfaction. The superiority of justice as impartiality as a distinctive conception of liberal neutrality can be brought out by contrasting its response to public decision-making with that of an argument such as Arneson's. First, however, Barry brings up a familiar charge against want-satisfaction theories, namely that they equate all manner of wants or preferences including bad or wicked ones. Arneson avoids this charge by focusing on rational or considered preferences. These

---

[8] R. Arneson, 'Neutrality and Utility', *Canadian Journal of Philosophy*, xx (1990), 215–40.
[9] Ibid., 220.

are preferences corrected by full information and appropriate reasonable deliberation. What such reasonable deliberation consists of I will leave to one side. It is, however, clear that Arneson is concerned to launder some preferences in order to make more likely a liberal outcome.

The more substantial arguments focus on the way utilitarianism and justice as impartiality differ in their understanding of votes on policies. These arguments take us through a review of a number of rival conceptions of voting and the weaknesses of the Contingent Valuation Method as a version of cost-benefit analysis. Barry considers the case of a referendum decision to build a dam within a constitutional system. The dam will bring public benefits such as work, power and recreational facilities. However, one consequence of locating the dam in a particular place will be the destruction of the environment of a small fish called a snail darter and its ultimate extinction.[10] How must the two rival theories respond to such a decision?

On the want-satisfaction theory some method will be used to aggregate wants in order to determine whether or not to build the dam. The majority decision will determine between building or not building. The want-satisfaction theory undoubtedly provides a justification for the decision, but is it a satisfactory justification? This issue can be assessed by comparing the decision with that which emerges from justice as impartiality. Both theories assume pluralism about ultimate ends, so there will presumably be both committed utilitarians and committed environmentalists with an ecocentric conception of the good among many other possible views about what is ultimately valuable. The want-satisfaction theory, provides a rationale for the ultimate decision by translating each individual's conflicting first-order conception of the good into the second-order conception of individual wants. The ultimate decision can therefore be justified by showing that it results in the best outcome in terms of the second-order theory of value. Consequently, if the decision goes against the snail darter, it will still need to be justified to the environmentalist in terms of the second-order conception of the good as bringing about more of that which is valuable. This, Barry argues with some plausibility, is a particularly demanding justification for the environmentalist whose view about the dam is that it is unquestionably bad from an ecocentric view point. Here the environmentalist is faced with a first-order claim that the decision is bad, and a second-order claim that the decision is good because it maximizes want satisfaction. Barry claims the problem is that unless you hold a want-satisfaction view of

---

[10] This was a real case; see *Tennessee Valley Authority v. Hill*, 437 U.S. 153 (1973), cited in Ronald Dworkin, *Law's Empire*, Cambridge, Mass., 1986, pp. 20–3.

the good, it does not seem that the majority decision has any purchase whatsoever. If we turn then to Barry's discussion of the weaknesses of the Contingent Valuation Method we find this dissatisfaction further compounded as one of the questions that the Contingent Valuation Method depends upon answering is how much a person would be willing to accept (WTA) in order to compensate for the destruction of a small fish like the snail darter? The problem with the Contingent Valuation Method is that it tries to measure the existence value of some creature in terms of the personal gratification that would be lost due to the extinction of the fish. But as Barry points out, most non-utilitarians would reject this whole way of trying to frame the issue, as what matters for an environmentalist is the damage to a species or ecosystem, not what effect this has on his or her level of gratification.

Barry then proceeds to argue that justice as impartiality can avoid these difficulties because once it has been agreed to consign the determination of this issue to a majority decision, there is nothing more that the theory needs to add. Therefore, the environmentalist is not required to change beliefs about the dam as a result of a majority decision. He can quite consistently accept that the decision is foolish and wrong whilst also acknowledging that it is reasonable that such decisions be decided in this way by majority vote. Justice as Impartiality does not require the agent to change his views about the good; a vote is just a vote, no more (p. 149). I will leave aside the question of whether or not this is a sufficient response to the need to sustain stable democratic institutions. I suspect it is not.

The problem with the want-satisfaction theory is that it gets the relationship between desire and valuation wrong and that it is too demanding. Justice as impartiality can avoid both problems altogether. How serious are these charges? Much of the plausibility can only be maintained by not treating the want-satisfaction and the contractualist theories fairly. To begin with, justice as impartiality is presented as being concerned with the derivation of a system of rules or procedures for determining controversial issues of public policy. The contractualist method is not applied directly to the issue of whether or not to build the dam. We can assume that agreement has been forthcoming on this issue, so there is no room for the regret that accompanies the utilitarian decision which is addressed directly to the outcome of building the dam and not the justification of a political process. We are not comparing like with like. Though Arneson's argument is ambiguous here, it seems perfectly permissible for him and other utilitarians to confine the direct application of the considered preference criterion to the choice of political procedures and systems of rules. Thus we might find a justification of a constitutionally constrained democratic majoritarianism in terms of its tendency to maximize aggregate preference satisfaction over a specified period of time. There does not seem to be any obvious reason why every single majority decision should be maximally beneficial. This requirement would only make the utilitarian justification prima facie implausible on the grounds that many people's wants might be poorly expressed in terms of the options any referendum or political system presents them with. Similarly it would require levels of information and participation that few democratic systems could reasonably expect or provide. Most decisions are not and could not be taken by referendum. As long as the time frame was not unreasonably long there does not seem to be anything wrong with framing the public justification of a procedure in terms of its tendency over time to maximize aggregate considered preference satisfaction. This admittedly still leaves the choice subject to the contingency that should a better way of determining aggregate preference satisfaction be discovered, an issue-by-issue decision might be more appropriate than confining the justification to the choice of procedure alone. Thus aggregate considered preference satisfaction does not provide a principled constraint to the extension of the criterion to single issues unless we factor in some appropriate 'stylized facts'. If we compare the justifications of utilitarianism and justice as impartiality at the level of choosing procedures then it does not seem that want-satisfaction theories must be any more counter-intuitive than contractualist theories. The problem for both theories in the context of pluralism over ultimate ends is in deciding what issues should be settled by majority decision and what left either outside the realm of politics or consigned to constitutional adjudication. It seems perfectly plausible to assume that the environmentalist will not be overburdened by a democratic majority only because we have already assumed that he is already prepared to attach priority to the desire to reach reasonable agreement. But if he is deeply committed to an eco-centric ethic it is not clear that the requirements of agreement presupposed by justice as impartiality will be any the less demanding than the requirements of a want-satisfying theory, as the participants of the reasonable agreement would seem to load the dice in favour of human rather than ecological or other species interests. I will return to this issue shortly.

II

Part of the claim that utilitarian theories result in counter-intuitive and burdensome demands depends on contrasting the way utilitarianism transforms ultimate ends with the way in which contractualism leaves them largely untouched. How seriously should we take this contrast? There is certainly something to be said for the view that want-regarding theories seem to misunderstand valuation. A person generally wants x because x is valuable in some way to him, as opposed to something being valuable because it is wanted. However, does a want-satisfaction theory such as Arneson's necessarily make this identification? There are two ways of approaching this issue which are obscured in Arneson's account. Firstly, we could approach it as a metaethical issue about the meaning of value concepts. Thus, something's being good is identified with preference fulfilment.[11] This is pretty clearly not Arneson's point, and if it was then Barry's criticism would have considerable force. The second way of construing the issue is to see the language of want-satisfaction (or more specifically considered preference satisfaction) as a way of providing a public language for arbitrating between ultimately conflicting conceptions of the good, in order to justify public decisions. This is viewing it as competing with justice as impartiality rather than with Scanlon's theory which attempts to provide a philosophical criterion of moral wrong. If we adopt the second view then clearly there is no requirement that any one person's conception of the good should be translatable into the language of wants or considered preferences without remainder, though there must be some degree of convergence. All we need to establish this convergence is a motivation to acknowledge the claims of maximal considered preference satisfaction as the best way of settling the choice of decision procedure or as a way of making specific decisions. There is no reason to believe that such a motivation suitably circumscribed is any less widespread or less appropriate than the desire to achieve reasonable agreement with those with whom one disagrees about fundamental issues. Indeed suitably defended and explained considered preference satisfaction might follow from the same motive.

This will still leave considerable scope for individual agents to feel regret at having to compromise on their views about the good, and so it should, for we have no reason to think that justifiable laws and public policies should not be completely unburdensome in a genuinely plural society. Of course the environmentalist may still think that a maximally beneficial outcome in terms of human wants or interests is irrelevant when considering the snail-darter case, but this does not undermine the claim that a want-satisfaction theory has nevertheless provided a public justification, even though one he will find both burdensome to accept and wrong in this case. This seems to me to parallel perfectly the situation of someone with a strong commitment

---

[11] Arneson does appear to make this claim when he says, 'In a sense, subjectivism is obviously non-neutral: it identifies the good with fulfilment of preferences', Arneson, 220. It is, however, clear from the context that he is not offering an account of the meaning of the good or value terms so I do not think too much can be read into this.

to a particular moral view in the case of justice as impartiality. Imagine a Catholic in a plural society confronted by a democratically sanctioned right to abortion, something that Barry thinks should be determined by majority decision (p. 92). Presumably this situation is faced by many Catholics in Britain who are opposed to liberal abortion laws but who, on the whole, avoid violent assaults on abortion clinics and murdering doctors who carry out such procedures. It does not seem to me implausible to claim that this person is in the same position as the environmentalist confronted by a want-satisfaction based justification for the policy. To say that the Catholic or environmentalist should view the outcome as just a decision seems to misunderstand the pluralism that Barry intends his theory to address. In fact it seems to me that Barry has a difficulty making his case against the want-satisfaction argument stick, for if he argues that the priority of the agreement motive in individual decision-making leaves no room for a sense of loss then his argument seems as counter-intuitive as his account of want-satisfaction theory, whereas if he allows for a significant sense of loss in accepting the majority decision which is the more realistic position, then how does his argument significantly differ from the want-satisfaction theory?

If we return to the case of the Catholic living in a liberal society like Britain where decisions on abortion are made by a free vote in Parliament, then it does not seem implausible to argue that such a person might well accept the burdens of the desire for reasonable agreement and retain the view that a majority decision in favour of a liberal law is fundamentally wrong. It would, however, be implausible to suggest that they do so without a considerable sense of loss at such a fundamental issue being decided in this way. To claim that there is no loss or sense of tragedy[12] would seem counter-intuitive and psychologically unrealistic. If, on the other hand, the Catholic does not accept the burdens of justification and thinks the whole idea of deciding issues of life or death by majority is repugnant then that is his or her prerogative, but it does not affect the rightness of using coercion to secure respect for the law. There is no reason to think that in controversial cases such as abortion or where serious environmental damage is a possible result, the outcomes of a contractualist agreement will leave the citizen without a sense of loss and possibly even tragic loss. That is not an argument against the policies emerging from such an agreement, but equally it means that the burdensomeness of accepting publicly justified practices is not a factor that distinguishes

---

[12] I use this term in the same way as Sue Mendus, who makes a similar argument about tragedy and loss in theories of justice such as Barry's, though I should point out she does so for very different reasons to my own. I am nevertheless indebted to her argument. See S. Mendus, 'Some Mistakes about Impartiality', p. 180.

want-satisfaction theories from contractualist theories. What would distinguish such theories is the expectation that an individual should be able to reduce his own conception of the good to a series of wants without remainder, but as we have seen there is no reason why a sophisticated utilitarian theory should require this. It no more follows that want-satisfaction theories expect agents to identify their main value commitments with subjective wants, than it follows that the appeal to moderate scepticism that Barry makes also transforms conceptions of the good into subjective preferences. All that utilitarianism needs is a motivation to accept maximal considered preference satisfaction overtime as a basis for public policy decisions. And it seems wholly unfair to deny this possibly widespread motivation whilst at the same time accepting as widespread the agreement motive that underpins justice as impartiality. How widespread each motivation is and whether they are in fact two distinct motives is not something I need consider here as it is not an issue that Barry thinks he need consider either. It is however, the issue that goes to the very heart of the difference between utilitarianism and justice as impartiality.

III

My argument thus far has been to contest Barry's claim to distinguish justice as impartiality from a version of utilitarianism which is concerned to justify liberal neutrality. This is because he has focused too much on want-satisfaction as a theory of the good rather than a procedure for determining the right. This problem is not Barry's but is rather an inheritance of the contractualist language which has dominated moral and political philosophy since at least Rawls's *A Theory of Justice*.[13] This legacy has been concerned to distinguish clearly between issues of the good and issues of the right. One thing that is certainly clear from modern utilitarianism is that it is exceedingly uncomfortable with such an unambiguous distinction. Much sophisticated modern utilitarian theory tends to conflate the right and the good so that the good to be maximized is often given in terms of what liberal theories would classify as the right.[14] It is only by forcing this somewhat artificial split upon utilitarian theories that one can generate some of the apparent defects that Barry has used in order to show the distinctiveness of justice as impartiality.

There is, however, a further issue that I put to one side which I now want to return to as it goes to the heart of the distinction between

[13] J. Rawls, *A Theory of Justice*, Oxford, 1972.
[14] See, for example, Griffin, *Well-Being*, and J. Broome, *Weighing Goods*, Oxford, 1991.

utilitarian and contractualist theories. The discussion thus far has concentrated on the Barry's contrast between utilitarian or want-satisfaction theories and justice as impartiality, because I wanted to show how the supposed difference between them only arises from forcing utilitarian arguments into an ill-fitting mould which serves to advantage contractualist theories. But if we challenge the status of contractualist theories as much modern utilitarianism does then we can see that there is a further crucial sense in which there is a continuity between some versions of utilitarianism such as Arneson's and contractualist theories such as Scanlon's and Barry's. Both classes of theory aim to provide an interpretation of equal treatment or fairness; this is obscured by Barry's treatment of utilitarianism which I have discussed above. If we go back to the burdensomeness of a decision in the snail-darter case, it will be remembered that the agreement motive (that is the motive to abide by a Scanlon-type agreement) would be enough to justify the decision to a person with an ecocentric conception of the good, as long as they had that motive. But even if the environmentalist has the requisite motive it is not obvious that a Scanlon-type agreement will motivate because the environmentalist might query the scope of the agreement and contest its implicit speciesism. The interpretation of 'fairness' and 'reasonable' carry with them commitments to the scope of the justification – that is, precisely to whom is it addressed. My point here is not to try and catch out Barry by showing that his theory does involve a conception of the good; rather it is merely to show that it is precisely on this issue that utilitarianism and contractualism compete and it is here that both *must* appeal to 'stylized facts' about motivation, reasonableness, and the burdensomeness of potential moral and political principles. Both offer rival views of who is to count and why in the distribution of benefits and burdens, so merely appealing to the outcome of Scanlon-type agreement will not serve as an adequate contradiction of utilitarianism.

Let me try and clarify this. In a famous and widely cited paper T. M. Scanlon offers a contractualist account of moral wrongness; his concern is to provide a philosophical account of the nature of morality. He claims:

An act is wrong if its performance under the circumstances would be disallowed by any system of rules for the general regulation of behaviour which no one could reasonably reject as a basis for informed, unforced general agreement.[15]

Scanlon's thesis is about the nature of morality. Barry takes up and

---

[15] Scanlon, p. 110.

modifies this theory to ground justice as impartiality, and on his account it forms the basis for a fair distribution as no one is burdened in ways that they cannot reasonably accept. Thus, it provides a way of achieving Rawls's objectives (p. 70), without the need for the original position. Barry's point is not to offer this as a definition of justice, but rather to offer it as a model of fairness and equal treatment. Fairness and equality are important here, because fair treatment is the only objective that can be universally hoped for in a society faced with the fact of the pluralism of ultimate ends. In the face of such circumstances the contractualist solution does appear to have considerable plausibility, especially if we think of rivals such as utilitarianism as offering merely one among a number of contested conceptions of the good. If, however, we think of utilitarianism as an attempt to respond to the same circumstances, then the obvious plausibility of contractualism over utilitarianism is at least questionable.

The plausibility of contractualism depends upon its serving as a model of fairness and equal treatment. It is supposed to be fair because it offers each person a strong veto against the imposition of burdens for the advantage of others, and therefore guarantees equal treatment. Its moral force against utilitarianism is that it rules out the sacrifice of some for the benefit of the majority. But utilitarianism can also be concerned with equal treatment. This is certainly true of Hare, Griffin, Singer and Arneson. Where they differ from contractualism is in the account they give of equal treatment. For Hare and Arneson at least, the egalitarianism is provided by a version of Bentham's dictum 'everyone to count for one, nobody to count for more than one'. In this case each considered preference is factored into the decision as having an equal status. This may not be an adequate account of equality of concern and respect, but whether it is so or not cannot be resolved by appealing to the intrinsic superiority of the Scanlon/Barry agreement. The issue between utilitarianism and justice as impartiality can therefore be resolved into the justification for the strong veto provided by the Scanlon/Barry agreement and the issue of who is included in the agreement. The first question of the strong veto has implications for whether the Scanlon/Barry agreement can really be said to give rise to an account of justice. The second issue of scope focuses on the question of whether morally contested issues such as abortion, population control or environmental destruction can be dealt with by the Scanlon/Barry agreement. I will say something about each in turn.

Barry uses the idea of a Scanlonian agreement to derive justice as impartiality. Utilitarianism is not considered as a rival theory of justice because it might place an unreasonable burden on a person and therefore it could not be justified as a principle of justice to that person. But this seems to beg the question because surely the question of whether utilitarianism is unduly burdensome must depend on what we take a fair burden to be. Unrestricted preference aggregation might well seem to tip the balance unfairly in one direction, by requiring agents to be indifferent to his own interests and wholly concerned with the general interest. But it is not obvious that justice as fairness does not tip the balance too far in the other direction with its strong veto on potential principles of distribution. The strong veto seems to weight the argument too much in favour of an individual's own self-interest as the cut-off point of utilitarian trade-offs. Any sacrifice which it is not in an individual's considered interest to accept would be ruled out. Any diversion of resources from a person who is faced with an expensive but life threatening illness could presumably be ruled out, especially if the resources were intended to maintain the arts or some other valuable but less urgent public good. Now it might seem that such trade-offs are quite obviously unacceptable, but given that they are made all the time in modern societies and if we think through the implications of the exercise of this strong veto, then it becomes less obviously incontrovertible.

Barry might respond that the conditions of reasonable agreement do not give a strong veto to even considered self-interest, but then the plausibility of his argument as a basis for any kind of agreement is going to have to make considerable appeal to 'stylized facts'. All that is not, of course, to suggest that the utilitarianism has a better answer, but it is at least to show that the argument does not go wholly in the direction of contractualism. A fair distribution cannot be so burdensome that nobody could accept it as some extreme utilitarian theory might be, but equally it cannot be premised on a veto that is so strong that it allows self-interest (even considered self-interest) to determine the outcome. Such a veto power would undermine the moral standing of any agreement; it would also seem to depart from our intuitions about equal treatment by subordinating the common interests of all others to the veto power of one. This might be seen as a departure from 'Bentham's dictum'. Neither theory can completely divorce its account of the obligations of justice from the claims of a plausible or realistic psychology.

Utilitarian arguments are not obviously any better than contractualist arguments at settling the issue of fair distribution, but were they are superior to contractualisms is in the fact that they are at least more honest by focusing on what kind of trade-offs can be morally justified. Contractualist arguments suggest that there is no issue here and that intuitions unambiguously follow a Scanlon/Barry-type agreement.

Where utilitarianism is perhaps better placed is on the issue of who should count, in that utilitarian arguments do not have to be species specific in the way that contractualist arguments are. Contractualist arguments only take account of those who can exercise a reasonable veto, but in so doing they create problems. If we think back to the abortion and environmental issues discussed earlier, both issues seem ill-suited to being discussed in terms of reasonable agreement. In the former case foetuses are excluded thus loading the argument against those who advocate a continuity of life between foetus and person; whereas in the latter, as we have also seen, the exclusion of other species from exercising a veto seems to load the argument in favour of human interests over those of other species. Now in both cases there may be good reasons for the exclusions, but they need to be stated and not assumed. Furthermore, it seems less likely that both committed environmentalists and 'right to lifers' could accept the 'justification' offered by justice as impartiality, and this weakens its claim to be an adequate principled response to the fact of pluralism. Utilitarianism, on the otherhand can give some weight to both foetal life and non-human animals. Whether or not it does so in a way that advantages the right to life argument or the protection of bio-diversity is another matter. But it is at least significant that by being flexible enough to accommodate the interests of the unborn or non-human animals it might therefore be in a better position to justify outcomes around which a consensus can be built.

What I have *not* done in this last section is show that utilitarianism has a superior answer to the issue of equal treatment than justice as impartiality, but what I think I have done is show that both Barry and Scanlon have not shown that justice as impartiality is an obviously superior theory to utilitarianism. To do more would require the development of a complete utilitarian theory. This is something I cannot do and am happy therefore to leave the matter to others. There is, however, an important moral to be drawn from this comparison between utilitarianism and contractualism, other than that utilitarianism is a genuine candidate as a third theory of justice, and that relates to the nature of justification and theory construction. Whether justice as impartiality does provide a superior account of justice and fairness depends upon its substantive content and not its method. Whether the principles of such a theory can be the focus of a reasonable agreement will depend upon what they look like and how they stand up to the contest with other rival theories. It cannot be decided independently of such a contest. Thus, whether a theory can provide the focus for a reasonable agreement is an independent issue from whether or not the theory gives rise to principles of justice. Utilitarianism, with its attempt to respond to outcomes, and its tendency to overcome criticisms by incorporating 'stylized facts' is a more appropriate model for theory construction and defence. There is nothing in principle which rules out some version of utilitarianism as the possible focus of reasonable agreement, but this is not the same as saying that such a theory could be the outcome of such an agreement. That the latter should be considered a potential defect of utilitarian arguments is a result of assuming the superiority of contractualist defences of justice and failing to take utilitarianism seriously.

5

The Priority of the Right Over the Good Rides Again[*]

RICHARD ARNESON

In 1973 Brian Barry wrote that 'a liberal must take his stand on the proposition that some ways of life, some types of character, are more admirable than others, whatever may be the majority opinion in any society'.[1] I cannot resist quoting Barry's memorable continuation of this thought:

Liberalism rests on a vision of life: a Faustian vision. It exalts self-expression, self-mastery and control over the environment, natural and social; the active pursuit of knowledge and the clash of ideas; the acceptance of personal responsibility for the decisions that shape one's life. For those who cannot take the freedom, it provides alcohol, tranquillizers, wrestling on the television, astrology, psychoanalysis, and so on, endlessly, but it cannot by its nature provide certain kinds of psychological security. Like any creed it can be neither justified nor condemned in terms of anything beyond it. It is itself an answer to the unanswerable but irrepressible question: 'What is the meaning of life?'[2]

This was written by way of objection to John Rawls's doctrine of neutrality on the good, and doubt about the role his doctrine played in his original position derivation of principles of justice. Now, almost a quarter of a century later, Barry has been converted to the Rawlsian neutralist camp. His conversion to neutrality has not eliminated his former allegiances without a trace. What has remained constant in Barry's work has been the conviction that conceptions of the good cannot be justified by arguments that would be compelling to all reasonable persons. Disagreement on the good is endemic. What has changed is Barry's view of the relationship between the right and the good. Barry had believed the liberal doctrine of right was derived from and dependent upon a liberal conception of the good. The position he now defends is that the liberal doctrine of right, which specifies the basic terms of fair dealing among persons, is a free-standing doctrine

[*] A version of this paper also appeared in *Ethics*, 108 (1997), 169–96, © University of Chicago Press.
[1] Brian Barry, *The Liberal Theory of Justice*, Oxford, 1973, p. 126.
[2] Ibid., p. 127.

that is justifiable independently of one's beliefs about the good, and about the meaning and purpose of human life.

Neutrality on the good according to Barry is an implication of a more fundamental conception which he calls justice as impartiality, and a theory of justice describes the motive for behaving justly, characterizes a criterion for deciding the content of just rules, and explains how people with the postulated motive will be led to conform to the rules that the criterion picks out as just. Barry's theory identifies the motive as the desire to be just. The criterion of just rules is that they can be 'freely endorsed by [reasonable] people on a footing of equality' (p. 52). He takes it to be unproblematic that if you are disposed to behave fairly, and you identify the reasonable acceptability test as determining what's fair, you will then be motivated to conform to the rules so selected. Justice as impartiality offers a coherent answer to the three questions, and this alone gives it a leg up on its main rival, justice as mutual advantage, the theory that each individual pursues her own good and that valid rules of justice are moral constraints that are mutually beneficial as compared to the baseline situation in which everyone pursues her interests without being bound by any constraint.

The importance of the claim about motivation Barry ascribes to justice as impartiality is that he postulates a capacity in humans to be moved sometimes to do what is fair because they see it's fair, even when conformity results in predictable damage to their own interests. The theorist of justice is not then limited to propounding social rules that each agent bound by the rules will have prudential reasons to obey.

THE SCANLON TEST OF REASONABLE REJECTABILITY

Barry finds the test for just rules in a form of contractualism developed by Thomas Scanlon, whereby

[A]n act is wrong if its performance under the circumstances would be disallowed by any system of rules for the general regulation of behaviour which no one could reasonably reject as the basis for informed, unforced general agreement.[3]

That is to say, consider a group of individuals all of whom desire to live under rules that are acceptable to everyone, the idea of contractualism is that the rules that people so motivated would reasonably choose determine what is morally right and wrong. Here the crucial word is 'reasonably'. The suspicion immediately arises that the rules that people would reasonably choose to regulate their affairs are the ones

[3] T. M. Scanlon, 'Contractualism and Utilitarianism', in *Utilitarianism and Beyond*, ed. Amartya Sen and Bernard Williams, Cambridge, 1982, pp. 103–28; see esp. p. 110.

that are best supported by moral reasons, and the contractualist formulation does not advance a single step towards determining what these most reasonable rules are. The contractualist idea is not utterly trivial in that it does restrict the type of considerations that can count as reasons when the issue to be settled is the choice of moral rules. Contractualism says that the only reasons that count are *moral* reasons, so that consideration of personal advantage and strategic calculations of relative bargaining strength are irrelevant to the issue. The fact that if we fail to reach an agreement we will fight and I will predictably win and get my way is not a reason in the relevant sense for you to accept the social rule that I propose. But although some types of considerations are ruled out, nothing in the contractualist formulation determines what is ruled in – what counts as a moral reason and where the balance of moral reasons concerning the choice of social rules actually lies. Barry writes as though his project is to derive substantive principles of justice from Scanlonian contractualism, but since Scanlonian contractualism reduces to 'One ought to conform to the moral rules that are best supported by moral reasons', the idea of deriving anything substantive from this purely formal and uninformative formulation is a non-starter.

Scanlon thinks contractualism has content; it implies the rejection of utilitarianism, because in some possible circumstances utilitarianism recommends the imposition of burdens on some people that they might reasonably reject. The resistance to an extreme utilitarian imposition of sacrifice on oneself for the sake of gains to others would not be 'disallowed by any system of rules for the general regulation of behaviour which no one could reasonably reject as a basis for informed, unforced general agreement'. Scanlon, is perhaps, thinking of cases in which imposition of severe deprivation on one or a few individuals is implied by utilitarianism so as to secure small benefits to a large number of already well-off persons. Generalizing from this sort of case, he proposes that the test of reasonable rejectability is to be applied by considering the condition of the losers under a proposed principle, and comparing their condition to what it might be under alternative principles, and to what those who lose in the move to the alternative principle have to give up in turn. Vague as this is, it seems to me clearly not an implication of the reasonable rejectability test itself, but of a purportedly reasonable supplement to it – 'the content of morality is what is morally reasonable, and utilitarianism is not morally reasonable'. Moreover, the suggested emphasis on how losers fare, and on the extent to which others will suffer setbacks if the losers' condition is improved, seems to ignore population size issues. Suppose a policy we might embrace imposes losses on all presently existing people but brings into existence many new people, who will lead wonderful lives and who would not have existed but for this policy. Scanlon's elaboration of his test appears to instruct us to ignore the gains for the extra people. This illustrates how the Scanlon test shows a tendency to slide from the trivial to the tendentious without any intervening argument.

In some of its formulations, Scanlonian contractualism limits what can be reasonably agreed to by imposing an internalist proviso. Internalism is the idea that moral obligation is necessarily connected to motivation, so that if someone is under a moral obligation then it must be the case that under appropriate circumstances he would be motivated to conform to it. The Scanlon test, with what can be reasonably accepted limited to the set of rules that those bound by the rules could be motivated to obey, now includes a genuine psychological requirement that limits what content the rules of morality can have. But Barry does not interpret contractualism as including internalism, for the sensible reason that it is entirely possible that someone should recognize that the rules of justice bind him to do a certain action and that he is really morally obligated to do that action – yet he is not in any way motivated to do the action. The thought 'this is what justice requires' leaves him entirely unmoved. So Barry's version of the Scanlon test is externalist. But then the position comes to this: the criterion of justice is what reasonable persons would agree to, with a 'reasonable' person being understood to be one who wishes to live with others similarly motivated on terms all can accept, and who agrees to the rules that are best supported by moral reasons. It remains mysterious why Barry, having interpreted the Scanlon test in this way, nevertheless thinks it is a substantive test that establishes the content of justice. Barry comes close to acknowledging this point (p. 113) and then states that at least the Scanlon test is useful in suggesting the empirical hypothesis that as the actual processes by which the fundamental legal rules of a society come closer to the process that the Scanlon test invokes – one in which reasonable persons choose without being swayed by any interested considerations except the force of the best moral argument – the rules selected by society should tend to approximate more closely to the requirements of justice. In other words, we should expect to find that a monarchy or an autocracy enforces social rules that are less just than those of constitutional democracies. But whether this broad empirical claim is true or false, why is this relevant to the value of the Scanlon test as a determiner of the substance of justice? As we will see, Barry also tends to think that the Scanlon test for justice leaves most political issues unsettled. Its determining power according to Barry is not great. But there is all the difference in the world between a weak constraint and no constraint at all. Barry hears faint guidance where (I claim) he should hear nothing at all. The best way to appreciate this is to follow through some of Barry's derivations to see what exactly is supposed to be derived from what.

Philosophers have debated J. S. Mill's harm principle – the idea that the only good reason to restrict someone's freedom, against her will, is to prevent non-consensual harm to others. This principle includes a prohibition on paternalism – the restriction of someone's liberty, against her will, for her own good. Barry disposes of the issue of paternalism in two sentences. He notes that 'it is not plausible for people to say that their lives are going to be blighted – in relation to their own conception of their good' (p. 87) – if they suffer minor paternalist impositions. End of story. The conclusion is that no one could reasonably reject the idea that whether paternalist legislation should be enacted should be left to the democratic political process to decide. The speed of the argument is breathtaking. The Scanlonian contract appears to be very strong indeed. But we should pause. Why is it the case that I cannot reasonably object to a paternalist imposition unless it is going to render my life blighted? Suppose I have a conception of the good which makes autonomous choice a condition of value, so being forced to do what would otherwise be good for me is not, by my lights, good for me. I might think paternalist imposition objectionable even if I expect the government to be unaggressive in implementing it, so my life will be only slightly worsened. Milquetoast paternalism is still paternalism. In practice the Scanlon test for justice in Barry's hands seems to be a licence to reach conclusions about justice on the basis of what Barry intuitively finds to be reasonable and unreasonable.

FROM THE SCANLON TEST TO NEUTRALITY ON THE GOOD

Barry thinks that the Scanlon test, and hence justice as impartiality, yield determinate implications for policy only within a narrow range of matters. Here there is generated a list of fundamental rights or constitutional essentials which any decent society must protect. (The phrase 'constitutional essentials' is slightly misleading, because Barry allows that in some contexts what I am calling the constitutional essentials might be protected by legislative not constitutional means, and that this sort of protection, if effective, would be unobjectionable. What matters is that society should uphold certain fundamental provisions by whatever means.) Beyond the constitutional essentials, for the rest of legislation and policy-making, justice as impartiality cannot specify substantive laws and policies, but instead determines that in a broad area where reasonable people will disagree about the morally best rules to regulate their common affairs, what is reasonable is to agree to reasonable procedures and to accept whatever is the policy selected by these procedures.

Barry does not specify where to draw the line between political issues on which reasonable people can be expected to agree and those on which we should expect continuing disagreement. He makes it clear that most of the stuff of ordinary politics – his example is setting the public school curriculum – will fall on the non-consensual side of the line. It is important to recognize the extent to which Barry's proceduralism constrains his espousal of a liberal neutrality doctrine. In Barry's view justice as impartiality both implies a certain ideal of neutrality on the good and sets limits to its reach. The idea of neutrality on the good that is required by justice as impartiality is that 'nobody is to be allowed to assert the superiority of his own conception of the good over those of other people as a reason for building into the framework of social co-operation special advantages for it' (p. 160). The idea is that any proposal to give special advantages to my particular conception of the good will be reasonably rejectable by those who do not share it.

Two thoughts converge to establish the limited reach of the neutrality doctrine. One is Barry's conviction that impartial reasons do not suffice to settle most ordinary political issues. The other is Barry's belief that the full range of a government's laws and policies cannot be neutral on the good. The resolution of this difficulty is that in the realm of ordinary politics justice as impartiality insists on neutrality at a higher level, at the level of procedures for deciding on public policy. The formulation of neutrality is itself cropped to forbid only 'building into the framework of social co-operation' advantages for one's conception of the good based on its claimed superiority. The framework for social co-operation encompasses the constitutional essentials including impartially fair procedures. Roughly, justice as impartiality insists on constitutional democratic procedures that give each member of society equal citizenship rights, including the equal right to participate in democratic politics by voting, advocacy and standing for office. Within the limits of fair procedures and the constitutional essentials, in Barry's view citizens are free to press for majority coalitions that will use state power to promote their favoured conception of the good. To use an example that is not Barry's, a public school curriculum might set evolutionary theory or religious creationism or a mishmash of the two views to be taught to high school students in biology classes.

Something has gone wrong here. The mere fact that the adherents of my particular conception of the good, which I might acknowledge as sectarian and reasonably rejectable from many morally innocent standpoints, can collect a majority of votes in a fair election does not suffice to qualify whatever sectarian social policy is thereby enacted as just. Nor should we find plausible the weaker claim that social policies brought about by fair procedures and not in violation of fundamental rights are at least not unjust. On the face of it, it is unclear why it should ever be acceptable to use state power for sectarian purposes, to give a privileged place to a particular conception of the good and its adherents.

In principle, arguments for one or another social policy within a diverse democracy should address all citizens with reasons that all can share. The mere fact that I have a strong taste or preference or a commitment to an ideology based on faith rather than reason does not rise to the level of acceptable argument in a democracy. The proposal to use state power to enact laws that cannot in principle be justified to all citizens whatever their tastes, preferences and faiths violates a democratic ideal of justification to all. In fact the ideal cannot be fully achieved. One reason this is so is even in good faith some citizens will draw the line between what does and what does not qualify as a reason that should be acceptable to all in the wrong place. Another difficulty is that even if all policies enacted are perfectly reasonable, citizens in fact vary in rational capacities, so some reasonable policies will be unreasonably rejected. But these are problems of implementation, not objections to the principle. Barry appears to scrap the ideal too readily.

Complications abound here. It might be the case that for a broad range of policy areas, it is better to have some collective policy than none, but reasons in principle available to all do not yield any determinate policy. In such cases we might all be better off in the long run if citizens are allowed to press their own sectarian conceptions of the good as public policy, under the proviso that majority coalitions are shifting so that although one can expect to lose some public policy disputes that turn on choice of a controversial conception of the good, over time one also wins sometimes, and everyone does better from her own standpoint to allow particular controversial conceptions of the good to be promoted by state policy within a specified domain by comparison with the alternative of having no public policies at all for this domain. But notice that this justification for allowing non-neutral policy itself has a neutral justification. This justification would fail to hold if majority coalitions are stable and some lose and some win time after time, or if there are pariah citizens who have equal democratic rights but are always shunned by other potential coalition partners and never are part of winning democratic coalitions. The point on which I would wish to insist firmly is that 'we are following fair procedures' cannot be an adequate answer to someone who complains that she is unfairly disadvantaged by sectarian state policy. To know what's fair here, one must evaluate the outcomes that purportedly fair procedures would tend to produce over the long run.

In a sense, Barry's version of neutrality is too weak. He allows conformity to fair procedures to license what we should regard as sectarian uses of state power. It appears that Barry feels driven to this proceduralism because he is assuming that uncontroversial impartial reasons and controversial conceptions of the good exhaust the space of reasons. These alternatives become exhaustive only by stretching the category of conceptions of the good. Why not hold that where uncontroversial reasons of fairness do not determine a policy, legislators should make their decisions on the basis of these considerations plus controversial, disputed reasons of fairness? Barry's taxonomy treats as equivalent an appeal to the Rawlsian difference principle or a libertarian theory of individual rights (assuming these are controversial doctrines) and an appeal to a sectarian religious revelation or to the personal tastes that are shared by a majority of voters. At one level, according to Barry, any appeal to notions of the good are barred, and at the level of ordinary politics, virtually anything goes. (Notice that an appeal to the difference principle or libertarianism need not involve any claim that one's own particular conception of the good is better than those of other people – unless the idea of a conception of the good is a residual category that collects everything except uncontroversial claims of right).

I suggest that a better interpretation of neutrality is that the policies enforced by a just state should always be justifiable in terms of neutral reasons, reasons that all citizens can share in so far as they are rational. These reasons can appeal to ideals of the good life as well as to ideals of fairness, provided these ideals generate reasons that all can share. However, I admit that the force of this criticism is lessened, the more compelling is the set of individual rights and social provisions that Barry finds to be justifiable to all and hence required by justice as impartiality.

In this connection consider Barry's treatment of the problem of a right to abortion from the standpoint of justice as impartiality. In contemporary democracies, the right of a women to choose an abortion is controversial. Some authors have proposed a principle of preclusion, which holds that if political issues turn on controversial religious and moral views, then unless 'everyone recognizes that some unified policy is absolutely necessary, legitimacy requires that individuals be left free, consistent with the equal freedom of others to follow their own paths'.[4]

Barry rejects this principle on the ground that it presupposes a

[4] See T. Nagel, *Equality and Partiality*, Oxford, 1991, p. 165.

strong presumption in favour of individual liberty which many reasonable persons will reject. At least as stated, the principle of preclusion is too strong. A moral principle may be controversial, and we may not be certain we are right to accept it, though the balance of reasons so far as we can now see tilts in its favour. The mere fact that the principle is not known with certainty, and that among the members of society the principle is controversial, are not by themselves good enough reasons to abstain from enforcement, and to support each person's right to act as she chooses with respect to its dictates. From the rejection of preclusion as a general principle Barry leaps immediately to the conclusion that justice as impartiality does not pick out any answer to the abortion debate as uniquely just – neither the woman's right to choose an abortion nor the foetus's right to continued life inside the womb of the pregnant woman. This leap goes too far, too fast. Even if the principle of preclusion is unacceptable as a general policy, maybe preclusion is right in this case. One has to look at the arguments. Neither Barry in his book nor I here can survey all the arguments on abortion, but I would have thought that for reasons outlined by Mary Anne Warren, it is incorrect to regard the foetus as a person endowed with the rights of persons.[5] Moreover, the claim that the foetus during the term of pregnancy is a full human person is the only claim that could plausibly rebut the presumption that the pregnant woman's right to her body entitles her to choose whether or not to have an abortion. Barry appeals to a parallel between the issue of abortion and the issue of the moral rights of sentient non-human animals. His thought appears to be that the two issues must be treated alike by justice as impartiality, and since it is obvious that laws forbidding inhumane treatment of animals might well be at least permissible from the standpoint of social justice, on pain of inconsistency one must regard abortion the same way. Hence he supposes that neither the right to abuse a foetus nor the right to abuse an animal belongs among fundamental individual rights that justice as impartiality shows to be reasonably rejectable. Both abortion rights and animal rights issues are to be left to democratic legislation. Justice as impartiality insists only on fair procedures. Barry himself reveals that his opinion is that inhumane treatment of animals (bear-baiting, cock-fighting, fox-hunting and so on) is morally wrong and that abortion by contrast is morally permissible, but this appears to him to be one of many matters which justice *per se* does not settle.

But for all that Barry says, it remains unclear why he regards

[5] Mary Anne Warren, 'On the Moral and Legal Status of Abortion', *The Monist*, 57 (1973), 43–61.

abortion as an undecidable issue so far as justice as impartiality is concerned. It is also unclear what the principle is that determines what matters are decidable from the standpoint of justice. Barry, here as elsewhere, seems to rely mainly on his raw intuition that any moral view must include reliance on some basic intuitions. My sense is that he resorts to these too frequently and before arguments have been fully explored. But I acknowledge that this is a judgement call of a sort that methodological discussion is unlikely to settle. One can only examine case by case the sceptical thought that further argument on the point at issue would be futile.

To return to abortion, the comparison with animal rights seems to me to strengthen rather than throw into doubt the Warren position on abortion. Any sentient creature has the right not to be caused to suffer gratuitously, and once the foetus is sentient, it too possesses the right not to have suffering inflicted on it without good cause. But a sentient creature which lacks cognitive capacities at or close to the level of humans does not have a fundamental right to life, and only the warranted assertion of the foetus's right to life could block the strong autonomy case for the women's right to choose whether or not to carry a pregnancy to term. This discussion passes many issues that would need extensive discussion in order to make a compelling case, but I am still at a loss as to how Barry, with less discussion, feels entitled to deny that justice speaks strongly in favour of a woman's right to choose. Barry spends more time discussing the pragmatic political issue, whether trying to settle the abortion issue in the courts, as a matter of constitutional essentials, is more likely to provoke widespread popular resistance to abortion rights than a strategic decision to leave the issue to the legislative sphere. But this speculation about strategy does not clarify the moral issue. Barry's treatment of abortion illustrates the odd mixture of scepticism about the power of rational argument and dogmatic confidence in his own strongly held moral convictions that inform the argument as a whole.

JUSTICE AS IMPARTIALITY VERSUS UTILITARIAN IMPARTIALITY

The problem for justice as impartiality is to discover fair terms of social order for individuals who disagree deeply about what sorts of life are good for the individuals who live them. Some theories of justice, notably utilitarian theories, do not suggest an adequate way of dealing with this problem. The utilitarian response is to translate conflicting conceptions of the good into commensurable aims. Each person's aspirations are regarded as wants or desires, and the satisfaction of these wants is utility. The degree to which each person's wants are satisfied under proposed social rules is for the utilitarian the ultimate criterion of deciding whether the rules are just. But according to justice as impartiality the utilitarian response to the diversity of opinion on the good fails to take seriously the depth of this disagreement. Many members of modern democratic society adhere to conceptions of the good according to which satisfaction of wants *per se* has no great value, so the reduction of people's values to wants cannot fairly represent everyone's view. The person who believes that society should protect and preserve great art does not believe that the fact that he wants great art to be preserved gives a reason for his fellow citizens to devote resources to preservation, or that if he had happened instead to desire the destruction of great art, his wanting that would have provided his fellow citizens with an equally sound reason to devote resources to destruction. Far from being the basis on which all can agree, the idea that the good is constituted by want-satisfaction is just another controversial conception of the good.

Justice as impartiality responds differently to the fact of diversity. The utilitarian response to diversity on the good is essentially to move the discussion to a higher plane of abstraction, where the disagreements do not show up. But the kind of description of values that is appropriate for social policy formation is itself a controversial social policy question. The mere fact that we need to move to a higher level of abstraction to undo disagreement on the good is not a sufficient justification. Here, according to Barry, neutrality has a crucial role to play in the formulation of an adequate idea of social justice.

THE JUSTIFICATION OF NEUTRALITY

Barry justifies his favoured version of neutrality by an appeal to scepticism. If one is motivated to seek terms of social co-operation that all members of society can freely accept who have this same motivation to live under rules that are acceptable to all, one will not insist on any special privileged position for any one conception of the good over others. One will not propose terms of social co-operation that could be justified only by appealing to the superiority of some conception of the good over others. The reason that this is so is that a careful study of the history of diversity of belief regarding the good shows conclusively that there is no tendency toward unforced consensus and that reasonable individuals tend to fan out into allegiance to a wide diversity of conceptions of the good. This means that any proposal of terms of social co-operation justified by appeal to the superiority of some conception of the good over others would be rejected by some reasonable persons who affirm other conceptions.

This argument from history is far from conclusive. One could have produced a similar argument in the year 1400 to show that physics would never become a progressive discipline with well established results. But even if the argument from history is accepted, and Barry's argument for scepticism along with it, all of that would fall short of justifying state neutrality on the good. Even if it is the case that there are many conceptions of the good that might elicit reasonable belief, it still undeniably remains the case that there are many conceptions of the good which are manifestly unreasonable. The premise that there is no unique winner among conceptions of the good is fully compatible with the fact that there are many losers. Elaborating on the character of his scepticism, Barry writes, 'no conception of the good can justifiably be held with a degree of certainty that warrants its imposition on those who reject it' (p. 169). But to get from there to the doctrine of neutrality on the good requires premises which he does not supply. For even if we accept the sentence just quoted, this is fully compatible with maintaining that some conceptions of the good are so lacking in internal coherence and plausibility that it would be ethically desirable that the state should take effective steps to campaign against them or in other ways to seek to block citizens from embracing them. After all, a posture of non-neutrality on the good is consistent with the assumption that many distinct and conflicting conceptions of the good are sufficiently defensible that reasonable persons might affirm them. A non-neutral policy might seek to root out weeds while acknowledging that there are many flowers any of which might be favoured.

This point does not merely concern logical possibilities. I believe that many religious doctrines, including many thriving Christian sects that command legions of adherents, are manifestly unreasonable. Such ideas as that persons are partly constituted by immaterial souls that can be expected to survive the death of the bodies in which they are housed and to proceed to some further existence in an afterlife are empirical claims for which there is not a shred of evidence, so a person who is being reasonable will not find them credible. Religious doctrines that derive prescriptions about how we should live our lives from assertions about the best way to maximize the chances of felicity in an afterlife are not credible. In saying that such doctrines are unreasonable I do not mean to deny that many intelligent people find them credible or that very clever arguments have been advanced on their behalf. Barry adduces the diversity of religious belief in the world and the utter absence of any discernible tendency over time toward convergence of people's religious beliefs as evidence for his scepticism. But it seems to me that this argument relies on an unstated premise to the effect that if a lot of ordinary non-feeble-minded people believe in some doctrine, their belief must be reasonable. This is a powerful premise.

Applied to the domain of empirical belief, it would show that astrology, flat-earth cosmologies, and hosts of mystical and superstitious claims are quite reasonable, for they all stably attract many adherents who are non-feeble-minded.[6] Unless you gerrymander the evidence by considering only the beliefs of a scientific elite, the evidence that Barry cites to show that we cannot adjudicate among competing conceptions of the good and find knowledge of the good that could be a non-arbitrary basis for state policy could be matched by evidence that would equally show that we cannot adjudicate among competing conceptions of the nature of the world we inhabit and find knowledge of empirical facts that could be a non-arbitrary basis for state policy.

My hunch is that the root of the difficulty is the idea, first propounded by Rawls, that liberalism is committed to a generalization from policies of principled religious toleration to a policy of neutrality not just with respect to religion but with respect to all conceptions of the good. I doubt the basis of principled religious toleration is the thought that any religious convictions affirmed by citizens can be represented as defensible and reasonable. One might characterize two routes to religious toleration, a right-based approach and a broadly utilitarian approach. The right-based approach defends toleration on the ground that the individual has the right to form her own religious beliefs, and worship or not in the manner she chooses. The right to freedom of choice in the domain of religion includes the right to worship false gods and form unreasonable beliefs. The utilitarian route to toleration resembles the right-based approach in that neither presumes that the religious beliefs likely to be affirmed by citizens are reasonable. The utilitarian position begins by noticing the strife that is occasioned by the attempt to impose religious orthodoxy in a setting where unorthodox religious beliefs have committed followers. The utilitarian also notes that the general case for freedom of expression applies to freedom of religion as a subcase. Third, although religions often affirm strange metaphysics and broad empirical claims unsupported by evidence, the practical advice given by religious faiths tends to be uncontroversially socially useful. Hence, all things con-

---

[6] In the context of recent debate as to whether prehistoric skeletons of ancestors of native Americans should be turned over to archaeologists for study or to native American people for reburial, Sebastian LeBeau stated: 'We never asked science to make determination as to our origins. We know where we came from. We are the descendants of the Buffalo people. They came from inside the earth after supernatural spirits prepared this world for humankind to live here. If non-Indians choose to believe they evolved from an ape, so be it. I have yet to come across five Lakotas who believe in science and in evolution.' This last claim sounds correct to me, and it is also very likely true that most non-Indians do not seriously believe in science and evolution. The quote is from George Johnson, 'Indian Tribes' Creationists Thwart Archaeologists', *New York Times*, 22 October 1996, p. C13.

sidered the gains from persecution look to be far outweighed by the gains from full toleration.

Neither the Lockean rights-based approach nor the utilitarian approach to religious toleration invokes the idea that it is epistemically impossible to discriminate among religious doctrines according to their plausibility. Hence, neither the Lockean nor the utilitarian case for religious toleration provides any reason to suppose that toleration should be generalized to encompass all conceptions of what is good and choiceworthy in human life.

Further light on Barry's argument from scepticism to neutrality emerges from consideration of his remarks on arguments for versions of neutrality advanced by Charles Larmore and Thomas Nagel.[7] Larmore argues that a principle of equal respect for all of one's fellow members of society militates against pressing for some government policy on the ground of the claimed superiority of one conception of the good over others. Barry's plausible reply is that it is not treating fellow citizens disrespectfully to press for a coercive state policy that favours one's own conception of the good over theirs if one reasonably believes that their conceptions of the good are demonstrably inferior and that if fully rational they would disavow these various inferior conceptions. Barry further notes that a principle of equal respect plausibly recommends neutrality only if one adds that in so far as one is rational one will have to acknowledge significant doubt as to whether one's own favoured conception of the good really is superior to its rivals. Absent scepticism, equal respect need not counsel neutrality. Nagel has held that a principle of 'epistemological restraint' (rather than scepticism) underpins neutrality by insisting that some reasons may be perfectly adequate to guide individual conduct but are unsuitable as a basis for a coercive government policy. My construal of a religious revelation may thus be a good and sufficient reason for me to affirm my religious faith but an inappropriate reason to adduce when what is in question is a collective decision on public policy. Why? Nagel is not very forthcoming about the nature of the distinction he invokes between public and private reasons. The idea is that some reasons are inherently private in the sense that they cannot be expressed in a way that is accessible in a public way that anyone in principle might attain. Barry's sensible response is that reasons are reasons; they cannot be cabined in a private domain; they inevitably are liable to cross over any boundary between public and private that is set up to contain them. The idea of a purely private reason is incoherent.

---

[7] See Charles Larmore, *Patterns of Moral Complexity*, Cambridge, 1987 and *The Morals of Modernity*, Cambridge, 1995. See also Thomas Nagel, 'Moral Conflict and Political Legitimacy', *Philosophy and Public Affairs*, 16 (1987), 215–40.

We can see that Barry is trying to thread the same needle as Larmore and Nagel. Take the example of religious belief, which appears to be driving the responses to the issue. If liberal neutrality tells religious adherents that their convictions should have no influence on public policy because they are unreasonable, this claim inevitably will have repercussions for reasonable private conduct. Since reasons are reasons, liberal neutrality would then be calling into question whether it can make sense to base one's private life on one's religious convictions. On the other side, if there are in fact good and sufficient reasons for the religious doctrines that I affirm, such that organizing my life around these beliefs is reasonable, then these reasons will spill across the divide between public and private and become reasons for adopting and for rejecting proposed public policies. The trick for neutrality is to block certain considerations from attaining the status of reasons in the public domain while allowing these same considerations to function perfectly legitimately as weighty reasons in the private domain. And what goes for religious convictions goes for other aspects of the good as well.

Despite their differences, Barry, Larmore and Nagel all pursue essentially the same strategy in the face of this difficulty. Barry names his own proposal 'scepticism' and describes it so: 'The answer that I wish to defend is that no conception of the good can justifiably be held with a degree of certainty that warrants its imposition on those who reject it' (p. 169). I have my reasons for affirming my own conception of the good, but I know that others have reasons for affirming their own views, opposed to mine, and I have no knock-down argument that shows they are wrong. The end result of arguments about the good is that I may well have good enough reasons to affirm my opinions on the good for myself and live my own life in accordance with them, but I do not have good enough reasons for using state power to impose my own conception on others.

It is important to Barry's argument that acceptance of liberal neutrality should be consistent with wholehearted affirmation by individuals of their conceptions of the good as guides to their private lives. If this result should fail to hold, and liberalism should require massive revision of individual beliefs about the good in the private sphere, then a significant advantage claimed for justice as impartiality over utilitarianism collapses. Recall that according to Barry the acceptance of utilitarianism as the theory of justice for a society requires individuals to reconceive their conceptions of the good in ways that are inconsistent with the utilitarian understanding of them. In marked contrast, it is supposed to be a plus for justice as impartiality that I can accept it without altering in any way my understanding of the character of the good life. Justice as impartiality requires only agreement on the proposition that neither my own conception of the good nor anyone else's is sufficiently strongly supported by evidence and reasons to warrant its imposition on others.

But what Barry calls scepticism will not do the work it is called on to perform in this argument. Let us concede that even after extended rational deliberation I will be somewhat uncertain that the doctrines about the good that now seem most reasonable to me are really correct. Let us also concede that the greater the consequences, for better or worse, of a policy choice, the more reasonable it is to expend resources to improve the quality of the choice. Furthermore, let us accept the plausible idea that generally speaking, weightier consequences will be at stake in public policy choice than in any individual life choice. But doubt that my conception of the good is really correct does not establish a conclusive presumption in favour of refraining from imposing one's conception of the good on others. After all, my doubt that my conception is correct may be cancelled out by greater doubts about the reasonableness of the process by which other persons chose their own conceptions.

Moreover, the expected value of a policy choice is reduced, other things being equal, by doubt that the benefits the policy would gain are really beneficial. But other things are often not equal, and when this is so, these factors can offset the reduced expectation generated by epistemic doubt about the relevant evaluations. If circumstances are such that the policy being contemplated is very likely to yield the desired results and if these results are sufficiently desirable (according to one's current, fallible judgements about these matters), then all things considered the policy may be worthy of selection even though there is some non-zero probability that the evaluations on which they are based are incorrect. For all that Barry has argued, I don't see that the decision to impose values differs in kind from the decision to build a bridge. One must reckon with the sceptical possibility that the science on which one's engineering calculations are based is radically defective, but the mere shadow of doubt does not render it reasonable to confine engineering judgements to the realm of private behaviour and to refrain from engineering commitments in the realm of public policy.

The thought that there should be a higher threshold of reasonableness required for imposing one's views on others than for acting on one's own views, when those likely to be affected are oneself and one's voluntary associates, seems to presuppose a moral presumption against imposing on others and in favour of individual liberty. Otherwise, why do epistemic worries about the likelihood that one's calculation of what to do is mistaken support a policy of inaction over action? After all, one's decision to refrain from intervening in someone else's life to help him attain a better quality of life could just as easily be mistaken as a decision to intervene.

Of course, if I am very doubtful that my practical deliberations concerning a policy that affects others are worth much, I always have the option of deferring to others who might be in a better position to judge. But one can defer to the authority of others when contemplating action that affects only oneself as well. Moreover, if one has reason to distrust one's own practical deliberation and some reason to trust the deliberations of others, this by itself does not counsel a general policy of letting individuals go their own way rather than imposing on them. The experts to whom one has reason to defer might just as easily be recommending imposition as abstinence from imposition. The mere fact that one distrusts one's own deliberations about the good as a basis for public policy does not *per se* induce any grounds for refusal to impose conceptions of the good on others.

Moreover, even if, contrary to what I have just argued, one agreed that it is reasonable to accept a presumption against imposition of a controversial view of the good on others, this agreement still does not suffice to justify neutrality. Reasonable presumptions can reasonably be overcome. It would be one thing to assert that a higher standard of proof is required to justify imposing on others than to justify acting for oneself or to justify letting others go their own way, and quite another thing to deny that this higher threshold is ever reached. Barry's argument, which consists just in pointing to the higher threshold, does not provide reason to think it can never be crossed.

I do not see how it could be the case that each of two or more persons could reasonably and persistently believe that his own conception of the good is superior to the conceptions of others. In ignorance, one might know of reasons to affirm one's own conception that in isolation sound persuasive. But once one is appraised of the existence of another person who is making the same claim for his own conception of the good, something has to give. If his conception differs from yours, at least one of you must be incorrect in claiming that your own is superior. If both of you persist in the claim to superiority, at least one of you is being unreasonable. If I have reasons to prefer an Episcopalian worldview, and she has reasons to prefer a Methodist worldview, if her reasons are as strong as mine, I cannot on pain of being unreasonable continue to insist that my beliefs are uniquely rational. The thought that from my perspective, my view is better supported by reasons, while from her perspective, her view is better supported by reasons, cannot lead to a stable position in which each of us affirms the superiority of our own view while recognizing the perspectivally justified claim to superiority of the other. If there is no decisive reason to regard my perspective as superior, then a symmetrical claim to superiority by each of us must give way to a withdrawal of any claim to superiority. Again, we both cannot reasonably claim superiority. The epistemic situation that appears to be favoured in the liberal neutrality scenarios is one in which each person privately affirms his own conception of the good but does not press this claim, and thinks it would be incorrect to press this claim as holding for the public sphere.

I might reasonably think that philosophical contemplation is a uniquely good mode of existence and organize my life around the conviction of its superiority yet feel my reasons are too weak to justify any proposal to use state power to impose this conviction on others who disagree. However, this nice liberal-sounding attitude does not make sense. It is not at all reasonable to affirm that philosophical contemplation is a superior human activity. At most there is reason to think that philosophizing along with a great many other human activities is worthwhile. And it is far from obvious that the reasonable conviction that philosophical contemplation along with a host of other activities is worthwhile somehow is debarred from being a legitimate reason for deciding on public policy.

Another question that arises in this connection concerns the alleged epistemic asymmetry between the right and the good. Why on earth suppose that beliefs about the right will be any less controversial than beliefs about the good? If the standard for imposing one's beliefs on others is certainty, then it seems that people's convictions about fairness and justice are very likely to be insufficiently supported by reasons to be legitimately imposed on others. Doctrines of reciprocity, libertarian natural rights norms, utilitarian and consequentialist maximizing principles, Rawlsian maximin and priority to the worst off views, norms of equal respect and equal consideration, and many other doctrines all compete for recognition as fundamental principles of justice. Even if one can claim that the balance of reasons tilts in favour of one of these conceptions of the right, any such claim will be controversial, and surely very far from certain. If one sets the threshold of supporting reasons for public policy at the level of certainty, it is doubtful that any proposed policy can pass, including conceptions of the right as well as conceptions of the good. Moreover, certainty seems to be an excessively demanding standard. If I am wondering how to treat people, and various opposed conceptions of fairness all have something to be said in their favour, it may then turn out that no conception of fairness will reasonably seem correct. But it is unreasonable to insist that a conception may legitimately be acted upon only if it is certain. If one lowers the bar below the too demanding level of certainty, then no reason has been suggested by Barry that should incline us to suppose that only some conceptions of the right and no

conception of the good can meet an appropriately lowered epistemological standard for public policy choice.

THE MENACE OF UNIVERSAL FIRST-ORDER IMPARTIALITY

Barry argues that justice as impartiality is a binding norm at the level
of society's institutional rules, but not at the level of individual choices
of how to live. He exploits this contrast between impartiality at the
level of rules and partiality at the level of individual behaviour to
defend impartiality against its contemporary critics who view it as an
inadequate philosophy of life, one that is both too insistent in its
demands on conduct and too grudging in not allowing the partialist
commitments and local loyalties of individuals to play an appropriate
role in determining how one should live. For the critics, the form of
impartiality that reveals its true colours is act-utilitarianism, the
doctrine that on each occasion of acting, one should always act so as to
maximize the aggregate sum of utility in the universe. Barry agrees
with the critics that a universal impartiality requirement on individual action would be excessive, but he denies that impartiality
rightly understood includes any such requirement.

Recall that the basic idea of impartiality is that 'just rules are those
that can be freely endorsed by people on a footing of equality' (p. 52).
Impartial rules are those that pass the Scanlon test. In this approach,
the correct moral perspective on individual actions is the one that
reasonable persons (concerned to live together on terms that all
who are similarly motivated and reasonable would find acceptable)
would accept for the assessment of their conduct. No version of act-
consequentialism would pass the Scanlon test, Barry supposes, as do
other contractualists. For this claim Barry adduces three reasons,
under the headings of control, co-ordination and compliance.

Barry observes that we all value a private sphere of conduct within
which we are free to pursue whatever we choose so long as we keep our
pursuits within the boundaries of familiar moral rules. We also value
having legitimate control over the course of our own lives. Barry
thinks the adoption of act-consequentialism would destroy such a
private sphere and deny that we should have any legitimate control
over our own lives. According to act-consequentialism, whenever we
act we should bring about the best consequences it is possible to bring
about. We are free to do what we like or to follow our own personal
commitments only to the extent that several acts we might perform
have expected consequences of exactly the same value, so we are free
to choose among them to break ties. Envisaging this scenario, and
finding it unacceptable, we should reasonably reject act-consequen-

tialism in a Scanlonian original position. Barry uses the formula, whether it would be reasonable to reject a candidate moral doctrine, but the basis for this claim seems to be the undesirable consequences of living in a world regulated by the doctrine, so in what follows I shall focus directly on the supposed undesirable consequences.

Barry's argument recalls an argument urged by Bernard Williams against utilitarianism. Williams argues that utilitarianism must misconstrue the value of integrity and cannot integrate concern for integrity into utilitarian calculation. Part of his argument goes as follows:

1. If utility is maximized, individuals pursue projects.
2. If individuals pursue projects, they are disposed to give them priority over the goal of maximizing utility when they choose actions.
3. If individuals are disposed to give their projects priority over the goal of maximizing utility when they choose actions, they are not motivated to behave as act-utilitarians.
4. If utility is maximized, individuals are not motivated to behave as act-utilitarians.

Integrity figures in this argument in so far as keeping faith with one's personal projects is taken to be the test of integrity. Williams makes the plausible assumption that the embrace of projects by individuals generates huge utility and then notes that to be committed to a personal project is among other things to give it more weight in one's decision-making than impartial utilitarianism would allow. So it seems utilitarianism both must and cannot countenance individual commitments to personal projects. Let us suppose that a parallel argument can be constructed against act-consequentialism, what follows? Barry wants to interpret such considerations as supporting the conclusion that the consequences of implementing universal first-order impartialism would be horrendous, and would be tantamount to giving morality despotic control over our private lives. If I want freedom to live my own life as I choose within broad limits, then I must accept the same freedom for others, and we are pushed back to the idea that the principle of justice as impartiality applies in the first instance to rules and institutions, and through them generates modest, not despotic, controls on individual discretion.

This conclusion may be correct, but it is too hastily drawn. Act-consequentialism holds that the right action to perform is the action, of those available, that brings about the best consequences. Williams's counter-claim is that if everyone accepted act-consequentialism and successfully conformed to it, the overall consequences would be less good than could have been reached if act-consequentialism had not been embraced, because the acceptance of act-consequentialism by itself limits the extent to which good consequences can be secured. If we were all motivated in a different way, and not motivated to do what act-consequentialism says we ought, we could expect to be better off. We might then identify the set of motives such that instilling them in people would induce them to behave in ways that would bring about better consequences than would be brought about if any alternative set of motives were instilled in them instead. This set of motives that secures best consequences will not be equivalent to the motive to conform to act-consequentialism, if Williams's argument about the nature of projects and commitments and their importance to securing a tolerable quality of life for persons is correct. We might further ask what set of legal and social rules would be most likely to promote best consequences in given circumstances. Let's suppose that the considerations raised by Williams and Barry dictate that the set of legal and social rules that is best from a consequentialist standpoint would allow wide discretion to individuals to plan their lives as they see fit.

What is still far from clear is how any of this constitutes an objection against act-consequentialism. Perhaps there are just different levels of assessment.

Consider a simple example. In a society regulated by consequentialism, an individual (Smith) approaches a stop sign along a desert highway late at night, with no traffic visible. The legal rule in force says one should always stop at all stop signs. So the legal rule says Smith should stop. Smith happens to be taking a seriously injured person to the desert hospital, Las Vegas General. Stopping at the stop sign will delay the rescue mission by only a few moments, but still, given the gravity of the emergency, the act-consequentialist calculation determines that the right act in this situation is that Smith should drive through the stop sign and get to the hospital fast. But sitting next to Smith is his grandmother, to whom he is very committed. His personal relation to his grandmother is one of his most important life projects. Granny hates going through stop signs. Factoring this into an act-consequentialist calculation, it remains that the right act is to drive through the stop sign. But Smith is not motivated always to do the right act. He has a character that is, let us assume, ideal from the consequentialist standpoint. His motives are such that his having them produces better consequences for the world than any other motives he might have. His motives strongly incline him to defer to Granny in this situation, to keep faith with a valued personal project, and that is what he will do.

Consequentialist assessment of the situation can proceed on at least three different levels: social rules and laws, motives and character, and individual acts. The three levels do not necessarily cohere, in the sense that the act that is dictated by the rules, the act that is the right act according to act-consequentialism, and the act that proceeds from the set of motives that is best to have according to consequentialist assessment, need not be the same act. But so what? The levels will generally cohere in this way, or else it won't be the case that the rules and motives specified are really the best possible.

The answer to Barry's worry about consequentialism versus control is that if granting individuals wide discretion to pursue their projects is a great source of good consequences, the legal and social rules that are best from a consequentialist standpoint and the motives it is best to promote and instil will reflect this fact. Moreover, the facts (1) that the legal and social rules protect discretion and (2) that individuals are motivated to value and exercise it will significantly affect the case-by-case act-consequentialist calculation of what it is right to do. Here I am supposing that the social rules that the society promulgates and enforces with penalties will be distinct from the moral principles that are taught, which in the society we are imagining reduce to the single act-consequentialist principle. Legal rules are enforced by legal penalties imposed by the criminal justice system, social rules are enforced by the informal sanctions of public opinion, and moral principles are enforced, if at all, by individual pangs of conscience and feelings of guilt. So if individual discretion is highly productive of good consequences, a society ruled by concern to maximize good consequences will make ample room for individual discretion. None of this guarantees that the rules, motives and principles that direct people's conduct will not require sacrifice of individual interests and projects for the greater good, but if my discretion and freedom are sacrificed, this will be for the sake of the good, including the freedom and discretion of others.

Barry's rejection of universal first-order impartialism is not well supported by his arguments. What holds for control holds even more obviously for co-ordination. Under this heading Barry worries that a tolerably well organized society must bring about socially useful co-ordination of the behaviour of its members in such matters as traffic rules, currency and banking conventions of politeness and so on throughout social life. Barry supposes that if the one supreme norm governing individual behaviour was that each should always do the act that is reasonably expected to produce best consequences, in many-person co-ordination problems and decision problems with an element of co-ordination individuals would predictably fail to stabilize their mutual expectations and would fail to co-ordinate, with consequences ranging from the unpleasant to the disastrous. But the considerations already adduced indicate how a society of act-consequentialists could solve this problem, and institute institutional rules, conventions and other devices that would get contracts made and enforced, promises kept, the language of speakers understood by hearers, truths told and lies avoided, drivers keeping to one side of the road, everyone agreeing on terms of address and farewell, and so on. Of course, it might turn out that the optimal level of compliance with institutions and practices of co-operation under these arrangements would be nowhere near either the levels that we now expect to encounter or the levels we now conventionally regard as ideal. But the issue here is not whether universal first-order impartialism is all things considered an acceptable doctrine, but whether any attempt to implement it must self-destruct as Barry alleges.

One might object that I have so far ignored one of Barry's arguments which appears to have considerable force. Barry in effect argues that to have individual discretion and freedom to live one's life as one chooses within broad limits is precisely to be free to choose among a wide array of options without any one option being singled out as morally required. The good consequences for human life that flow from individual discretion are lost if a universal impartialist first-order morality is adopted, because such a morality is incompatible with wide discretion.

In reply: whether the adoption of a universal first-order morality in practice eliminates all human discretion, or the benefits that now accrue from individual discretion, depends on how heavily or lightly moral requirements sit on individuals who are deciding what to do. Whether individuals are substantially constrained in their choice of life by the principles of right conduct depends not just on how stringent the conception of right conduct is but also on the extent to which individuals are free to behave wrongly. This level of freedom depends on other features of the culture including its legal and social rules and the motivational patterns and character types it promotes. As the story of Smith and his grandmother illustrates, the extent of freedom provided for individuals can be substantial. Even if one were to hold that we should not call an action wrong unless we thought that an individual should be punished for failure to comply (unless there is some special excuse for non-compliance), a theory of right conduct might meet this condition but prescribe light punishment by conscience for wrongful conduct in many circumstances, and might in addition incorporate a generous doctrine of excuses that further dulls the pangs of conscience. Act-consequentialism can be upheld by a loose or a strict consequentialist regime, and Barry's worries apply only to the latter.

One might also be suspicious of universal first-order impartialism on the ground that people tend to be unintelligent or at least less than fully rational, prone to selfishness, and likely to be ignorant or confused on matters of fact that are relevant to policy decisions they must make. So requiring people always to reason from first principle before they act may lead in practice to avoidably bad decisions. This standard worry has a standard reply, namely that we should distinguish act-consequentialism (or any other version of universal first-order impartialism) as a criterion of right action and as a practical guide to decision-making. Accepting act-consequentialism for the former role is compatible with rejecting it for the latter role.

On compliance, Barry's point is simple and apparently powerful: any universal first-order impartialist morality would be incredibly demanding on individuals and would conflict with very powerful human drives and impulses, some of which are very likely biologically rooted, such as an impulse to be partial in one's choices and to favour kin over non-kin, neighbours over strangers, my tribe over members of other tribes. Hence universal first-order impartialism would be unfeasible, because the difficulties of ensuring compliance to its code would be too great. Here Barry invokes a doctrine of the mean. Unlike Nozickean libertarianism, which makes too few demands on individuals in the name of impartial rules to help thy neighbour, and universal first-order impartialism, which makes far too many such demands, justice as impartiality makes demands that are just right or at least in the neighbourhood of the correct level.

In reply, one might argue that Barry may be living in a glass house and be well advised not to throw stones. Against theorists of justice as mutual advantage, Barry appeals to the empirical premise that people can be motivated sometimes to do what is fair just because they perceive it to be fair. If that premise is correct, it is not clear why the advocate of universal first-order impartialist morality cannot help herself to it in defending the feasibility of an impartialist political system. If it is not correct, or needs qualification, the qualifications may threaten the feasibility of second-order justice as impartiality as much as the feasibility of first-order impartialist systems.

Leaving this point aside, I doubt that ensuring full compliance with impartialist morality is crucial to the stability and feasibility of such a society. To be stable, society needs a decent system of legal and social rules and sufficient willingness on the part of members of society to acquiesce in those rules. A society can survive quite handily even if its aspirational morality is observed mainly in the breach. These points apply to the society that postulates act-consequentialism as the standard of right conduct just as they apply to any other type of society. No doubt it would be nice, from a consequentialist standpoint, to bring about more rather than less compliance with the act-consequentialist principle, other things being equal (this *ceteris paribus* clause incorporates the consideration that there is an optimal trade-off among compliance with legal and social rules, action proceeding from ideal motivation and performance of right acts). The consequentialist will say that so far as implementation is concerned we should do the best we can. But I do not so far see that the compliance issue is especially pressing for the act-consequentialist in the sense that it points to any decisive known obstacle to setting up a society that upholds act-consequentialism in the course of establishing a society that is ideal from a consequentialist standpoint.

Barry also has a direct argument against the moral doctrine of act-consequentialism. He develops his argument by considering the views of Shelly Kagan,[8] who asserts that our response to cases in which one can save the life of another at small cost and risk to oneself shows that we accept that independently of any special relationship or obligation connecting one to a potential beneficiary there is always *pro tanto* a moral reason to bring about the greater good, which reason might be defeated by countervailing reasons. Kagan then argues at length that there are no such countervailing reasons that can defeat the presumption that we ought to do whatever will produce the greater good. Barry responds by offering an alternative explanation of why we regard ourselves as obligated to help in the lifesaving case, which does not involve acceptance of a *pro tanto* reason always to bring about the greater good, and so which prevents Kagan's argument from getting off the ground. Barry writes: 'An obvious alternative to a duty to maximize the good that would generate a duty in the case as stated is a duty to prevent harm' (p. 25). Moreover, this invocation of a duty to prevent harm rather than a general duty to bring about the good makes sense, because in modern societies we find wide and stable disagreement concerning the good, whereas there is wide agreement as to what constitutes harm, so a duty to do good is inherently deeply controversial in a way that a duty to prevent harm is not. Barry finds in this move not only a way to fend off Kagan but also to develop a positive moral argument against act-consequentialism. Given pluralism of belief about the good as a stable fact of life in modern society, an 'injunction to maximize the good is therefore bound to lead people to pursue incompatible aims. It is thus a formula for mutual frustration and conflict. Of course, there is no incoherence in an injunction to everybody to maximize some specific conception of the good' (p. 26), but any such specific injunction will be morally arbitrary, will give a privilege to one conception of the good over others that are equally reasonable.

The claim that reasonable people cannot agree on the good cannot be turned into a quick refutation of act-consequentialism of the sort that Barry tries to construct. First and most important, the claim is strictly

[8] Shelly Kagan, *The Limits of Morality*, Oxford, 1989.

irrelevant in a discussion of act-consequentialism, because this doctrine leaves entirely open how to evaluate the goodness of consequences. There are versions of consequentialism that would count the extent to which important individual rights are respected or violated as the relevant standard for assessing consequences as better or worse. The assessment of consequences can be done entirely in terms of considerations of justice and fairness, if one is a sceptic like Barry about agreement on the good. Kagan himself makes it clear that his phrase 'the greater good' is a blank cheque to be filled in by any theory of good consequences, and does not suppose that the cheque must be filled in by any doctrine of the good, much less a controversial or sectarian particular conception of the good. Barry fails to establish the asymmetry between the right and the good that is the starting point for his argument, but even if we accept the asymmetry claim, it gives no help to the attempt to refute act-consequentialism.

A second objection is that the worrying features of an act-consequentialist doctrine that relate to the stringency of its requirements would still be present in the doctrine if we interpreted achieving good consequences as preventing harm. Given the great unmet needs of the bulk of the world's population and the existence of mechanisms in place that can alleviate these needs by individual contributions, there is no practical limit to the extent to which one can effectively sacrifice one's interests, if one is a citizen in an affluent society, in order to bring about the prevention of significant and uncontroversial harms to impoverished people around the globe. The prevention of harm, like the achievement of greater good, is a sink that can drain virtually all our resources if we are willing. So the move from achieving good to preventing harm does not make a difference to the stringency of act-consequentialism.

Finally, Barry suggests that we can explain our attitude to the opportunity to rescue by invoking a duty to prevent harm instead of a duty to maximize the good. There are two contrasts here, harm versus good, and *prevent* versus maximize. Maybe accepting a duty to prevent harm does not mushroom into a duty that can demand virtually all of one's personal resources as a duty to *maximize* the good seems to do. But he does not argue for avoidance of the language of maximization. If saving one life is good, is not saving two lives better, and in general, is not more harm prevention better than less? So we are back to a maximization doctrine. My conclusion is not that Kagan's argument succeeds or that act-consequentialism is the correct theory of morality, but merely that Barry's arguments jump too swiftly to a conclusion he evidently judges reasonable. The details passed over may be consequential: after all, it is reported that God is in the details.

Barry's dealings with universal first-order impartialism are in some ways characteristic of his arguments throughout his book. He has an attractive vision of a certain kind of liberal society, and a good nose for philosophical threats to it. We learn many lessons about the project of contemporary philosophical liberalism from his attempts to repel these threats, whether or not we regard the attempts to be successful.

Although I have registered disagreement after disagreement, in conclusion, I wish to stress the philosophical good sense, humane and cosmopolitan sensibility, and penetrating intelligence that inform Barry's writing. He engages with central issues in political philosophy, and adds significantly to our understanding of them. Even when Barry's arguments strike the reader as excessively swift, they very often cut quickly to the heart of the issue. Barry combines high moral purpose, a capacity for indignation and exasperation, and a wry sense of humour. On the central issues of contractualism, impartiality and neutrality, Barry makes undeniable progress toward dispassionate analytical understanding. Those who disagree with Barry's conclusions now have their work cut out for them, for his arguments set a high standard.

6

Impartiality and Liberal Neutrality

SIMON CANEY

It is a commonplace that in many societies people adhere to profoundly different conceptions of the good.[1] Given this we need to know what political principles are appropriate. How can we treat people who are committed to different accounts of the good with fairness? One recent answer to this pressing question is given by Brian Barry in his important work *Justice as Impartiality*. This book, of course, contains much more than this. It includes a powerful and incisive discussion of several accounts of distributive justice (justice as mutual advantage and justice as reciprocity), a critique of other attempts to defend liberal neutrality and a rebuttal of those who are critical of the ideal of impartiality. In this chapter I wish, however, to focus on Barry's defence of liberal neutrality. The paper falls into three parts. Section I outlines the thesis that Barry wants to defend and gives a brief sketch of the argument he employs to defend it. Barry's argument makes two claims – what I have termed the Sceptical Thesis and the Agreement Thesis. Section II therefore critically assesses Barry's defence of the sceptical thesis and Section III examines the agreement thesis.

I

Let us begin with Barry's account of liberal neutrality. What political ideal is Barry defending? In *Justice as Impartiality* Barry affirms the following view:

(C) Impartiality requires that: (i) Principles of justice should be neutral between conceptions of the good (p. 172), and (ii) Political decisions not concerning matters of justice should be made by a fair procedure *but* may appeal to ideas of the good (pp. 109–10, 132, 143–5, 161).

[1] Earlier versions of this paper were given at the Department of Politics at the University of Glasgow (December 1995) and University College London (April 1996). I am grateful to the participants at both for their helpful suggestions. I am also grateful to Andrew Mason and Joseph Chan for helpful comments on an earlier draft of this chapter.

Several points should be made about this claim. First, we need to explain what is meant by the term 'neutrality'. Barry, like other anti-perfectionists, uses the concept of neutrality in the following sense: principles of justice are neutral if they are not predicated on claims about the good life. Principles of justice may not rest upon assessments of the worth of different conceptions of the good (pp.12, 83–5, 160, 172 and 177).[2] It is also important to have a clear understanding of the term 'conception of the good'. This term is used to denote an individual's judgements concerning which activities or ideals are valuable and rewarding: it denotes his or her views about what makes life worthwhile and important (pp. 29–30). Barry makes a useful distinction between first and second-order conceptions of the good. First-order conceptions of the good are people's particular and concrete judgements about which activities are rewarding and which worthless. Second-order conceptions of the good, by contrast, are more general and less particular accounts of the good. Barry gives two examples of second order conceptions of the good which help to illustrate the distinction. One is the view that want satisfaction is valuable (p. 133): this does not give people detailed accounts of what activities they should pursue and is compatible with a large selection of different specific (first-order) conceptions of the good because people have different desires. None the less it is a certain way of regarding what makes life meaningful. A second example of a second-order conception of the good is the belief that 'autonomy' is valuable (p. 129): this too is compatible with a large array of more concrete (first-order) conceptions of the good. One can value autonomy (in the sense of valuing the capacity to make choices and to act on one's own choices) and be an artist, merchant banker, shepherd, pimp or doctor. On Barry's view the state – when constructing principles of justice – should abstain from both first- and second-order conceptions of the good.

To understand Barry's type of liberalism it is helpful to contrast it with other liberal positions. First, we ought to distinguish Barry's position from what might be called *full neutralism* where the latter states that all political principles (and not just principles of justice) should be neutral between conceptions of the good. Full neutralism thus rejects (Cii). Like Rawls, Barry explicitly rejects full neutralism (p. 143).[3] Thus on his view the state may legitimately appeal to ideas about the good in order to enact legislation protecting beautiful land-

---

[2] See also 'In Defense of Political Liberalism', *Ratio Juris*, vii (1994), 326. For other helpful accounts of the nature of neutrality see Will Kymlicka, 'Liberal Individualism and Liberal Neutrality', *Ethics*, ic (1989), 883–4; Charles Larmore, *Patterns of Moral Complexity*, Cambridge, 1987, pp. 43–7; and John Rawls, *Political Liberalism*, New York, 1993, pp. 190–5.

[3] Ibid., pp. 214, 227–30.

scapes, promoting the arts, and preserving ancient buildings since none of these concern matters of justice (p. 161).

Barry's position should also be contrasted with what might be termed *liberal perfectionism*. According to the latter, the state has a duty (a) to protect the freedom of the individual, and (b) to further rewarding and fulfilling conceptions of the good. Like Barry's theory, liberal perfectionism recognizes and respects standard liberal freedoms. It differs, however, from Barry's theory in two regards. First, it does not insist that principles of justice should never appeal to ideas of the good: it thus rejects (Ci). Second, it dissents from Barry's justification of (Cii). For a perfectionist, political procedures in which citizens can draw on their ideas about the good have value partly insofar as they advance valuable conceptions of the good. On Barry's view, however, this is irrelevant: the justification for allowing people to appeal to their judgements about the good when deciding issues not concerned with matters of justice is that doing so is 'intrinsically fair' (p. 110). Now a liberal perfectionist and Barry might actually agree on the procedures to be adopted and a perfectionist can agree with Barry that procedures have value in part because they are intrinsically fair. But the two approaches differ in that the perfectionist approach, unlike Barry's, is also concerned with the quality of the outcomes of the procedure. It is concerned that the procedure described in (Cii) furthers valuable conceptions of the good.

Now that we have an account of the thesis that Barry is defending we can consider the argument that he gives in its defence. Why should we accept (C)? Barry's answer makes two claims, namely:

(P1) the Sceptical Thesis: All conceptions of the good could be reasonably rejected (pp. 168–73).

(P2) the Agreement Thesis: (i) Principles of justice may be implemented only if no reasonable person could reject them (pp. 164–8); and (ii) Issues not concerning matters of justice should be decided by a fair political procedure but can be predicated on claims which could be reasonably rejected (pp. 109–10).

Now Barry infers from (P1) and (P2) the conclusion, C, that political decisions concerning matters of justice should be neutral between conceptions of the good and that political decisions not concerning matters of justice may appeal to ideas about the good and must be made by intrinsically just procedures.

Barry then uses this argument to derive certain basic rights. He dwells in particular on two specific freedoms. First, he considers disagreements about which religion, if any, is true. What should the state do here? He says we should find a description of the good in question that is neutral between all the disputants. The neutral description in this case is 'being able to pursue one's religion': now once we have identified this as the good that is at stake he says that the only way to distribute it is equally. Therefore everyone has the right to pursue his or her own freedom (pp. 82–3: see also p. 143). He then proceeds to consider disagreements about sexuality. Again reasonable people disagree about which sexual practices are worthwhile and which demeaning. If we are to reach a description which is neutral between all sides we cannot therefore describe the good at stake as 'engaging in worthwhile sexual practices' because different sides disagree about what this means. The only neutral description of what is at stake is to refer to 'the freedom to pursue one's own sexuality'. If this is the good at stake all reasonable people would agree that everyone is entitled to it. Therefore each person has a right to engage in the sexual practices of their choice (including homosexual sex) (pp. 84–5: see also p. 143).

At this point it is worth considering the extent to which Barry thinks that his conclusions should apply to societies other than contemporary liberal democracies. By contrast with Rawls in *Political Liberalism*, Barry does not proclaim that his liberal principles should apply only to liberal democracies. Furthermore, several considerations suggest that he believes that all states should adopt his principles of liberal neutrality. In the first place, he explicitly adopts a universalist perspective, arguing that there is 'a universally valid case in favour of liberal egalitarian principles' (p. 3: see also pp. 4–7). Furthermore in the first volume of *A Treatise on Social Justice* Barry argues that almost all humans think it important to justify one's conduct to other people.[4] Barry might then argue that all political systems – and not just liberal political systems – are marked by a lack of agreement about the good. Indeed he remarks that the belief that some societies are united in their moral beliefs is a gross exaggeration (pp. 4–5). Of course, some societies may be more homogenous than others but there might still be controversial issues in these societies and therefore a need for a neutral theory of justice. I shall, therefore, tentatively assume that although Barry's main concern might be drawing up principles of justice for liberal democracies he nonetheless thinks that his principles apply to all societies. (None of my criticisms of Barry rely on this assumption and I make it only in order to have a complete picture of Barry's account of liberalism).

Now that we have some understanding of the nature of Barry's liberalism, we need to assess the plausibility of the two premises on which his argument relies.

---

[4] Barry refers, e.g., to 'the virtually unanimous concurrence of the human race in caring about the defensibility of actions in a way that does not simply appeal to power', Brian Barry, *Theories of Justice*, London, 1989, p. 285. See also ibid., pp. 284, 363.

II

I shall begin with the sceptical thesis. This affirms that disagreement exists among reasonable people on the question of which conceptions of the good are worthwhile and which are impoverished or meaningless (pp. 12, 27, 168–9). Barry refers to this as 'scepticism'. By this he does not mean to deny that some conceptions of the good are better than others: he is not sceptical in this sense. Rather his claim is that it is never possible to know with certainty which conceptions of the good are better than others. His claim is grounded on the observation that in spite of discussions about the good life that have taken place over several centuries we are still nowhere near reaching a consensus (pp. 168–72).

How defensible is the sceptical thesis? Four points should be made. The first is that there is something prima facie odd about Barry's scepticism. It is odd in two respects. (a) It supposes that scepticism applies to some areas of moral philosophy but not others. It affirms therefore what might be termed 'restricted scepticism'. This brand of scepticism may well be correct but it requires some explanation because it is not clear why scepticism, if it applies at all, should apply to some areas in moral philosophy but not others. Without an explanation as to why some areas are immune to the influence of scepticism, restricted scepticism appears rather mysterious. (b) Moreover, even if we accept restricted scepticism, we need to know why it applies to all judgements about the good but not to judgements about justice. Why assume that the distinction between what can be known with certainty and what cannot maps onto the distinction between the right (which can be known with certainty) and the good (which cannot)? Restricted scepticism does not entail that reasoned argument can resolve with certainty issues concerning matters of justice but not issues concerned with the good. It is compatible with a position which states that reasoned argument can resolve some (but not all) disputes about justice and some (but not all) disputes about the good. Again therefore an explanation is required: without it we have no reason to think that all judgements about the good can be reasonably rejected.

In addition – and this is my second point – it seems implausible to claim that every judgement about the good is subject to reasonable disagreement. Consider, for example, the following activities and pursuits:

(a) membership in religious cults: consider the numerous cults that have proclaimed that the end of the world is nigh only to have these proclamations proved false. Or consider those (including David Icke) who have declared themselves to be the Son of God.

(b) astrology: consider those who take the claims of astrology seriously and reverently follow the statements of charlatans even though there is no scientific basis for the descriptive, explanatory and predictive claims made by astrologists

(c) mind-numbing labour: consider jobs which consist simply of the ceaseless repetition of the same monotonous task all day six or seven days a week. Such jobs allow for no creativity, contact with other human beings, intellectual stimulation, emotional reward or financial compensation. Is it reasonable to argue that this life of drudgery represents a worthwhile and fulfilling life?

(d) community and love: consider the claim – shared by all religious as well as secular outlooks – that community and love are valuable. Most would agree that a life of loneliness and lacking in warm personal relationships is, other things being equal, thereby impoverished.

(e) materialism and egoism: consider Scrooge's lifestyle prior to his conversion. How plausible is it to deny that his life went better when he renounced his callous, miserly, misanthropic ways? Surely we think not simply that he was a fairer man afterwards but also that he led a more worthwhile life.

(f) alcoholism: consider someone with great talents and ability but who, because of his or her alcoholism, wastes them. Their addiction destroys his or her talents (to be a great footballer say) without bringing any benefits.

(g) drug addiction and solvent abuse: consider someone who has the potential to be a great musician but who starts taking hard drugs thinking he or she can handle it. That person becomes addicted and becomes obsessed with getting enough money to sub-sidize the habit. As a consequence, he or she loses work. Friends who have tried to help gradually become alienated. So that person ends up without fulfilling his or her tremendous potential, without control over his or her life and without friends. Surely this is not a rewarding or enriching life?[5]

---

[5] Andrew Mason has suggested one possible response to this line of argument. As he points out, one might make a distinction between particular 'judgements about the good' and 'traditions of thought about the good', where the former denote individual judge-ments about particular activities and the latter denote systems of ethical beliefs. He then suggests that scepticism about the latter (that is, bodies of thought about the good) is more plausible than scepticism about the former (that is, individual judgements about particular pursuits). See Mason, 'Justice, Contestability and Conceptions of the Good', *Utilitas*, 8 (1996), 298, n. 8.

Two responses can be made to this suggestion. First, it is not clear to me that scepti-cism about *all* 'bodies of thought about the good' is a plausible position. Consider, for example, the views discussed in examples (a) and (b) above. Can we plausibly argue that affirmation of these sets of beliefs about the good is reasonable? Alternatively consider a variation on example (e): consider someone whose whole outlook on life is focused simply on acquiring power, money, and status, and mixing with the rich and famous. Now this is not simply an individual judgement but a body of beliefs about the good that

In all of these cases, I would argue, Barry's scepticism is difficult to maintain. Would not most people accept these claims about the good?[6] If, however, we reject Barry's sceptical claim his argument is powerless against perfectionist theories of justice which incorporate some of the above judgements about the good. Consider, for example, a perfectionist theory of distributive justice which incorporated judgements about the meaningfulness of a person's labour. When assessing their entitlements it would take into account the nature of their work and those with boring meaningless jobs would be compensated (financially, say) for this.[7]

Two additional points should be made about (P1). Barry's sceptical thesis appears persuasive because much of *Justice as Impartiality* focuses on religious disagreement and it is clear here that many intelligent and thoughtful people do disagree profoundly about religious issues (pp. 29–30, 115, 163–4, 169–71). This disagreement is significant but it is important not to be distracted by it and consequently to overlook the wide agreement on other matters of the good.

In addition, we ought to distinguish scepticism from what might be called pluralism.[8] The latter affirms that many specific conceptions of the good are worthwhile (and that others are not). It denies scepticism (since it claims that we can establish what is worthwhile). It also rejects any monist view which proclaims there to be but one worthwhile conception of the good. A pluralist would argue that people have different talents and abilities and therefore that the good for one person may differ from the good for someone else. Now the distinction

governs decisions such as who one should befriend (those who can help promote your career) or marry (someone wealthy) or what one should wear, where one should holiday, what pursuits one should adopt, etc. (i.e. in short, how one should lead one's life). My suggestion is that it is implausible to claim that this is a worthwhile 'body of thought about the good'.

Second, it is worth noting that if Barry adopts the position Mason describes then it is not clear how, if at all, his position would differ from the perfectionist position affirmed by philosophers like Joseph Raz (cf. *The Morality of Freedom*, Oxford, 1986), since both would allow principles of justice to be informed by judgements about the good. For an instructive discussion of related issues see Joseph Chan, 'Aristotelian and Liberal Conceptions of Political Community: Political Perfectionism vs. Liberal Neutrality', unpublished paper, pp. 14–19.

[6] Suppose that someone denies these claims. Here it might be appropriate to observe that some of our judgements about the good are unreasonable. Judgements about the good might, for example, be unreasonable because of their reliance upon one or more of the following defects: incorrect beliefs, inadequate information, selective information, invalid logical reasoning, self-deception, or wishful thinking.

[7] I am not committed to the claim that all the above judgements should be incorporated into a theory of justice. My claim is only that scepticism does not provide a good reason for excluding them. There may, of course, be other reasons for not including them.

[8] See the characterization of pluralism given by Joseph Raz, 'Liberalism, Scepticism and Democracy', in *Ethics and the Public Domain: Essays in the Morality of Law and Politics*, Oxford, 1994, pp. 103–4.

between scepticism and pluralism is worth making because the claim
that individuals in liberal democracies adhere to different ideals of the
good might seem to support Barry's sceptical thesis. But the observation that individuals pursue different personal ideals is quite
compatible with the pluralist claim. The existence of variety is not
equivalent to, nor does it imply scepticism. This argument should not
be misunderstood. It is not making the (implausible) claim that there
are no disagreements about the good. Its suggestion is only that much
of the diversity of different conceptions of the good can be explained
not by scepticism but by pluralism.

In conclusion, therefore, the sceptical thesis is too sweeping. Before
we accept Barry's claim he needs to explain why we should adopt
restricted scepticism and why this restricted scepticism applies to all
conceptions of the good. In addition the sceptical thesis is contradicted
by many counterexamples in which it is implausible to claim that some
judgements can be reasonably rejected.

III

Suppose, however, that we accept (P1). Before we accept Barry's claim
that the state should adopt neutral principles of justice we need to
have good reasons for endorsing (P2). (P2) affirms that decisions concerning matters of justice should be made on 'terms that nobody could
reasonably reject' (p. 168). This second premise is inspired by Thomas
Scanlon's paper 'Contractualism and Utilitarianism' in which he
argues that moral rules are those rules that no-one could reasonably
reject.[9] Barry adapts this theory and applies it to principles of justice,
arguing that rules are just if they cannot reasonably be rejected. At
this stage it is worth pausing to examine what Barry means by this.
What is the exact nature of the relationship between the claim that 'X
is just' and the claim that 'X could not be rejected by a reasonable
person'?

We can distinguish between (at least) two different interpretations
of the claim that a principle is just if no-one can reasonably reject it,
namely:[10]

the equivalence version: according to this version, a just principle
is defined as a principle which no-one can reasonably reject. The

---

[9] 'Contractualism and Utilitarianism' in *Utilitarianism and Beyond*, ed. Amartya Sen
and Bernard Williams, Cambridge, 1982. Scanlon writes that 'An act is wrong if its
performance under the circumstances would be disallowed by any system of rules for the
general regulation of behaviour which no one could reasonably reject as a basis for
informed, unforced general agreement', ibid., p. 110.

[10] The following discussion is indebted to the instructive but different taxonomy of
different types of contractarianism outlined by Chandran Kukathas and Philip Pettit,
Rawls: 'A Theory of Justice' and its Critics', Cambridge, 1990, pp. 27–35.

relationship between the claim that 'X is just' and that 'X cannot be reasonably rejected' is one of identity. The two statements are identical.

the justificatory version: according to this version, a principle is just because no-one can reasonably reject it. The reason why 'X is just' is that 'X cannot be reasonably rejected'. The relationship between the two terms is therefore not one of identity. Rather one term (the claim that a principle cannot be reasonably rejected) is morally basic and grounds the other.

Now it is important to distinguish between these two different versions since the second, but not the first, is vulnerable to two powerful objections. Consider, first, what might be termed the *back-to-front objection*. Judith Jarvis Thomson makes this objection against Scanlon, arguing that it gets things back to front to argue that torturing babies is immoral *because* reasonable persons would reject it. As she rightly suggests, surely reasonable people would reject it because it is wrong.[11] Now this is a powerful objection to the justificatory version but (as she is willing to accept) does not damage the equivalence version since the latter does not say that the reason why it is wrong is that reasonable people would reject it. Consider, also a second objection, namely what might be termed the *circularity objection*. This common line of reasoning maintains that it is misconceived to argue that a rule is just because a reasonable person could not reject it, because what standardly happens is that notions of fairness and justice are built into the definition of reasonableness. Given this, it is circular to argue that a rule is just because a reasonable person could not reject it because a reasonable person is characterized as someone committed to just principles.[12] Now this objection is most forceful as a criticism of the justificatory version: if true, it shows that the argument begs the question. It is, however, powerless against the equivalence version. If two terms are equivalent then of course there will be circularity.

These two reasons strongly suggest, therefore, that the equivalence version is more plausible. We should, however, consider two objections which might be levelled against the equivalence version. The first maintains that it is implausible to claim that just rules are those rules that could not be reasonably rejected because there are some rules

---

[11] Judith Jarvis Thomson, *The Realm of Rights*, Cambridge, Mass., 1990, p. 30 n. 19. Thomson's objection is against the Scanlonian claim that *moral rules* are correct because no one can reasonably reject them but her objection is as forceful against the contention that *rules of justice* (like prohibitions of murder or torture) are correct because no one can reasonably reject them.

[12] See, ibid., pp. 188–9 n. 5. For other objections to Scanlon's method see Ronald Dworkin, 'Foundations of Liberal Equality', *Tanner Lectures on Human Values*, xi (1990), 28–31.

that could not be reasonably rejected which are not plausibly
construed as rules of justice. No one could reasonably reject the claim
that I ought (*ceteris paribus*) to help an elderly man cross the road but
we would not claim that this is a principle of justice. The claim that X
could not be reasonably rejected is therefore not equivalent to the
claim that X is just. Many acts of kindness and benevolence (i.e. acts
not demanded by justice) could not be rejected by reasonable persons.
Scanlon was right, this objection suggests, to claim that moral rules
(and not specifically rules of justice) are those that could not be
reasonably rejected. Barry can, however, respond to this objection by
reformulating his claim slightly. Instead of claiming that a principle is
just if no one can reasonably reject it, he might claim that a principle
governing the distribution of burdens and benefits is just if no one can
reasonably reject it. On this revised account, to say that 'X is just' is to
say that 'X is a principle governing the distribution of burdens and
benefits which cannot be reasonably rejected'.[13] Once reformulated in
this way Barry's position is not committed to the implausible conclusion that justice requires that one should help elderly people cross
the road.

At this point, a critic might raise the following objection to the
equivalence thesis: if the two terms ('X is just' and 'X cannot be
reasonably rejected') are equivalent then what point is there using
both? If A equals B then surely one of the two terms can be dispensed
with: it is redundant. We should therefore simply appeal to what is
just and do not need to invoke what reasonable people cannot accept.
The concept of reasonable rejectability, according to this objection, is
superfluous.

This conclusion is, however, premature. Indeed, Barry himself gives
a response to it which strongly suggests that he endorses the equivalence as opposed to the justificatory version. Barry's central point is
that if two terms, A and B, are equivalent then one can learn more
about the nature of A if one learns more about the nature of B (p. 113).
Drawing on this point, Barry argues that if we accept that just rules
are rules that well-informed equally-placed people could not reasonably reject then one way of finding out what justice is is to see what
people do not in fact reject in situations which approximate the conditions embodied in Scanlon's contract. Thus Barry writes, 'as empirical conditions approach those of an ideal Scanlonian original position,
the observed outcomes will tend to be those that could not reasonably

---

[13] I shall assume in what follows that the principles to be discussed are concerned
with the distribution of burdens and benefits. This enables me to employ the shorter
statement that 'X cannot be reasonably rejected' in place of the more cumbersome statement that 'X is a principle governing the distribution of burdens and benefits which
cannot be reasonably rejected'.

be rejected in such an original position' (p. 113). This Barry terms the 'empirical method' (pp. 195–9). The concept of 'reasonable rejectability' is therefore not superfluous because it can play an epistemic role. The fact that reasonable people living in a society which embodies Scanlon's conditions reject a proposition is therefore evidence (albeit not conclusive evidence) that that proposition is unjust.

*

It is perhaps appropriate here to sum up. I have argued that the justificatory version of justice as impartiality is susceptible to two powerful objections, neither of which has force against the equivalence version. I have also argued that two additional arguments against the equivalence version are unsuccessful. It is not easy to say which version Barry himself endorses since he does not invoke the distinction I have made but there is no evidence to suggest that he is logically committed to the justificatory version. Furthermore, his appeal to the 'empirical method' provides some support for the assumption that his position is best captured by the equivalence version. In what follows I shall assume, therefore, that Barry endorses the equivalence version.

With this in mind, we can now consider whether justice as impartiality (as construed above) is a defensible account of justice. Why should we think that just rules are those that cannot be rejected by any reasonable person? Barry does not provide a clear answer to this question. Nonetheless within his work, we can find two suggestions. First, he suggests in chapter one of *Justice as Impartiality* that (P2) usefully expresses an intuitively plausible egalitarian perspective. Thus he writes that principles of justice which cannot be rejected by reasonable people 'are impartial because they capture a certain kind of equality: all those affected have to be able to feel that they have done as well as they could reasonably hope to' (p. 7). He adds:

the whole idea that we should seek the agreement of everybody rests upon a fundamental commitment to the equality of all human beings. This kind of equality is what is appealed to by the French Declaration of the Rights of Man and of the Citizen and by the American Declaration of Independence. Only on this basis can we defend the claim that the interests and viewpoints of everybody concerned must be accommodated' (p. 8: see also p. 113).[14]

Given this, we might therefore defend (P2) on the grounds that Scanlonian contractualism models the idea of equality by taking each person's views into account. It allows people to 'veto' principles which do not treat them fairly.

This line of argument is, however, not conclusive. It is true that one way of treating people equally is to ask what reasonable people would

---

[14] See also *Theories of Justice*, pp. 288–9, 348–9.

accept. But it is also true that there are other ways of spelling out the egalitarian view which do not rely on Scanlonian contractualism. Consider the view affirmed by Ronald Dworkin and Will Kymlicka. They argue – very persuasively – that the state respects its citizens equally to the extent that it shows equal respect to everyone's interest in living a fulfilling and meaningful life. As they point out, we wish to live worthwhile lives and wish to avoid boring, trivial or worthless conceptions of the good.[15] On this view therefore correct principles of justice should protect and promote this interest in well-being. Now this, like justice as impartiality, is an egalitarian theory which aims to show its citizens equal respect yet, unlike justice as impartiality, it is not committed to Scanlonian contractualism. A commitment to the equal moral standing of each person does not therefore logically imply a commitment to the agreement thesis because there are other ways of developing the egalitarian principle. Whilst it might be correct to claim that one can accept the agreement thesis only if one accepts an egalitarian conviction about the moral equality of all persons (p.8), it is incorrect to claim that if one accepts the egalitarian perspective then one must accept the agreement thesis. We therefore require additional moral arguments before we can accept Barry's claim that political principles should command the support of all reasonable persons.

Later in *Justice as Impartiality*, Barry appears to make a second suggestion. He argues that people have a strong wish 'to live in a society whose members all freely accept its rules of justice and its major institutions' (p. 164). Following Scanlon, Barry maintains that people wish to adopt principles which they can justify to other reasonable human beings (see p. 165). People, he claims, are moved by what he terms the 'agreement motive' (pp. 164–8). Let us call this the *psychological fact*. Barry's suggestion is that the *psychological fact* lends support to the thesis that a principle is just if no person could reasonably reject it.

This line of reasoning is, however, open to two objections. First, a critic might object to Barry's argument as follows: it is not clear how a psychological claim can generate a normative conclusion. Even if humans have this desire (namely, a desire to justify one's principles), this, in itself, fails to establish that it is a worthy desire and that a theory of justice should be constructed to satisfy it. That individuals are moved by the 'agreement motive', the objection continues, does suggest that Barry's theory of justice is not utopian (assuming that people do not have desires which conflict with the agreement motive

[15] See Ronald Dworkin, 'Foundations of Liberal Equality': Will Kymlicka, *Liberalism, Community and Culture*, Oxford, 1989, pp. 10–12; Will Kymlicka, *Contemporary Political Philosophy: An Introduction*, Oxford, 1990, ch. 2, § 2, esp. pp. 14–16, and ch. 6, esp. pp. 202–3.

and which are more powerful). If Barry's claim that people have this desire is correct, institutions governed by his principles stand a good chance of being feasible. But we need to know more than that it is feasible. We need to know that it is just and an appeal simply to what people desire is not enough. All the *psychological fact* shows is that people are likely to comply with Barry's political system: it does not show why they should nor that it is just.

Barry can, however, deal with this objection relatively easily by re-phrasing his argument slightly. Instead of grounding his theory of justice on the observation that we have a wish to justify our conduct to others, he might instead argue that we have a widespread intuition that principles of justice should be justifiable.[16] This reformulated version of his argument appeals not to people's desires but to people's common sense moral values. It suggests that justice as impartiality is intuitively plausible and appealing.

Barry's argument is, however, vulnerable to a second more powerful objection. Even if we have this intuition (or are moved by this desire), it is clear that we have other intuitions which compete with it. Con-sider, again, the theory of justice advocated by Dworkin and Kymlicka. Their claim that citizens have an interest in living meaningful lives seems undeniable. Given this, surely a theory of justice should take this interest into account. To see this consider two proposed theories of justice. Suppose that under one people live miserable impoverished lives, whereas under the other people live fulfilling lives. It seems undeniable that the second theory of justice is preferable to the first. Once we accept this, however, it follows that any plausible theory of justice must take into account its effects on people's interest in well-being. A straightforward appeal to people's intuitions does not estab-lish the correctness of justice as impartiality since the latter omits any reference to one of the most important interests of all citizens. It is therefore not plausible to stipulate that justice should be defined simply in terms of what people cannot reasonably reject. A plausible theory of justice would incorporate both (i) a commitment to people's interest in well-being and (ii) a commitment to policies which com-mand widespread assent.[17]

Neither consideration therefore supports (P2). Barry makes power-

---

[16] This raises the question of why Barry does phrase it in the way he does. The most likely explanation is that Barry wishes to counter any suggestion made by advocates of justice as mutual advantage that the only reason we have to do something is that it furthers our self-interest. Barry's point is that we recognize other reasons for action. See *Theories of Justice*, pp. 284–5.

[17] This account of justice, it should be noted, is compatible with a perfectionist pos-ition. A perfectionist can plausibly argue that a perfectionist state best enables people to flourish (and therefore meets condition (i)) and can do so by adopting procedures which command widespread support (and therefore meets condition (ii)).

ful objections to justice as mutual advantage and justice as reciprocity but we lack a convincing argument in defence of justice as impartiality.

*

Barry's agreement thesis is also open to a second objection. Not only do we lack convincing arguments for (P2): we also have good reason to reject it. To see this we should examine in greater detail what Barry means by 'reasonableness'. Barry does not give a precise definition of reasonableness but his usage of the term suggests that for someone to be reasonable she must, among other things:

i)   not advocate principles of justice which are based on incorrect beliefs (p. 69: an epistemic condition),

ii) not advocate principles of justice solely on the grounds that they favour her self interest (p. 8: a moral condition),[18]

iii) seek to reach agreement with other reasonable persons.

The problem with the ideal of reasonableness once it is characterized in this way is, however, that it is unduly stringent. Let us call this the *stringency objection*. This problem arises because it is evident that reasonable disagreement exists on many issues concerned with matters of justice. Consider the profound disagreement about the legitimacy of redistributive taxation, the nature of a just war, the appropriate way to treat terrorists, legitimate principles of punishment and in particular capital punishment, the justifiability of reverse discrimination, the nature of a just electoral system, the value of freedom of expression, and the nature and extent of our obligations to future generations and members of other states. Now in many of these cases there are no principles of justice which could gain the acceptance of all reasonable persons. But given Barry's claim that principles of justice should not rely on claims which someone could reasonably reject it follows that there can be no principles of justice on many of these matters. But this is surely a highly implausible conclusion. The claim that principles of justice must never be predicated on claims which can be reasonably rejected is therefore too demanding.

Someone might respond to this argument as follows: ideally, principles of justice should not be predicated on claims which reasonable persons can reject. Where this is not possible, however, principles of justice may rest on premises and arguments which can be reasonably rejected. Barry, however, cannot make this response without compromising his commitment to liberal neutrality. If he concedes that

[18] Barry unpacks this moral component in *Theories of Justice*. He writes 'Flatly asserting "It's contrary to my interest and that's why I oppose it" will be ruled out. It is simply not a valid move in the game. Beyond that, we must invoke a requirement of good faith: that people will not put forward frivolous or tendentious arguments for a position that they actually hold only because it is personally advantageous', p. 352.

principles of justice may appeal to controversial considerations, then it is difficult to see why they may not appeal to, among other things, controversial judgements about the good. If principles of justice can depend upon disputed beliefs about the right we need an argument explaining why they cannot also depend upon disputed beliefs about the good. The *stringency objection* thus remains intact.

*

At this point it is worth considering an additional problem with Barry's argument. Suppose that one accepts Barry's claim that principles of justice are correct if they cannot be reasonably rejected. Barry assumes that if reasonable people disagree about which conceptions of the good are worthwhile then principles of justice which are predicated on conceptions of the good could be reasonably rejected. This assumption is, however, questionable. In particular, it overlooks the possibility that principles of justice which incorporate controversial claims could command the agreement of all reasonable persons if they came about by a *procedure* which no one could reject. Barry accepts that principles not concerned with matters of justice could enjoy legitimacy because of the way they were chosen.[19] But if this is true of non-justice-related principles which embody controversial claims then surely it could also be true of principles of justice which embody controversial claims. A concern to reach principles of justice which no reasonable person could reject does not therefore entail that principles of justice should eschew controversial claims.

It is important here to recall Barry's formulations of the ideal affirmed by justice as impartiality. According to Barry, '[w]hat the theory of justice as impartiality calls for are *principles and rules* that are capable of forming the basis of free agreement among people seeking agreement on reasonable terms' (p. 11: emphasis added). This, however, is compatible with a political system in which reasonable people accept a political procedure (it forms a 'basis of free agreement') and therefore accept its decisions even though the decisions on matters of distributive justice, say, rest on claims which some reasonable people dispute. Barry writes that justice as impartiality demands 'a consensual basis for the ground rules of social life' (p. 30) and 'a set of rules for living together that are capable of attaining the free assent of all' (p. 191). Both of these, are however, compatible with a political system in which reasonable people accept a political procedure (affirming the 'ground rules of social life' and 'a set of rules for living together')

---

[19] For an outline of political procedures which would bestow legitimacy on the principles chosen, see Simon Caney, 'Anti-Perfectionism and Rawlsian Liberalism', *Political Studies*, xliii (1995), 255–6.

but in which people determine what is just by appealing to their conceptions of the good.[20]

*

I now want to suggest a reason why principles of justice, if they are to be plausible, should rely on controversial claims. In *Justice as Impartiality* Barry does not discuss what resources he thinks should be distributed to individuals. Many anti-perfectionists, like John Rawls, believe that the state should distribute primary goods (like liberty, powers, opportunities, wealth, income and social bases of self-respect).[21] Such goods are helpful for a diverse array of conceptions of the good and can therefore be adopted by a neutral state. A problem arises, however, because there are cases where these primary goods conflict and a choice needs to be made about which should hold sway. There might, for instance, be a conflict between liberty and economic wealth. Suppose that we could improve the overall level of wealth by limiting people's freedom. Given a conflict between primary goods we need a criterion to enable us to choose. It is difficult, however, to see how a neutral theory of justice can help us make the choice. One plausible response is that, when this occurs we should assess which primary good is more important here by appealing to a more specific account of the good. In other words, the state when constructing principles of justice should invoke claims about the good to resolve such conflicts. Barry, however, is prohibited from making such a claim and it is difficult to see how he could plausibly deal with such trade-off decisions.

*

Having considered Barry's defence of the claim that principles of justice should not rest upon controversial ideals, it is worth turning our attention to his treatment of other political principles. Barry, recall, argues that whilst matters of justice should not rely on controversial claims other political issues can. Let us call this the *asymmetry claim*. The asymmetry in the way that Barry treats claims about justice (which must eschew controversial premises) and claims about non-justice-related matters (which need not) needs to be explained and

---

[20] Consider also Barry's claim that '[t]he essential idea is that fair *terms of agreement* are those that can reasonably be accepted by people who are free and equal' (p. 112: emphasis added). Again this does not require that principles of justice must not rely on claims which reasonable persons reject. It is compatible with a political system in which decisions concerning matters of justice are the product of a political procedure (which reasonable people endorse) in which people may appeal to their ideals of the good (even if they are claims which could reasonably be rejected). People could accept the 'terms of agreement' because of the way in which the decision was made.

[21] See Rawls, *Political Liberalism*, pp. 75–6, 178–90.

justified. It embodies two claims. The first is the conceptual claim that one can separate matters of justice from other political issues; the second is the normative claim that principles of justice, unlike other political principles, must command the consent of all reasonable persons. Let us begin with the normative claim.

This normative point stands in need of justification. One might call it into question in two ways. First, if the argument showing that principles of justice should eschew controversial claims is persuasive (as Ci claims) why does it not also show that all political principles should eschew controversial claims? Or to put the same question a second way: if we can appeal to controversial claims to resolve those political issues that do not raise issues of justice (as Cii claims) then why can we not also appeal to controversial claims to resolve matters of justice? What, in other words, explains the asymmetry in the treatment of controversial claims about justice and controversial claims about non-justice-related issues?

Barry's work does suggest a response to this objection. He reasons that unlike issues concerning justice many other 'issues unavoidably turn on conceptions of the good' (p. 122 n. a). His suggestion is that it is impossible to deal with some political issues without relying on judgements about the good. He writes, for example, that the content of the curriculum taught in state schools must inevitably appeal to ideas of the good:

decisions about what the publicly run schools are going to teach must obviously involve a view about the value of learning some things rather than others. (So must the imposition of minimum scholastic standards on private education.) It would be absurd to suggest that there is some way of determining a curriculum that is neutral between all conceptions of the good, and it is significant that those who support the idea of legislative (as against constitutional) neutrality have never attempted to lay out a neutral curriculum. (p. 161)

Two points should, however, be made in response to this. First, Barry's claim is that it is not *possible* to construct an educational curriculum and be neutral between conceptions of the good. Is this, however, true? Recall that, according to Barry, a political principle is neutral if it is not predicated upon an assessment of the worth of some specific conceptions of the good. Given this definition a state's educational curriculum is neutral as long as its content does not reflect the state's judgement of what is worthwhile. A state could therefore construct a neutral curriculum by adopting the following measures: some subjects are taught which all conceptions of the good value (like mathematics or geography). On more contentious matters, like religious studies, imagine a scheme in which parents are given a panoply of choices (Christianity, Islam, humanism etc.) from which they must choose

which subjects their children are to study. Under such an arrangement
the state is not making a judgement about which religion (if any) is
valuable. Alternatively consider the suggestion made by some libertarians that parents should be allocated educational vouchers which
they can then employ to choose which schools their children attend.
One could thus imagine a market system of schools, offering different
subjects, and in which the choice as to what is studied reflects the
choice of parents. In both of these systems the state does not make
assessments of the worth of the different conceptions of the good since
the choice is made by the parents. Now my argument here is not that
this kind of educational system is desirable; it is simply that it is
possible for the state to construct a neutral curriculum. It is, therefore,
incorrect to claim that it is 'absurd to suggest that there is some way
of determining a curriculum that is neutral between all conceptions of
the good' (p. 161).[22]

Secondly, Barry's argument does not fully address the objection to
the *asymmetry claim*. If successful, Barry's argument shows that the
state cannot be neutral concerning some matters (like education). But
it does not show why this is particular to some issues (like education)
but not to others (such as those concerning matters of justice).

Barry has therefore failed to justify his asymmetrical treatment of
principles of justice (which must be neutral) and other political principles (which should not). At this point, someone might make the following argument on Barry's behalf: it is not possible for the state to be
neutral between conceptions of the good on matters like education
since, whatever curriculum is adopted, different conceptions of the
good will enjoy different levels of success. The educational systems
arrived at by either of the methods suggested above are not neutral
because the curriculum chosen will have the consequence that some
conceptions of the good are more successful and other conceptions are
less successful.

But Barry should not accept this argument for three reasons. First,
it employs a different concept of neutrality to that which Barry is
defending. According to Barry, a political principle is neutral if it is not
predicated on a judgement about the good (p. 123, 142, 160). Whether
the principle has the consequence that some conceptions of the good

---

[22] One suggestion (made to me by Brian Barry and Peter Jones) is that neither of the
proposals described above can accurately be described as an 'educational' system since
the latter, by its very nature, must incorporate judgements about the good. A full
neutralist can, I think, plausibly reply that this *definitional* move is too hasty and that
we can define education in terms of providing a general preparation for life (whatever
one's conception of the good) and an understanding of one's society and the world. On
this broad definition of education, both of the neutralist schemes described in the text
could count as educational systems.

are more successful than others does not jeopardize its neutrality. The attempt to defend Barry's asymmetrical treatment of principles of justice and other political principles thus relies on a quite alien concept of neutrality. Secondly, Barry is right to reject the concept of neutrality employed in the last paragraph (p. 77, 123). As many anti-perfectionists have pointed out, this concept of neutrality is both (a) unattainable and (b) undesirable.[23] It is unattainable because some conceptions of the good conflict with others and therefore either one or the other succeeds: it is not possible for both to fare equally well. It is undesirable because it would mean restricting popular and successful conceptions of the good to ensure that less popular conceptions of the good fare equally well. Finally, like the previous attempt to defend the normative component of Barry's *asymmetry claim*, it fails to explain why it is both impossible for the state to be neutral between conceptions of the good when dealing with issues unconcerned with justice *and* possible for the state to be neutral between conceptions of the good when legislating about matters of justice.

Both attempts to defend the asymmetry in the treatment of principles of justice and other political principles are therefore unsuccessful. If Barry's defence of a neutral theory of justice is successful it implies that he should reject (Cii) and embrace full neutralism.

*

Thus far Barry's distinction between political issues concerning justice and political issues not concerning justice has been accepted without question. It is worth, however, also examining the conceptual component of the *asymmetry claim*, namely the contention that one can separate issues of justice from other political principles. It is not clear, however, whether this distinction can be sustained.[24] The problem arises because those matters Barry deems not to raise issues of justice frequently require financial support and thus inevitably raise issues of distributive justice. To see this consider some of Barry's examples – legislation protecting areas of great natural beauty, furthering the arts and maintaining historic sites (p. 161). Barry's claim is that such legislation (unlike legislation concerning the just allocation of resources) may legitimately be informed by citizen's views about the good. But each of these policies brings with it a financial cost, namely the cost of supporting the arts and ancient monuments, and the opportunity cost of not using the protected land for other purposes. And these costs will

---

[23] For (a) see John Rawls, 'Fairness to Goodness', *Philosophical Review*, lxxxiv (1975), 539, and Rawls, *Political Liberalism*, pp. 193–4. For (b) see Kymlicka, 'Liberal Individualism and Liberal Neutrality', pp. 884–5.

[24] I am grateful to Michael Lessnoff for suggesting the following line of argument.

standardly require taxation. People's entitlements (their share of resources) are being affected by these other good-based policies. Judgements about the good are therefore influencing who gets what. The
neat distinction between issues concerning justice and issues that are
not concerned with matters of justice – on which Barry's theory of
liberal neutrality relies – is therefore unconvincing.

Barry's denial of the linkage between these other political issues and
issues of justice is dependent on a specific view of the nature of just
institutions. In the first volume of *A Treatise on Social Justice* Barry
discusses whether the state should subsidise opera and he argues that
whether or not it does so does not raise any issues of justice: 'it is an
example of a public policy issue to which justice is essentially irrelevant'.[25] Barry's conclusion rests on the following line of reasoning:

> In cases where the distribution of benefits and burdens is incidental to the
> rationale of an institution, asking whether the institution is just or unjust may
> be somewhat beside the point. An obvious example is that of the public sub-
> sidization of grand opera.[26]

His argument is that whether an institution is just or unjust depends
on the rationale underlying its distribution of goods. Since the in-
tentions underlying policies of subsidizing the opera are not redistributive they do not raise any issues of justice.

But this is a highly questionable account of justice. Surely what
matters when assessing the justice of an institution is how advantages
and disadvantages are, in fact, distributed regardless of the 'rationale'.
Suppose that money is spent on subsidizing opera (the rationale being
that this promotes a fulfilling and exalted conception of the good) and
that consequently less is spent on meeting the basic needs of the poor.
Surely an adherent to a theory of justice committed to meeting basic
needs can describe this state's actions as unjust. The point therefore
remains: subsidizing valuable conceptions of the good costs money and
therefore normally involves taxes and thereby affects the distribution
of advantages and disadvantages.

IV

It is time to sum up. I have argued that neither Barry's sceptical thesis
nor his agreement thesis are compelling. The former fails to explain
why scepticism is restricted to issues about the good and is difficult to
sustain given some judgements about the good. The agreement thesis
is also questionable. We lack any convincing argument for the agree-

[25] Barry, *Theories of Justice*, p. 356.
[26] Ibid., p. 355.

ment thesis and it is also susceptible to a powerful objection (the *stringency objection*). In addition, I have suggested that perfectionist theories of justice can satisfy the agreement thesis if they are implemented by a fair political procedure. Finally, I have called into question Barry's asymmetrical treatment of principles of justice (which should be neutral) and other political principles (which should not).

7

What's 'Wrong' in Contractualism?

MATT MATRAVERS

Brian Barry's *Justice as Impartiality* is an important book, one of its contributions to the discipline is a characteristically clear presentation of what follows if one accepts a commitment to equality and the reasonableness of continuing and profound disagreements about the nature of the good life (the reasonableness of pluralism). I take the argument of *Justice as Impartiality* to be an important next step in the attempt to give an account of the content of justice which is impartial, fair, or neutral[1] between conceptions of the good, and engaging with it has the great advantage that many of the criticisms that can be made of Barry apply to other liberal contractualist theories of social justice. It is faintly ironic that it is one of Barry's great virtues, his clarity, that makes it easier to see the problems inherent in the attempt to complete the impartialist project. I have not attempted below to offer a systematic summary and critique of Barry's book or any particular section of it. Instead I have opted to try to engage with the ideas that drive it at a more fundamental level.

At the heart of Barry's theory, as the title of his book suggests, is the idea that in a world characterized by the reasonableness of pluralism the rules of justice must be such that they appeal to no particular conception of the good in their derivation or justification – they are to be impartial. The strategy of this paper is to investigate that claim, specifically, to investigate whether Barry invokes or needs thick ethical commitments in order to complete his project; commitments which undermine his claim to impartiality. To anticipate the argument: In the first section of my comments I give a brief synopsis of Barry's argument and argue that he builds on a commitment to equality and the reasonableness of pluralism. Further, Barry believes that if one combines scepticism (his response to the reasonableness of pluralism), with equality and what he calls 'the agreement motive', then justice as impartiality is revealed as the unique solution to the problem of

---

[1] As will become clear, I take these terms to describe the same project, which has taken contractualist form over the last twenty-five years.

finding public, reasonable, rules of justice. I argue that this is not, in fact, the case. Justice as mutual advantage is an acceptable solution unless Barry moralizes his conception of equality. If he does this, however, it casts doubt on his claim to impartiality. In the second section, I argue that it is an implication of contractualism (as I define it), that the notion of 'doing wrong' is reduced to 'taking unfair advantage'. Barry is aware of this problem and in *Justice as Impartiality* and in some subsequent comments he has tried to argue for a different account of doing wrong based on the notion of harm. My claim is that Barry is committed to an account of wrong which depends upon a conception of the person as having an essential interest in the avoidance of harm and that this grounds a moral theory independent of his favoured Scanlonian contractualism. In the remainder of the second section and in the third, I argue that this understanding of wrong threatens the distinction between moral theory and theories of justice; a distinction which is crucial to Barry's claim that his account of justice is impartial. In the final section I offer some concluding comments. In short, justice as impartiality wins out over justice as mutual advantage only because Barry is committed to a moralized conception of equality. In addition, Barry's insistence that some things are wrong in themselves undermines his contractualism and his distinction between the questions of how each of us ought to live and how we can and ought all live together. If true, both of these claims undermine the impartiality of Barry's theory and this, given the nature of Barry's account, represents a serious problem.

EQUALITY AND THE REASONABLENESS OF PLURALISM

That equality is at the bottom of Barry's theory is not a contentious claim: 'the whole idea', he writes, 'rests upon a fundamental commitment to the equality of all human beings' (p. 8). The reasonableness of pluralism is equally crucial to Barry's account. Commenting on what the project is about, he notes that 'justice as impartiality is not designed to tell us how to live. It addresses itself to a different but equally important question: how are we to live together, given that we have different ideas about how to live' (p. 77, italics suppressed). That we have different ideas about how to live – that there exist multiple conceptions of the good life – is not simply a sociological or anthropological fact (as Rawls's phrase 'the fact of pluralism' might suggest), but nor does Barry treat it as a metaphysical claim (as it is in Larmore's *Patterns of Moral Complexity*).[2] Rather, what matters is the

---

[2] C. Larmore, *Patterns of Moral Complexity*, Cambridge, 1987, p. 23. 'There are many viable conceptions of the good life that neither represent different versions of some single, homogenous good nor fall into discernible hierarchy'.

epistemological claim that 'no conception of the good can justifiably be held with a degree of certainty that warrants its imposition on those who reject it'. This Barry calls 'scepticism' (§ 27).[3]

While equality and the reasonableness of pluralism provide the background to Barry's theory, much of the work is done by Barry's account of motivation, which is taken from Scanlon's 'Contractualism and Utilitarianism'.[4] Each of us is assumed to be motivated 'to find terms for living together that could not reasonably be rejected by other people who were similarly motivated' (p. 165). Our concern for other people is grounded in the commitment to equality, and scepticism tells us that no-one can reasonably insist on his or her own conception of the good as the basis for these terms. Thus, the terms of agreement – the rules of justice – that emerge will be independent of any (and in that sense neutral between) particular conceptions of the good. Impartiality emerges as 'the only fair, and thus generally acceptable, way of dealing with ... the unresolvability of disputes about the good' (p. 13).

However, that the rules of justice need to adhere to what Kymlicka calls 'justificatory neutrality'[5] does not in fact entail that they need to accord with the theory of *Justice as Impartiality*. Scepticism and the agreement motive do not, by themselves, result in justice as impartiality. A justice as mutual advantage theorist may correctly claim that terms of agreement that mirror relative bargaining strength but that are to the advantage of all (compared with a baseline of non-cooperation) are compatible with such neutrality.[6] Barry has two options here, both appeal to the commitment to equality. He opts to rule out justice as mutual advantage as incompatible with the uncoerced nature of the agreement. This is, in effect, to argue that the agreement motive demands that one desires to justify one's actions to others on grounds that they could not reasonably reject *from a position of equal bargaining power*. Equality here is doing much more than merely demanding that everyone has a veto, it is determining that each person has a veto of a particular kind (one based on equal bargaining

---

[3] Scepticism *à la* Barry is, I take it, compatible with a monistic metaphysics of value.

[4] T. M. Scanlon, 'Contractualism and Utilitarianism', in *Utilitarianism and Beyond*, ed. Amartya Sen and Bernard Williams, Cambridge, 1982, 103–28.

[5] W. Kymlicka, 'Liberal Individuality and Liberal Neutrality', *Ethics*, ic (1989), 883–905. Kymlicka distinguishes 'consequential neutrality' which commits the state to 'seek to help or hinder different life-plans to an equal degree' from 'justificatory neutrality' which 'allows that government action may help some ways of life more than others but denies that government should act in order to help some ways of life over others ... the state does not justify its actions by reference to some public ranking of the intrinsic value of different ways of life, for there is no public ranking to refer to', 884–6.

[6] I am grateful to John Charvet for this point. As Charvet puts it in an unpublished paper, '"to each according to his relative bargaining power" ... is a completely impersonal principle. It applies to everyone quite impartially'.

strength). The second option (which Barry does not take)[7] is to maintain a weak conception of equality and accept that justice as mutual advantage is a theoretically plausible interpretation of what follows from such a commitment (given scepticism), but to argue that it is inferior to justice as impartiality both because it has internal deficiencies and because it is intuitively a less satisfactory theory for capturing the significance of our belief in equality.[8] By rejecting this option and offering instead a thicker, moralised, conception of equality Barry avoids justice as mutual advantage but at the cost of jeopardizing his claim to impartiality.

THE AGREEMENT MOTIVE AND DOING WRONG

For Barry, then, the agreement motive is supposed to do the work of the missing veil of ignorance; it is supposed to rule out bargains based on relative threat advantage. Barry is quite explicit about this, indeed, it underpins his argument for the superiority of the Scanlonian original position over that of Rawls. Rawls begins with something like the assumptions of justice as mutual advantage; with self-interested agents who aim to get more rather than fewer primary social goods. As a result, Rawls needs a thick veil of ignorance to eliminate the possibility of the rules of justice reflecting relative bargaining strength. The introduction of the thick veil of ignorance, however, effectively transforms the original position from a multi-person bargaining situation into a single choice made in conditions of uncertainty, and this lies at the heart of Barry's (and many others') dissatisfaction with Rawls's contractualism.[9]

One of the advantages of justice as impartiality, then, is that it has an entirely different structure. By beginning with agents motivated to find terms of reasonable agreement from a position of equal bargaining strength, justice as impartiality avoids the conflict between self-interest and morality. Whilst this motivation has a built in ethical component, however, it is not unconditional. Rather, the agreement motive is conditional on other people being similarly motivated. In

---

[7] He cannot, because he takes it as given that an agreement based on relative bargaining strength is 'coerced' (see, e.g., p. 50).

[8] This latter type of argument resembles that offered by Kymlicka in his comments on Nozick's entitlement theory. Kymlicka argues that Nozick is most plausibly read as trying to show that the entitlement theory follows from an initial commitment to treating people with equal respect. Kymlicka goes on to show that not only is the theory internally flawed, but that when the consequences of its practice are taken into account it fails to capture what matters to us about the initial commitment, W. Kymlicka, *Contemporary Political Philosophy: An Introduction*, Oxford, 1990, pp. 118–25.

[9] See *Justice as Impartiality*, ch. 3, and Barry's *Theories of Justice*, Hemel Hempstead, 1989, pp. 196–201.

contrast with justice as mutual advantage, which has the structure of a prisoner's dilemma (the motivation to defect from the agreement is continuous with the motivation underlying the agreement), in justice as impartiality,

the criterion of just rules and institutions is that they should be fair, and the motive appealed to is the desire to behave fairly. ... Justice as impartiality ... has the structure of an assurance game. If I am motivated by a desire to behave fairly, I will want to do what the rules mandated by justice as impartiality require so long as enough other people are doing the same (p. 51).

The question which concerns me in this section is, what is it to do *wrong* given this understanding of the grounds of just rules and this account of motivation?

For the moment let us consider only those wrongs which are also (in the relevant sense) injustices.[10] In such cases, when an agent fails to regulate his actions in accordance with the demands of justice, he does wrong because he takes advantage of his co-participants' regulation of their self-interest in accordance with such demands (that is, the demands of rules that would be agreed to in a suitably constituted hypothetical choosing position). In a comment on some remarks by Neil MacCormick on *Justice as Impartiality*, Barry gives the following formulation:

it is wrong to behave unjustly because, where the mutual constraints are such as would have constituted the terms of a (hypothetical) fair agreement, and others are in general keeping to those terms, that would be to take unfair advantage of the forbearance of others.[11]

I should add that this seems to me not only correct of Barry's (or Scanlon's) contractualism but of any contemporary contractualism.

Strangely enough, this characterization of the nature of wrongness in contractualism has been a matter of discussion more in the literature on the philosophy of punishment than in that concerned with distributive justice. In penal philosophy it is commonly the starting point for so-called 'fair play' theories of punishment. It is also commonly found unsatisfactory (including by some of its early proponents). The core objection is that 'it distorts the essential character of crime'.[12] This is because it requires that we think of what wrong is

---

[10] This is to avoid, for the moment, difficulties that arise in Barry's application of Scanlon's formula (which concerns our understanding of morality) to the problem of justice.

[11] Brian Barry, 'A Commitment to Impartiality: Some Comments on the Comments', *Political Studies*, xliv (1996), 329.

[12] R. A. Duff, 'Penal Communications: Recent Work in the Philosophy of Punishment', *Crime and Justice: A Review of Research*, xx (1996), 27. This account of the function of punishment can be found in H. Morris, 'Persons and Punishment', *The Monist*, lii (1968), 475–501; J. Finnis, 'The Restoration of Retribution', *Analysis*, xxxii (1972), 131–5; J. G. Murphy, 'Marxism and Retribution', *Philosophy and Public Affairs*, ii (1973), 217–43;

as the taking of unfair advantage and this may be plausible for a restricted class of actions (like parking one's car illegally), but it seems counter-intuitive for others, such as murder and rape. We do not normally think that crimes such a murder or rape are wrong because someone, the murderer or the rapist, has acted unfairly.

Barry is aware of these criticisms and he is dismissive of such an understanding of wrong and along with it the fair play theory of punishment. He writes (in characteristically robust terms) that

> it would be eccentric to say that what makes murder or grievous bodily harm wrong is that they are unjust in virtue of their taking unfair advantage of the forbearance of others. Some philosophers have, admittedly, said this; but all that shows is that some people will say anything.[13]

The philosophers he has in mind are those of the fair play school. So, it must be the case that what Barry means by wrong when we describe some acts – *mala prohibita* – is that they take unfair advantage of others. When describing other acts – *mala in se* – as wrong, however, he means something quite different.[14] The question is, what? Barry's suggestion is that we rely on harm. 'What makes these things [*mala in se*] wrong is precisely their inflicting harm on the victims'.[15]

In *Justice as Impartiality* the concept of harm plays a small but important role. Whilst Barry rightly rejects Mill's harm principle as a theorem of justice as impartiality (that is, he rejects the idea that all legislation which cannot be justified on the grounds of preventing harm is *a priori* unjust), he endorses a positive harm principle; 'justice requires ... the prohibition of acts that themselves cause harm directly to others' (p. 88). Barry is clear, both in *Justice as Impartiality* and in

---

A. von Hirsch, *Doing Justice: the Choice of Punishments*, New York, 1976; W. Sadurski, 'Distributive Justice and the Theory of Punishment', *Oxford Journal of Legal Studies*, v (1985), 47–59, and 'Theory of Punishment, Social Justice, and Liberal Neutrality', *Law and Philosophy*, vii (1989), 351–73; G. Sher, *Desert*, Princeton, 1987, ch. 5; R. Dagger, 'Playing Fair with Punishment', *Ethics*, ciii (1993), 726–52. For subsequent retractions see J. G. Murphy, 'Retributivism, Moral Education, and the Liberal State', *Criminal Justice Ethics*, iv (1985), 3–11; A. von Hirsch, 'Proportionality in the Philosophy of Punishment: From "Why Punish?" to "How Much?"', *Criminal Law Forum*, i (1990), 259–90, esp. 264-9, and *Censure and Sanctions*, Oxford, 1993, pp. 7–8. For a good summary of many points of criticism see R. A. Duff, *Trials and Punishments*, Cambridge, 1986, ch. 8.

[13] Barry, 'A Commitment to Impartiality', 329.

[14] Cf. Aristotle, *The Nicomachean Ethics*, Oxford, 1980, Bk. V, i–ii (esp. 1129a25–1129b6 and 1130b10).

[15] Barry, 'A Commitment to Impartiality', 329. They are also, therefore, injustices because doing harm is contrary to the demands of justice. This is the position which Richard Dagger also endorses in his defence of fair play theory. Dagger, like Barry, believes that an account of wrong as unfairness cannot accommodate certain wrongs. 'All crimes', he writes, 'are in some sense crimes of unfairness. They may be *more than* crimes of unfairness, as rape, robbery and murder surely are'. Dagger, 479. Emphasis in original.

his later comments[16] that the prohibition of harm is a rule of justice. That is, it emerges from the Scanlonian original position (nobody could reasonably reject a proposition designed to protect people from gratuitous harm). In *Justice as Impartiality* he writes that 'a rule of justice prohibiting the injuring of other people is therefore something that can be easily agreed upon by people with a wide diversity of overall conceptions of the good' (p. 88). Barry's view is that a certain number of things (which he calls 'vital interests'),[17] are required for protection against harm and that such protection is needed for 'the furtherance of virtually any conception of the good'. That is why nobody could reasonably reject a proposition defending such interests (and why we virtually[18] all have good reason to promote such protection). Our 'vital interests' are:

security against the deliberate infliction of injury and death by other people, and the provision of sanitation, potable water, shelter and heat (as required by climate), ... medical care ... A supply of food adequate to provide for normal growth, work at full capacity, enjoyment of leisure, pregnancy and child-rearing.[19]

A problem arises, however, because if this is a rule of justice – something which is the subject of agreement in the choosing situation – then it is subject to the analysis above. To do harm to another is to fail to regulate one's behaviour in accordance with a rule that would have been agreed in a hypothetical, fair choosing position (when others are so regulating their behaviour); it is to act unfairly. *If* it is to underpin a different account of wrong it must be the case that doing harm to another person is just wrong, it is to do something *mala in se*. The positive account of harm must stand independent of the hypothetical agreement and the contractualist account of motivation and must, then, be independently justified.

To see why this is important it is necessary to take a short diversion through the idea of contractualism. I take a contractualist argument to be an attempt to generate rights through a hypothetical agreement. A (for want of a better term) natural rights theory uses rights in the design of the choosing situation. Broadly, one can assess how con-

---

[16] Barry, 'A Commitment to Impartiality', § 3.

[17] Ibid., 332.

[18] Barry correctly notes the need for this proviso; some people regard suffering as part of their conception of the good (Barry notes that 'Mother Theresa thinks that suffering is a great gift from God', ibid., 332). Ian Shapiro has pointed out to me that people committed to a conception of the good which we might characterize as a commitment to 'martial virtue' may also be such that they not only believe that suffering is a great good but that inflicting suffering is also of value. The importance of this point is made clear below in note 26 and the text surrounding it.

[19] Barry, 'A Commitment to Impartiality', 332.

tractualist a theory is by asking how little (or how 'thin'[20] is what) it builds in to the design of the choosing situation. The more that is assumed, or the thicker the assumptions, the less contractualist the theory.[21] If the prohibition of harm is a *product* of the choosing situation what that means is that nobody in a correctly-constituted choosing situation could reject a rule that protects against harm. If it stands independently, what that means is that what makes a choosing situation correctly- rather than incorrectly-constituted is that it includes amongst its conditions the prohibition of harm.

If Barry wants to say simply that some wrongs are only injustices (*mala prohibita*) and others are much more, they are wrongs because it is wrong to harm another human being (*mala in se*), he has to accept that his theory is looking less and less contractualist. To combine this result with that of the first section: What is going in to the contract (rather than emerging from it), is that our commitment to justifying our actions to others on grounds that they could not reasonably reject has an ethical dimension, the principles to which we appeal to justify our actions should not be able to be reasonably rejected by others from a position of equal bargaining power. Secondly, independent of the contract it is wrong to do harm to another, and this wrong presumably has an accompanying non-contractualist, and thus non-conditional, motivation. It is wrong to do harm to another person even if the injunction not to do harm does not command universal, or near universal, obedience.

---

[20] I have come to the conclusion after many conversations with colleagues and students that liberals would do well to adopt the language of thickness and thinness and drop that of neutrality, fairness or impartiality. The reason for this it that, despite the valiant attempts of Kymlicka and others to distinguish justifiatory and consequential neutrality, it still seems natural to allege that liberalism is not really neutral (because it treats Nazis, child-molesters etc. poorly). Likewise claims that Rawls and other 'liberal impartialists' try to build on neutral foundations are misleading. Adopting the thick/thin terminology has the great advantage that it makes it more difficult to mis-understand the aspirations of liberal theory. The sentence 'But is this really thin to Nazis?' comes, in my experience, far less quickly to the mouths of students than the same sentence (or variants of it) using the language of fairness, neutrality or impar-tiality. Similarly, asking 'how thin are Rawls's (or Barry's) assumptions?' I have found attracts far better responses – from both students and colleagues – than asking the same question using the idea of neutrality.

[21] Thus, I am using 'contractualist' to mean an approach to the questions of political philosophy that may be contrasted with 'realist' and 'relativist'. This is why I think that there is an intimate link between 'liberal impartialism' and 'liberal contractualism'. Hobbes and Locke are not contractualist (in my sense). They both use the contract to explain obligation but both build on independently given accounts of morality. Any reader who thinks I am not entitled to the rights of Humpty Dumpty (to give meanings to words just as I wish) may simply replace 'contractualist' with 'constructivist' in my paper. I choose not to do so because it tends to result in (even more) inelegant sentences.

BUT SO WHAT?

Anyone familiar with the early critiques of Rawls's *A Theory of Justice*, might be beginning to wonder why I think I am saying anything new. It was, and remains, a standard criticism of Rawls that he was 'smuggling in' that which he was trying to prove and that, therefore, his theory was circular.[22] Such criticisms were, and are, misplaced: Rawls's *A Theory of Justice* is not, I believe, an attempt to generate an account of justice from a completely neutral, non-controversial or rationalist original position (cf. pp. 7–8). Rather, as I have suggested, the relevant questions are 'how thin are the assumptions in the original position?' And, 'are they sufficiently thin for the theory to complete the project of giving an account of justice which respects the ethical significance Rawls gives to the fact of pluralism?' But once one begins to think in this way it is not sufficient just to allege that the answers are 'built in', one has to argue that what is built in is so 'thick' as to undermine the impartialist pretensions of the theory. The question is, then, whether my criticisms of Barry are not similarly misplaced.

I do not believe that any reader of *Justice as Impartiality* would think its contractualism orthogonal to the main argument, nor do I believe that Barry makes it explicit just how thick his idea of equality really is. It may be the case, however, that Barry would be happy to accept much of what I have said above; what *Justice as Impartiality* is about is convincing people of what follows if they accept 'fundamental equality'. The argument is, then, that with respect to justice, what follows is that if other people are obeying the rules that would be agreed to in a fair hypothetical bargaining position, then you ought to do the same. With respect to some other questions of morality, under normal conditions[23] you ought not harm another person, independent of whether this is a generally obeyed injunction.

This satisfies Barry's desire to be true to common sense morality (for common sense does tell us that there is a difference between parking offences and murder). However, it does not fit Barry's general scheme for the relationship of justice and morality (see pp. 75–9). The attraction of justice as impartiality is that it accepts that each of us may believe in a set of moral commands which (we believe) have a different source from those of justice, but justice as impartiality 'set[s] the legitimate limits to the pursuit of any particular moral system's precepts' (p. 77). So, the Thomist may believe that usury is immoral but

---

[22] See, e.g., the essays in Part I, 'The Original Position' in *Reading Rawls: Critical Studies on Rawls' A Theory of Justice*, ed. N. Daniels, New York, 1975; and Barry's own *The Liberal Theory of Justice*, Oxford, 1973.

[23] That is putting aside questions of self-defence and punishment.

he has little chance of getting this accepted in debates over public policy and no chance of having it established as a basic rule of justice because the position from which it is derived (belief in a particular God and an interpretation of that God's commands by a particular person) may be reasonably rejected. The Aztec, likewise, who believes in the goodness of human sacrifice may continue to believe this but he is not to act on this belief because justice as impartiality limits what injunctions from his moral code he may pursue. Justice as impartiality is concerned with the agent's actions in relation to others, not his beliefs. However, what follows from this is that if the Aztec did sacrifice someone what he would be doing wrong is ignoring the demands of justice as impartiality, but this is precisely the account Barry now believes is insufficient. What Barry is now saying is that the act of sacrifice is *wrong* (*mala in se*), not that pursuing this particular precept of Aztec religion[24] is wrong because it is incompatible with justice as impartiality.

This raises the difficult problem of the relationship in an impartialist society between the rules of justice and the public morality embodied in its positive law and morality. This question is raised because it seems that there is a way out of the above problem if one says that the Aztec acts *unjustly* in acting on the command to harm another and, in addition, he acts *immorally*. This is essentially the 'Dagger solution' (see note 15), the Aztec does two wrongs; in acting unjustly he does something that is unfair and in harming another he does something immoral. But, if we have an account that tells us that the denial of any vital interest to any person is wrong it seems we no longer need justice as impartiality to justify our outlawing such practices. Of course, the Aztec is going to fare badly whether his actions are outlawed because they are unjust or because they are immoral, so does it matter (to anyone but theorists of punishment) that the Aztec is prevented from performing certain acts because those acts are immoral, unjust or both? Yes, because the attraction of justice as impartiality is its justificatory neutrality. In an impartialist society the Aztec is entitled to have his beliefs treated as any other set of beliefs, he is condemned for *acting* in such a way as to violate principles which would be agreed in a suitably constituted hypothetical choosing situation. If he is condemned for acting immorally, independently from the contractualist procedure, then the sense in which the impartialist society is justificatorily neutral (is impartial), is extremely restricted. Of course, it is open to Barry to conclude that the Aztec's beliefs are so at odds with equality as to place the Aztec 'out of bounds' (someone not

---

[24] I should add that this 'Aztec' is created to make a point, it is of no relevance whether historical Aztecs did believe in a religion that commanded human sacrifice.

seriously to be considered in moral argument),[25] but what applies to the Aztec applies to any set of beliefs which command actions, or omissions, that harm another where 'harm' is defined as the denial of any vital interest. Considering Barry's list of vital interests this would seem to include many positions currently espoused in contemporary political theory and practice. Barry's antipathy to Robert Nozick's arguments in *Anarchy, State, and Utopia* is well known, but I take it that the doctrines defended in that work are not to be declared immoral (and, thus, unacceptable) before the contractualist procedure even begins.

In essence, my argument is that Barry is caught in a dilemma. If he wants to maintain his contractualism and his claim to impartiality I believe he must accept that what we mean by doing wrong is captured by the idea of acting unfairly. As he believes this claim to be false, he must accept that introducing a moral theory independent of the contractualist procedure undermines not merely his contractualism but also his claim to impartiality. On Barry's original argument concerning the relationship between justice and morality, the Aztec does poorly (from the point of view of furthering an Aztec society) in a society characterized by justice as impartiality, but this is not a problem. Justice as impartiality does not claim to treat everyone equally (it is not a theory of 'consequential neutrality') and 'those who start by making the most oppressive demands must naturally expect to have them cut back the furthest' (p. 77). But it does matter that the rules of justice adhere to justificatory neutrality, that all conceptions of the good are treated equally (in the sense that all are ignored) in the derivation of the rules of justice. However, if Barry adopts the second non-contractualist argument the Aztec is not so treated, his conception of the good is ruled out prior to the contract and this will be true for any doctrine which involves the denial to some person of a (or some) vital interest(s). In this case, justice as impartiality looks increasingly as if it addresses the question of how *we* are to live together, given that *we* all agree on all the basic moral questions.

[25] Barry has, on occasion, expressed a distaste for the use of fanciful examples in moral philosophy. However, the Aztec seems to me no more outrageous than the orthodox Thomist whose claims Barry is prepared to consider seriously. However, the point is a theoretical one and it holds independently of how we class the Aztec, Thomist, pursuer of 'martial virtue', or Nozickean. The point is that any account of the good that includes a proposition of the form 'it is morally permitted/obligatory to harm another' (other than in exceptional circumstances) is, on the Barry account of morality, false (for it is wrong to do such a thing). Acting upon such beliefs is doing something immoral. Both of these claims stand independently from the contractualist procedure and both need independent justification.

CONCLUSION

Put as bluntly as possible, I have argued (in Section I) that Barry cannot avoid the possibility of justice as mutual advantage as *an* impartialist theory and (in the remaining sections), that he cannot distinguish between wrongs of unfairness and wrongs-in-themselves, without undermining his claim to justificatory neutrality. I believe that if any of the above arguments is right that Barry needs to rethink, or be more explicit about, the nature of his project. In fact, I believe that much of *Justice as Impartiality* could survive such a re-thinking. It has become a standard criticism of liberal contractualism that the pretensions of contractualists to provide an alternative grounding of morality are disingenuous; contractualism must either conceal thick – perhaps, realist – ethical commitments (e.g., the early Rawls and Barry), or it must depend on the shared values of a particular public political culture (the late Rawls being the most explicit in making this move), in which case it is nothing but a sophisticated version of the Walzerian project of articulating shared understandings. Barry, in reflecting on the nature of his project, distances himself from the second of these alternatives, pouring scorn on the idea that political philosophy is about working out the shared beliefs of discrete communities which confront one another in mutual incomprehension. Shared understandings are insufficient because even a society in which the underlying beliefs of people were liberal must not leave itself lacking 'any resources for arguing with those who rejected these shared understandings' (p. 4). Barry's arguments provide some resources for the liberal but, if I am right (and, perhaps, even if I am not – Barry himself admits that he cannot offer decisive arguments in favour of either fundamental equality or scepticism), those resources are either thick, undefended, ethical assumptions or they are, indeed, deep commitments that we share.[26] Neither of these options is attractive to me and I cannot believe either is all that appealing to Barry. The only third possibility, however, is to defend a genuine contractualist theory which neither assumes equality nor recoils from the implication that whatever the difference between speeding and murder is it is not that the latter is *malum in se*, for nothing is wrong-in-itself. I believe that this can be done, but that is another story.

---

[26] It often seems to me that Barry writes in a way that suggests that he believes the basic premise of liberalism (which he takes to be fundamental equality) is widely shared by (at least some) people in all (or almost all) cultures and, therefore, working out the consequences of *this* shared understanding is a proper task of political philosophy.

8

Mutual Advantage and Impartiality*

DAVID GAUTHIER

Brian Barry contrasts his preferred theory of justice as impartiality with 'the most simple approach, which will for ever be associated with the name of its greatest expositor, Thomas Hobbes' (p. 31), and which Barry denominates justice as mutual advantage. 'David Gauthier', we are told, is 'the contemporary champion of justice as mutual advantage' (p. 42). It may, therefore, be appropriate for me to seek to rescue this approach from the criticisms Barry heaps upon it. But to do this it is necessary to identify the view which Hobbes and I champion. This is not a matter safely left to the hands of its enemies, such as Barry, and predictably his account is a distortion. So what is justice as mutual advantage? Barry proposes 'that a theory of justice may be characterized by its answers to three questions. First, what is the motive ... for behaving justly? Secondly, what is the criterion ... for a just set of rules? And thirdly, how are the answers to the two questions connected?' (p. 46). How does justice as mutual advantage answer these questions?

Hobbes tells us that 'A just man ... is he that taketh all care he can that his actions may be all just'.[1] The just or righteous man is contrasted with the unrighteous man whose 'will is not framed by the justice, but by the apparent benefit of what he is to do'. The just man, then, is moved to act justly by the thought that his act would be just, and not by the thought that his act would be advantageous. I think we may extend Hobbes's account to suppose that the just man would be moved to act justly by the thought that his act would satisfy some description under which it would be just. Justice, Hobbes tells us, lies in keeping one's covenants. So according to Hobbes, a just man would be moved to act by the thought that he would thereby be keeping his covenant.

Now Barry says that according to justice as mutual advantage, 'the

* This chapter was written while I was visiting Research Fellow at the Australian National University, to which I am grateful for support.
[1] Thomas Hobbes, *Leviathan*, ed. R. Tuck, Cambridge, 1996, pp. 103–4.

motive for complying with the constraints imposed by rules of justice is that this is, taking a long view, a more effective way of advancing one's conception of the good than is not complying with these rules' (p.46).This is not the account that we have found in Hobbes. But Barry is not altogether wrong. What the theory of justice as mutual advantage claims is that a person whose will is, in Hobbes's phrase, 'framed by the justice ... of what he is to doe',[2] may expect to do better overall in advancing his conception of the good than one whose will is always 'framed by the apparent benefit'[3] of his action. We may put this in slightly different terms. The theory of justice as mutual advantage characterizes a just man as one who takes the justice of an action to provide a motivating reason for performing it. The theory then claims (A) that (with some qualifications) in taking the justice of an action to provide the motivating reason for performing it, an agent maximizes the extent to which she may rationally expect to realize her good. Very roughly, the underlying argument, to which I shall return, is that such an agent may be trusted by her fellows in ways that others may not, and that being so trusted affords her opportunities for (mutually) beneficial interactions with her fellows that others are denied. And the theory also claims (B) that in virtue of (A), a just man *correctly* takes the justice of an action to provide a motivating reason for performing it.

Leaving (A), and the qualifications to which I have referred, for further attention later, let us turn to Barry's second question. What does justice as mutual advantage claim to be the criterion for a just set of rules? The underlying idea is that if society is to command the rational support of its members, then it must be a 'co-operative venture for mutual advantage',[4] to employ Rawls's ever-useful phrase. The absence of social practices, rules and institutions would lead, if not to the extreme of Hobbes's war of all against all, yet to a mutually suboptimal state of affairs. In such a condition, each person would find it beneficial, in terms of her own conception of a good life, to enter into an agreement with her fellows, accepting a structure of institutions and rules that would facilitate co-operation, supply public goods and remove public evils, even though the institutions and rules would curb her direct pursuit of her own good. And so I say that 'the principles of justice are those principles for making social decisions or choices to which rational individuals, each seeking to co-operate with her fellows in order to maximize her own utility, would agree'.[5] I should now prefer

[2] Ibid., p. 104.
[3] Ibid.
[4] John Rawls, *A Theory of Justice*, Oxford, 1972, p. 4.
[5] David Gauthier, 'Justice as Social Choice', in *Morality, Reason and Truth*, ed. D. Copp and D. Zimmerman, Totowa, NJ, 1984, p. 255.

to replace 'maximize her own utility' by 'advance what she judges good' but this emendation leaves the basic structure of the theory unchanged.

Agree under what conditions? Since, as I say, 'the principles are to provide a basis not only for making future social decisions but also for evaluating past decisions and existing institutions and practices',[6] it follows that the agreement should not be 'influenced by actual social circumstances'. Were we 'to consider an agreement in which each person assumes his existing social position, then we should ... allow the *status quo* to constrain the choice of principles of justice, although we should have no reason to suppose ... [it] to be ... mutually advantageous or just'.[7] Furthermore, agreement should not 'be affected by ... the ability each person has to advance his interests in the context of making agreements with others', so that the process of agreement must 'exhibit procedural equality and maximum competence among the persons who are to agree on the principles of justice'. However, since each person aims to advance what she judges good, each 'must be expected to take his capacities and interests into account', although 'no one is thereby able to tailor principles to his own differential advantage, since each is equally able to demand that his capacities and interests be recognized in the content of agreement'.[8] Thus justice as mutual advantage treats principles as just in so far as they would be agreed to by persons, aware of their conceptions of the good and each equally effective in advancing his own conception, deciding *ex ante* on how to make social choices – deciding, we might say, the terms on which they would interact.

I have quoted at some length from my own account of justice, since Barry has been kind enough to treat me as a contemporary champion of justice as mutual advantage. But I do not think that I am departing in any serious way from Hobbes in insisting on equal recognition, since he insists 'That every man acknowledge other for his Equall by Nature'[9] and 'That at the entrance into conditions of Peace, no man require to reserve to himselfe any Right, which he is not content should be reserved to every one of the rest'.[10]

It should be clear from what I have said that justice as mutual advantage does not hold that a principle is just because it would be mutually advantageous for persons, in their existing social situation, to agree to it or to act on it. Nor does it hold that a principle is just simply because it would be mutually advantageous for persons to

[6] Ibid., p. 256.
[7] Ibid., p. 257.
[8] Ibid., p. 258.
[9] Hobbes, *Leviathan*, p. 107.
[10] Ibid.

accept it, were they jointly choosing their terms of interaction *ex ante*. There are many principles that would be mutually *advantageous* – benefiting each in relation to the absence of rules – without being plausible candidates for rational mutual *agreement*. I shall not embark here on a full discussion of rational terms of agreement, but only suggest that in a co-operative venture for mutual advantage, procedural equality will ensure that these terms afford each the opportunity to benefit in the same proportion to his contribution as every other person. Justice as mutual advantage will then propose, as the criterion for a just set of rules, that it affords the members of society maximal equal opportunities to benefit from the co-operative interactions which the rules make possible in proportion to the contribution they make to those interactions.

Barry objects to the theory of justice as mutual advantage in that its claim 'to provide a basis for peaceful interaction is undermined by its necessarily encouraging a constant struggle for positional advantage' (p. 48). But positional advantage plays no role in the account I have offered, except in so far as one associates a person's position with the contribution he makes to co-operative interaction. And seeking this sort of positional advantage – contributing more so that one may receive more – in no way undermines peaceful interaction. Barry seems to think that the ephemeral treaties between Europeans and North American Indians which punctuated the process of conquest exemplify agreements which the theory would consider just (cf. p. 41). It must be acknowledged that Barry can find some support for this view in Hobbes, who claims that justice lies in the keeping of (valid) covenants,[11] and that a covenant between conqueror and conquered is valid.[12] But in *Morals by Agreement* I argue that just principles of interaction require a non-coercive baseline.[13] The outcome of a coercively extracted agreement has no claim to be just.

If Barry were to accept my answer to his second question as canonical for the theory of justice as mutual advantage, he would, I think, insist that it would make even more glaring what he takes to be the primary internal inconsistency in the theory. This inconsistency becomes evident in considering the third question – how the motive for behaving justly is connected to the criterion for a just set of rules. Barry wants to argue that the motive identified by justice as mutual advantage fails to support conformity to the rules denominated just by that account (p. 47). Now this argument does not apply directly to the account of justice as mutual advantage which I have offered, given my

[11] Ibid., p. 100.
[12] Ibid., p. 138.
[13] David Gauthier, *Morals by Agreement*, Oxford, 1986, pp. 192ff.

account, following Hobbes, of the motive to just behaviour. But it is easy enough to rephrase Barry's objection, so that it becomes the charge that the claim identified above as (A), that in taking the justice of an action to provide a motivating reason for performing it, an agent maximizes the extent to which she may rationally expect to realize her good, is patently false. And if (A) is false, then (B), that a just man *correctly* takes the justice of an action to provide a motivating reason for performing it, is also false. The ultimate currency in which the theory of justice as mutual advantage deals is provided by an agent's good, and in that currency justice, as characterized by the theory, need not pay.

I have never claimed that it is always appropriate for an agent to have her will framed by the justice of her acts, or to regard justice as giving her an adequate motivating reason for acting. I have insisted that the claim must be qualified. I agree with much of Hume's analysis of the circumstances in which justice is appropriate. What I do claim is that in a society whose practices and institutions are more or less just, each person should recognize the advantage to herself in being willingly accepted by her fellows as a party to co-operative interaction. Each should then recognize that to be so welcomed, she must be thought by her fellows to be a just person, and that the most reliable and reasonable way to be thought a just person is to *be* a just person. Each person then has reason to expand her initial conception of a good life, whatever it may be, to include justice, provided only that her good is such that it may be advanced by the co-operative interactions possible in a just society. In the Humean circumstances of justice, the just person will correctly take the justice of an action to afford her a motivating reason adequate for performing it.

And if the circumstances of justice do not obtain? It may be that some persons do better for themselves than they could expect in a just society. Even if some of the fruits of mutually advantageous co-operation are lacking, their share of the goods provided by coercive interaction may exceed what they could hope to gain from such co-operation. But coercion is an unstable basis for society, at least among persons who are not ideologically corrupted. Those who believe, correctly, in justice as mutual advantage, will recognize that the practices and institutions of their society do not satisfy the criterion it proposes. They will not take themselves to have any reason to conform to the rules of their society, where these fail the test of justice, save that afforded by their coercive imposition. And coercive imposition, on its own, does not provide political stability. Consider what happened in the Soviet Union, and in South Africa, when the supporters of the regimes ceased to believe their official rationales, whereas the Europeans who overcame the native Americans had little doubt about the basic justice of their cause, a justice that, as they understood it, had little to do either with mutual advantage or Barry's preferred impartiality. So I remain convinced that those principles, practices and institutions that satisfy the criterion proposed by justice as mutual advantage constitute a stable basis for society, whose rationale can be appreciated from both the perspective of a hypothetical *ex ante* agreement on the conditions of interaction, and the outlook of an individual seeking the fruits of co-operation in order to advance what she judges good. If these two standpoints do indeed fit together, then Barry's charge of internal inconsistency fails.

A serious criticism remains, that 'the criteria for just outcomes generated by justice as mutual advantage can fail to correspond in crucial respects to what is normally considered to be just' (p. 48). In particular, justice as mutual advantage fails to afford any moral basis to the claims of those who lack the capacity to be productive participants in society (cf. p. 42). I put the criticism in these terms because I have no choice but to accept it. The deep role of mutual advantage in my account of justice is given by the idea of society as a co-operative venture for mutual advantage. If society is such a venture, then each person must be, or at least expect and be expected to be, both a beneficiary of and a contributor to society. Or at least, a person is eligible to be a beneficiary if and only if she is a contributor. And this is assured if the criterion of a just set of rules is that it affords the members of society maximal equal opportunities to benefit from the co-operative interactions which the rules make possible *in proportion to the contribution they make to those interactions*. Those who make no net contribution, then, are entitled to no net benefit.

Barry finds this conclusion unacceptable. He claims that his preferred alternative to justice as mutual advantage, justice as impartiality, avoids it. But does it? To answer this question, we need to know the criterion for just outcomes according to justice as impartiality. 'In rough terms', Barry tells us, 'the criterion of just rules and institutions is that they should be fair' (p. 51). So what does fairness require? I am unable to find any straightforward answer to this question in Barry's text, but I think it would not falsify his view to say that fair rules and institutions are ones that satisfy Scanlon's test, and so are rules that 'no one could reasonably reject as a basis for informed, unforced, general agreement'.[14]

Consider now what I have called the extended Lockean proviso.[15] Let a and b interact in a way that benefits a in relation to the outcome he

---

[14] T. M. Scanlon, 'Contractualism and Utilitarianism', in *Utilitarianism and Beyond*, ed. Amartya Sen and Bernard Williams, Cambridge, 1982, p. 110.

[15] Gauthier, *Morals by Agreement*, pp. 201–5.

would expect in b's absence, but is costly to b in relation to the outcome he would expect in a's absence. For example, suppose a seizes the crops b has grown; then a does better than he would have expected in the absence of b (and so of the crops grown by b), and b does worse than he would have expected in the absence of a (and so of the seizure of his crops). Then a violates the proviso. Proviso violations need not be wrong. For suppose a to be caught in a sudden winter storm, and to come upon a locked cabin built and owned by b, and to take shelter by breaking into the cabin. Here a clearly does better than he would have expected to do in the absence of b (and so of the cabin), and b does worse than he would have expected in the absence of a (and so of the break-in). Thus a violates the proviso. Although we should expect a to compensate b if he were able to do so, we should not think that a acted wrongly in breaking into the cabin, quite apart from compensation. But when proviso violations are not wrong, they are not what I call deep violations. For given the great benefit of being able to take shelter in an emergency and the small cost of affording shelter, rational persons would agree to permit taking shelter as mutually advantageous. Deep proviso violations are ones that could not be part of a mutually advantageous agreement – such as the unilateral seizure of crops in non-emergency conditions.

Now I claim that any rule allowing a deep violation of the extended Lockean proviso can be reasonably rejected as a basis for informed, unforced general agreement. A deep violation unilaterally sacrifices the interests of the violated party. And it seems that Barry must agree, for he says 'that nobody should accept a rule that would require a unilateral sacrifice of their interests' (p. 70). But a rule that extends social benefits to those who do not contribute to the benefits of co-operative interaction licenses deep violations of the proviso. For those who gain the benefits do better than they could have expected to do in the absence of those who do contribute, whereas those who contribute do worse than they would have expected to do in the absence of those who receive but do not contribute to producing the benefits, since in their absence the benefits would have accrued to those who do contribute. It follows that such a rule can be reasonably rejected as a basis for informed, unforced general agreement by those who recognize that their interests would be unilaterally sacrificed.

The advocate of justice as impartiality will understandably seek to undermine the argument I have just offered, since it threatens to render his position effectively equivalent to the view of justice as mutual advantage which he finds objectionable. How might he do this? One possibility would be to claim that the appeal to informed, unforced general agreement is to be understood primarily in relation to *rights*. The idea is that the rules characterize society in terms of the rights of its members, and that it would be reasonable for anyone to reject rules affording her lesser rights than her fellows. Social co-operation is then characterized in terms of the exercise of individual rights, as well as natural capacities. Thus each member of the society contributes to the benefits realized by co-operative interaction, in so far as her exercise of her rights is a necessary, though not in itself a sufficient, condition for such interaction and so for the resulting benefits. And so everyone has a claim to some share of these benefits.

We need to distinguish two contrasting views of society – as a co-operative venture for mutual advantage, and as a structure of rights and duties governing interaction. If we accept the first view, then we are led to justice as mutual advantage. But if we accept the second view, then we allow room for a conception of justice concerned primarily with the fairness of the structure of rights and duties. And we may then introduce a feature of the theory as justice as impartiality which seems crucial to both Barry and Scanlon, but which so far has played no role in my account – 'the desire to find and agree on principles which no one who had this desire could reasonably reject' (p. 68).[16] So far I have considered agreement only as determining the criterion for a just set of rules. The *desire* for agreement concerns the motivation for just behaviour. The idea, as I understand it, is that we think of persons as motivated to seek agreement on terms of interaction, abstracting from any direct consideration of the benefits that may be attained and the costs that must be imposed by inter-action. What each person wants is for her actions to be justified in the eyes of her fellows (cf. p. 165) – a matter to which I shall return. And this desire does indeed give rise to a very different understanding of justice than if society is thought of primarily as a co-operative venture for mutual advantage.

Barry claims that 'Justice as mutual advantage is unstable because it has the structure of a prisoner's dilemma. What is in my interest is that everybody else … adheres to rules that are mutually advantageous if generally adhered to and I break them whenever it is to my advantage to do so. Justice as impartiality, however, has the structure of an assurance game. If I am motivated by a desire to behave fairly, I will want to do what the rules mandated by justice as impartiality require so long as enough other people are doing the same' (p. 51). This contrast is both illuminating and misleading. It is illuminating in so far as it focuses on the problem to which justice may be seen as the solution. It is misleading in so far as it identifies the problem with the solution. Or so I shall now argue.

A world of persons, each with her own conception of the good life, will

---

[16] Scanlon, 'Contractualism and Utilitarianism', p. 111.

tend to have the character of a multi-person prisoner's dilemma. Although co-operative, mutually advantageous interaction is in principle possible, yet each, pursuing what she judges good, is naturally led to behaviour that is beneficial to her but costly to others, so that the overall outcome is suboptimal, disadvantageous from everyone's point of view. Such an outcome is asocial, a state of nature, and is contrasted with society, which is conceived as realizing the possibility of mutually advantageous co-operation. Each person stands to benefit from society. Each has a reason therefore to agree to principles, practices and institutions that would realize mutual advantage, and just arrangements are those that would obtain the agreement of everyone. But do not these arrangements replicate the prisoner's dilemma which they are intended to resolve? Would not each person wish to have her fellows adhere to them while seeking to violate them herself? Advocates of justice as mutual advantage – or at least some of them including Hobbes and myself – deny this; they claim that each does best to be accepted by her fellows as a sincere adherent to these arrangements, and that the best way to be so accepted is to be such a person. And from the standpoint of such a person – a *just* person – adherence to just arrangements has the character not of a prisoner's dilemma but an assurance game. Each is disposed to adhere in so far as she expects the general adherence of her fellows.

Contrast now a world of persons each as before with her own conception of a good life and so as potentially facing a multi-person prisoner's dilemma, but suppose in addition that each has the independent desire to interact with her fellows on terms that no one with such a desire could reasonably reject. To resolve their interaction problem, they do not proceed directly, but appeal to this shared desire for agreement, which transforms their situation so that it has the shape of an assurance game. The problem to be solved by just arrangements is to provide an agreed basis for interaction. Each is directly motivated by her desire to interact with others on such a basis, to adhere to it provided she may expect the general adherence of her fellows. In the absence of such an expectation, of course, she would not be motivated to adhere. Her desire is not that she act on a basis that persons seeking agreement could not reasonably reject, but that everyone act on that basis. And so persons do face an interaction problem, but its structure makes it inherently more tractable than it would be were the independent desire for agreement absent.

And would that it were so, we might say. But I am not persuaded. I do not deny that there are persons who desire to interact with their fellows on terms that no one with such a desire could reasonably reject. And one may consider what such terms would be. But those without this desire may reasonably ask what such terms are to them. Not that they do not recognize the need for terms of interaction. As Barry says, 'every society needs ... a common system of guidance operating on the members of society by internalization, the pressure of others' opinions, and diffuse sanctions ...' (p. 34). But, our objectors may ask, why should we accept a system of guidance which presupposes a desire for agreement? Why not a system which is addressed to the problem we actually face – the problem of interaction among persons with differing views of the good life, and which then addresses this problem directly, speaking to each person in relation to her own view? Why not begin from the stake each person has in the terms of interaction?

I have said that the theory of justice as mutual advantage characterizes a just person as one who takes the justice of an action to provide a motivating reason for performing it, and claims that in so doing, an agent in the circumstances of justice maximizes the extent to which she may rationally expect to realize what she judges good. But it is quite compatible with this to suppose that for many persons, taking the justice of an action to provide a motivating reason for performing it is also supported by a desire for, or perhaps better, a concern with fairness in realizing mutual advantage. Rather than supposing that persons characteristically have a desire to interact with their fellows on terms that no one with such a desire could reasonably reject, we may suppose that persons characteristically have a desire to interact with their fellows *when such interaction may be mutually advantageous* on terms that no one with such a desire could reasonably reject. We might suppose that viewing other persons as participants in a joint venture for mutual advantage elicits the desire that the terms of the venture be freely acceptable to all. This is speculative moral psychology. But I suggest that it is more plausible to think of persons as concerned with fairness within the context of mutual advantage than to suppose, as Barry and Scanlon must do, that persons are concerned with mutual advantage within a prior context of fairness. The theory of justice as mutual advantage recognizes the centrality of moral reasons and emotions in human life, but it integrates these moral considerations into the overall concerns of human beings. Thus it accepts society as providing a structure of rights and duties governing interaction, but it sees this structure as integrated into the core concern with society as a co-operative venture for mutual advantage.

I have suggested that justice as mutual advantage and justice as impartiality differ in their view of society. I now want to consider another fundamental difference between the two theories, which focuses on their accounts of justification. We may get to the heart of the issue by asking: what stands in need of justification, and to whom? From the standpoint of justice as mutual advantage, rational agents naturally deliberate about their own actions and act in the light of their deliberations without any further question of justification arising. An agent will judge what it makes sense for her to do, but she may answer this by determining her own good and the means for realizing it. Others may respond to her actions in terms of what makes sense for them to do, but she is not accountable to them for her actions nor they to her for theirs. Interaction is naturally non-moral. But as we have noted, the suboptimal character of the outcomes provides a rationale for agreement on principles and practices governing interaction. From the point of view of each individual, these principles and practices give rise to constraints on her deliberation – they introduce considerations about what makes sense for her to do over and above those afforded by what she directly judges good. According to justice as mutual advantage, these constraints stand in need of justification, which must be addressed to the constrained individual. She must be shown why she should introduce these constraints into her deliberations. We have already considered the answer that justice as mutual advantage offers – those constraints are justified that would be agreed to by rational individuals agreeing on their terms of interaction, since in the circumstances of justice an individual who deliberates and acts in accordance with them may expect to realize what she judges good more effectively than one who ignores them.

That some justification must be offered in support of deliberative constraints to the constrained individual is at the core of what I call contractarian moral theory, of which justice as mutual advantage is part. Replying to Simon Blackburn, Bernard Williams has said that 'moral philosophy has been concerned with the justification of the ethical life *from the ground up*',[17] and it is this concern which is at the core of contractarianism. Of course Williams is pessimistic where I am optimistic; he finds no adequate justification in Aristotle or Kant whereas I claim to find one in Hobbes. And I believe that it is essential to the ethical life, or at least that part of it which is the province of justice, that justification be available. For in governing the interactions of persons quite apart from any ties of kinship or friendship they may or may not have, justice has nothing to appeal to but deliberative rationality. The idea that its appeal might be free standing seems to me chimerical.

Yet it is exactly this idea which is required by justice as impartiality. For consider what, on this view, stands in need of justification, and to whom. The desire that persons are supposed to have to interact with their fellows on terms that no one with such a desire could reasonably reject should not be interpreted on a par with the desire, say, for tasty and nutritious food, important as the latter is. Scanlon argues that

[17] B. Williams, 'Reply to Simon Blackburn', *Philosophical Books*, 27 (1986), p. 206.

'the idea of general agreement ... is ... what morality is about',[18] and the desire addresses this. We are then to think of *moral* agents as those who have this desire, and we may suppose that it expresses their need to justify their actions to their fellows by relating them to principles on which all moral agents can agree. According to justice as impartiality, then, one's actions stand in need of justification, and this justification is addressed to those affected by the actions, and addressed to them in their capacity as moral agents. An agent accepts deliberative constraints on the pursuit of her good, not because these constraints are justified to her, but because adhering to these constraints ensures that her actions will be justified to her fellows.

The idea that persons stand in need of justifying their actions to others strikes me as bizarre. One can of course make sense of it by assuming the context of co-operation for mutual advantage, in which each wants to be received by others as a participant in co-operative interaction and so wants others to find her actions acceptable. But it is then a derived need, and not the ultimate need postulated by justice as impartiality. And one can make very different sense of it by treating it as the secularized residue of the doctrine that persons seek to justify their actions before God. But once the residue is recognized for what it is, it surely loses all credibility. And so justice as impartiality lacks a plausible view of justification.

I have argued that the theory of justice as impartiality, as presented by Barry, requires a different view of society, and a different account of justification, than justice as mutual advantage. And I have argued that in both cases, the different view of justice as impartiality is not a plausible one. But I want now to recall that I began this discussion of differences in an attempt to show how justice as impartiality might avoid finding itself identified with justice as mutual advantage. If it can do this only by embracing implausible views of society and justification, then perhaps we should abandon the attempt, and recognize that a viable theory of justice as impartiality coincides with the theory of justice as mutual advantage, at least in the form in which, largely following Hobbes, I have propounded it.

Now this is to stand Barry's position on its head (or, as I prefer to say, on its feet), since he claims that 'We need look no further than justice as mutual advantage to find a theory that rejects the impartialist objective'(p. 193). He concedes that it shares 'the premise that the goal is a basis for general agreement', but insists that it 'rejects the key feature of justice as impartiality: the idea that constraints should be accepted freely as reasonable'. The charge has no basis whatsoever in

---

[18] Scanlon, 'Contractualism and Utilitarianism', p. 128.

the accounts of the theory to be found, whether in Hobbes or in my own writings.

In justice as mutual advantage, as I have insisted, we are to think of persons as if they were in a position to decide by unanimous agreement on their terms of interaction. The default position, if no agreement is reached, is that each acts to advance what she judges good, taking into account of course her expectations of how others will act to advance what they judge good. This default position – state of nature – is, as Hobbes and I have insisted and as Barry fully acknowledges, mutually costly in relation to other terms of interaction, which are then candidates for voluntary or free agreement. Each is motivated to agree in order to advance what she judges good. But not all candidates for voluntary agreement will seem reasonable to everyone. For in so far as some terms of interaction are seen as more favourable to some persons that to others, in terms of securing the benefits of agreed interaction, then those terms will not seem reasonable to those to whom they seem less favourable since they will see no reason why they should benefit less from a voluntary and unanimous agreement than do their fellows.

Thus, as I have already noted, Hobbes says *'That at the entrance into conditions of Peace, no man require to reserve to himselfe any Right* [by which he means only a liberty of action] *which he is not content should be reserved to every one of the rest'*.[19] For, he tells us, 'If Nature ... have made men equall; that equalitie is to be acknowledged: or if Nature have made men unequall; yet because men that think themselves equall, will not enter into conditions of Peace, but upon Equall termes, such equalitie must be admitted'.[20] Since as we have seen, Barry introduces Hobbes as the 'greatest expositor' of justice as mutual advantage, he can hardly refuse to acknowledge what Hobbes says as canonical. So the idea that the criterion for a just set of rules is that it be a possible outcome of free agreement on terms of interaction that each accepts as reasonable is entrenched at the very core of the theory. And indeed, advocates of justice as mutual advantage will say, how could it be otherwise? For on what basis other than the advantage of each person, conceived broadly in terms of the advancement of what she judges good, could persons be expected to agree freely on terms of interaction, or to find such terms reasonable? You may coerce me to accept terms that give you the lion's share of social benefits; you may, indeed, if you have my life or the lives of my loved ones in your hands, induce me to accept terms that leave me worse off than if I had nothing to do with you (the offer I can't refuse), but such terms cannot be freely

[19] Hobbes, *Leviathan*, p. 107.
[20] Ibid.

accepted by me as reasonable; no more, according to justice as mutual advantage, can they be just.

A good illustration of Barry's misunderstanding and misrepresentation of justice as mutual advantage is found in his discussion of the situation of homosexuals. Barry suggests that 'Protestants and Catholics might agree to set their differences aside and allow freedom of worship, and then combine to condemn homosexuals to death amid appalling torments' (pp. 163–4). And he seems to think that this casts some light on the relation between homosexual rights and justice as mutual advantage.[21] Specifically he claims that mutual advantage might underwrite the agreement, but would not protect the homosexuals. Now this of course might be true; in a particular social situation, two groups, themselves opposed, might recognize the futility of their own struggle, and might consider it mutually advantageous to join forces so that they could vent their hatred on a third, relatively powerless group. But invoking a reference to mutual advantage does not bring justice on the scene. What justice as mutual advantage says is that the situation of these persons would be just if but only if, supposing *all* of the persons to be in a position to determine together their terms of interaction, their situation would be a possible outcome of their agreement on such terms. But the situation described is patently not such a possible outcome.

When Barry presents his theory of justice as impartiality, he is at pains to insist that attacks on particular instances of first-order impartiality are not an attack on the theory, and that 'the appropriate role for impartiality is supplied by the theory of justice as impartiality' (pp. 256–7). He seems not to have noticed that by parity of reasoning, attacks on particular instances of first-order mutual advantage are not an attack on the theory, and that the appropriate role for mutual advantage is supplied by the theory of justice as mutual advantage.

The question of homosexual rights raises deeper issues than Barry considers, and it will be illuminating to consider them in relation to both theories of justice. Let us then suppose that the dominating religious groups in a society are united in their condemnation of homosexual practices. They will of course represent their condemnation in moral terms; they will insist that homosexual practices are wrong, and that they condemn them – and those who engage in them – because they are wrong. Now I suggest that whether these groups embrace justice as mutual advantage or justice as impartiality, they will refuse to accept homosexual rights and will consider themselves justified in their refusal. Let us take justice as mutual advantage first.

---

[21] See for confirmation the index entry referring to this passage: 'justice as mutual advantage: homosexual rights and' (p. 302).

They – let me call them the homophobes – would insist that there is no basis of mutual advantage which could lead to agreement on terms of interaction between homosexuals and themselves. Thus homophobes would deny that they stand in the circumstances of justice, in their relations to homosexuals. Indeed, they would insist that, homosexuality being morally wrong, to seek mutually advantageous arrangements with homosexuals would be wrong.

Recall the extended Lockean proviso – the idea that it is wrong to advance what one judges good through interaction with other in ways that make one better off than one would be in their absence and the others worse off than they would be in one's own absence. The homophobes would insist that in tormenting and executing homosexuals, they were not advancing what they judged good in relation to how things would be in the absence of homosexuals. They would insist that the presence of evil, as manifest in homosexuality, was a cost which they could only seek to minimize by rooting it out wherever it may be found.

Now I trust I need not say that I find this homophobic view abhorrent. But notice that it requires a view of morality quite different from, and actually opposed to, that implicit in justice as mutual advantage. Rather than treating moral constraints as enabling persons to interact in mutually beneficial ways, it treats them as determining what is allowed to count as mutually beneficial. It imposes a prior, allegedly moral standard on the circumstances within which justice is allowed to operate. And so the homophobes will see no injustice in their treatment of homosexuals – and if their condemnation of homosexuality were sound, they would be right. Justice as mutual advantage will not yield answers that we find acceptable if it is applied within the context of an opposed moral doctrine.

What of justice as impartiality? Barry recognizes that his argument for it 'presupposes the existence of ... the desire to live in a society whose members all freely accept its rules of justice and its major institutions' (p. 164). It insists that 'no conception of the good should be given a privileged position' (p. 160). Now the homophobes may have the desire to live in a society whose members all freely accept its rules of justice, but not in one which gives no conception of the good a privileged position. For they have the desire to live in a society in which there are no homosexuals – and in such a society all of the members may indeed freely accept its rules of justice. They will insist that to be impartial among all conceptions of the good would be morally wrong, and so they will accept justice as impartiality only within a clearly circumscribed sphere. Their view of morality is not only opposed to but incompatible with that implicit in justice as impartiality, for their view requires that a heterosexual view of the good be privileged (or a homosexual view condemned). Thus they will suppose that justice as *unconstrained* impartiality is morally unacceptable, and will insist that when justice as impartiality is properly constrained by prior standards of moral rightness, their conduct proves in no way unjust.

The homophobes can accept justice as mutual advantage, but their 'moralized' view of mutual advantage will constrain its operation so that they will see the persecution of homosexuals as falling outside the circumstances of justice. They cannot accept justice as impartiality in its pure form, but their 'moralized' view of impartiality will lead them to treat their persecution of homosexuals as falling outside its proper scope. Barry may see an important difference here. He may insist that justice as mutual advantage affords no basis for attacking the homophobic view, whereas justice as impartiality does. But this is true only in that one of the premises of justice as impartiality – that no conception of the good be privileged – must be rejected by the homophobe, whereas no strict premise of justice as mutual advantage need be rejected by him. The real criticism of the homophobic view has to proceed in terms of its substantive claim that homosexuality is evil, and this is an issue that must be addressed outside the province of theories of justice.

Suppose that this criticism succeeds, so that the homophobes come to doubt their condemnation of homosexual practices as evil. They may continue to find some of these practices personally repellent, but they recognize that their desire to persecute those who engage in them is sadistic rather than moralistic. They can now acknowledge that persons contribute to the benefits of co-operative interaction regardless of their sexual orientation, and so come to regard homosexuals as fellow participants in a co-operative venture for mutual advantage. They can envisage interacting with homosexuals on terms that persons with a desire for agreement could not reasonably reject. And so whether they view justice as mutual advantage or as impartiality, they will condemn the persecution of homosexuals as unjust. Advocates of justice as mutual advantage will argue that homosexuals are entitled to benefit from society in the same proportion to their contribution as their fellows, and will note that there is no general correlation between social contribution and sexual orientation. Advocates of justice as impartiality will argue that homosexuals are entitled to interact with their fellows on terms that no one with a concern for agreement could reasonably reject. Barry's supposition that what he understands as impartial justice would afford homosexuals greater protection than mutually advantageous justice seems to me baseless.

Indeed, the advocate of justice as mutual advantage will insist that the principles he endorses treat homosexuals with strict impartiality, looking only to the contributions they make to society as entitling them to benefits from society in the same proportion as all other persons. He will argue that no one could reasonably reject such principles as a basis for agreement, and that everyone has reason to want such agreement in so far as the benefits of society depend on it. Contributions and benefits alike are evaluated from the perspective of the recipient, and so in terms of her conception of the good life. Thus the advocates of justice as mutual advantage will insist that no conception of the good is given a socially privileged position. At this point the advocate will surely insist that the theory of justice as mutual advantage incorporates impartiality and determines its appropriate role. Justice demands impartiality among persons conceived as joint participants in a co-operative venture for mutual advantage. And so justice as mutual advantage, properly understood, does not reject, but rather realizes, the impartialist objective.

One of the great achievements of modern social thought and practice has been to recognize and to a previously unprecedented extent actually realize the possibility of persons with very different conceptions of the good life interacting in mutually beneficial ways. The ideal society may then be seen, not as one in which a privileged conception of the good is realized, but as one in which individuals are enabled and encouraged to develop and pursue their own conceptions of the good, in circumstances which ensure that, so far as possible, each contributes to and benefits from the activities of her fellows. Justice as mutual advantage takes the place of a substantive good as the constitutive ideal for such a society. I remain convinced that in a world freed by rational thought from the enchantment of myths and ideologies, it is the only ideal which can gain our allegiance and belief.

9

Reasonable Agreement: Political not Normative*

RUSSELL HARDIN

THEORIES OF DISTRIBUTIVE JUSTICE

There have been three main competing normative political theories in our time: libertarianism, justice as fairness and utilitarianism.[1] Brian Barry proposes a revision or variant of justice as fairness, which he calls justice as impartiality. There is a sense in which he is not proposing a new theory but is rather cleaning up the analysis and vocabulary of what he takes 'to be the standard contemporary liberal theory' (p. 124). The cleaning up, however, is substantial. There are three central elements of Barry's theory that I wish to discuss. The first and simplest is that it is a second-order theory about institutions for achieving distributions for individuals, not a first-order theory for individual choice or individual outcomes. The second and third are that the content of its recommendations depends on impartiality and on reasonable agreement, terms that have manifold meanings.

Because of its general importance to virtually all discussions of justice, I will briefly consider the nature of second-order theories immediately below. Then, after canvassing some of the background of Barry's contribution to theories of justice, I will discuss what he takes to be his main alternative category of theories: mutual advantage theories. Finally, I will turn to the two relatively novel claims of his own theory: impartiality and reasonable agreement. Almost all the

* This paper began as a commentary on Brian Barry's *Justice as Impartiality*, Oxford, 1995, given at the American Political Science Association, San Francisco, 30 August 1996. I am grateful to the participants on that panel, including Brian Barry, and to Chandran Kukathas for discussions of an early draft.

[1] Libertarianism is represented in D. Gauthier, *Morals by Agreement*, Oxford, 1986; J. Narveson, *The Libertarian Idea*, Philadelphia, 1988; and R. Nozick, *Anarchy, State, and Utopia*, New York, 1974. Justice as fairness, which now has many exponents, is the original thesis of John Rawls, *A Theory of Justice*, Oxford, 1972. The articulate exposition of utilitarianism as a political theory has a very rich history, with major contributions from Jeremy Bentham, John Stuart Mill and many political economists of the past two centuries and with proto-contributions from Thomas Hobbes, Bernard Mandeville, David Hume and others before the terminology of utilitarianism gained vogue.

play in Barry's account turns on that glorious word, reasonable. Surely all theorists think they are reasonable. Presumably, we may infer from Barry's persuasive redefinition of that term that most of them are, in some sense, unreasonable. I should perhaps note up front that I am, in his sense, an apparently unreasonable utilitarian.

SECOND-ORDER THEORIES

The central insight in second-order theories of the foundations of social institutions is that of Rawls in 'Two Concepts of Rules'.[2] In this paper, Rawls wrote to defend utilitarianism as a two-stage theory against certain silly objections once popular.[3] (Alas, in a discipline in which nothing is ever finally learned, these objections are still popular.) First we establish a principle of what outcome we want to achieve and then we design an institution that will help us achieve it best. Those with roles in the relevant institutions *act according to the rules of their roles*, not directly according to the supposed utility of their actions. At the level of the social actor who is not a role-holder in a particular institution we might recast this problem as one of resolving a collective action dilemma or a co-ordination problem. Each of us wants the generally good result but none of us might be motivated to act so as to achieve it, either by altering a co-ordination or by contributing to a collective provision. Our institution constrains or motivates our behaviour in relevant ways so that we do achieve it.

Utilitarianism is a two-level theory: both first and second order, that is to say, both moral and political. As a political theory it is a second-order theory in the sense in which impartiality and justice as fairness are second-order theories. In a second-order theory, the result we wish to achieve on the ground in the lives of individuals (the first order) determines the nature of the institutions for organizing society (the second order). As a political theory utilitarianism prescribes institutions or constraints on institutions.[4] Utilitarianism is additionally a first-order theory in the strong sense that it directly prescribes ranges of behaviour for individuals. The chief difference between the second-

---

[2] John Rawls, 'Two Concepts of Rules', *Philosophical Review*, 64 (1955), 3–32.

[3] For example, that a sheriff should participate in or allow an unjust lynching of an innocent person if that lynching would calm a mob and prevent it from doing even worse things. The conclusion of this silly morality tale is supposedly that utilitarianism violates justice.

[4] For one view of utilitarianism as a political theory, see Russell Hardin, *Morality Within the Limits of Reason*, Chicago, 1988, chs 3 and 4. It is sometimes supposed that if everyone acted as a utilitarian there would be no need for institutions. This supposition is probably false because, for example, co-ordination problems often require institutional resolution. But, in any case, the point is irrelevant for practical life because we cannot expect everyone to be moral.

order (institutional) and the first-order (personal) applications is merely the differing natures of strategic interaction at the two levels. Indeed, it is strategic interaction that defines the two levels.[5] At both levels utilitarianism is incomplete in so far as assessments of welfare or causal understandings are incomplete.

Barry and Rawls do not suppose their theories apply as both moral and political theories. Barry says impartiality is a second-order theory *only* (pp. 77 and 194, and part III *passim*). Clearly fairness is not a full moral theory in the way that utilitarianism is – presumably no one seriously holds that morality is merely a matter of fairness. Barry and Rawls both suppose that good institutions will at least partly lead individuals to be just in the sense of working for just institutions and policies, but they do not hold that fairness is a general moral theory.

THEORIES OF JUSTICE

In proposing a theory of justice grounded in impartiality Barry's purpose is, like that of Rawls, to construct a theory of justice as fairness with a strong element of mutual advantage. In *Theories of Justice*, the first volume of his larger *Treatise*, Barry canvasses these two main grounds, fairness and mutual advantage, on which contemporary theories of justice are based.

Much of the fair division literature is about how self-interested players can achieve fair results. Barry discussed this issue at compelling length in *Theories of Justice*. This is a problem for a Rawlsian theory of justice only in the design of the institutions that are to implement it. It is not the problem of establishing the principles of justice that are to govern the purpose of those institutions. What we need at this prior stage is a principle of fairness *per se*. The fair division literature generally takes for granted what this principle is, since that literature generally deals in interpersonally comparable utiles of something nearly indistinguishable from what in ordinary parlance is called money. A fair division of x utiles or dollars among n persons is, *ceteris paribus*, x/n utiles per persons. In the standard fair division literature, what is to be distributed is determined *ex ante*, so that the distribution is the only issue at stake.

In a real society, in which most of what is to be distributed must be produced, a rigorous fairness theory that required equality of distributions might run up against deep problems of motivation for those who produce what is to be distributed. Hence enforced egalitarianism might mean that overall production would be severely depressed, so that all would be equal but, alas, equally miserable. Somehow, then,

---

[5] Ibid., ch. 2.

if incentives for production matter, we must consider introducing inequalities that lead to greater overall welfare, as in a mutual advantage theory.

Thomas Hobbes is the first great theorist of mutual advantage. Because his concern was only with order and welfare and not with justice, he was not interested in a normative notion of mutual advantage, in which essentially all are better off with respect to some alternative. He often wrote as though essentially all were better off with any order than with disorder, but he acknowledged that religious fanatics and glory seekers (certain aristocrats) might not be, so that his mutual advantage theory was essentially sociological rather than merely normative. David Gauthier's theory of morals by agreement is largely a mutual advantage theory, but Gauthier requires supplementary moral principles to make his system work.[6] Libertarian theories might often be cast as mutual advantage theories, although they are often grounded in supposed natural rights to property. A strictly ordinal utilitarianism is a mutual advantage theory. But, as such, it is inherently incomplete in what it can specify as the utilitarian outcomes because ordinal welfare cannot be aggregated in determinate ways.[7] It shares this problem with the criterion of Paretian improvement, in which any change in allocations must make at least one person better off while not making any person worse off. Often there are many such changes that could be made, but some are better for me while others are better for you, and neither the Pareto criterion nor ordinal utilitarianism can help us choose which of these to make.

The recent turn to resourcism in discussions of distributive justice may be motivated by an effort to reduce our problem to a similarly simple prima facie move to divide up something that is easily measured, as we may suppose that, at a first approximation, dollars are the measure of resources. A game theoretic account of mutual advantage shows the resourcist hope not to be generally coherent. There are, however, circumstances in which it may be straightforwardly meaningful. By somewhat tendentiously stipulating that some goods do not weigh in our welfare until other goods have been counted first, Rawls makes his Difference Principle sound like a principle of mutual advantage. But it is not really that, not least because mutual advantage is inherently indeterminate. It is his lexicographic invocation of egalitarianism that yields determinacy, at least in principle. Hence, his theory is fundamentally dependent on both mutual advantage, or welfarist, and on fairness considerations, although

---

[6] Gauthier, *Morals by Agreement*.
[7] Hardin, *Morality Within the Limits of Reason*, ch. 4.

many commentators and Rawls himself often refer to it as merely a fairness theory.

Resourcist theories seem to be inherently fairness theories. Contractarian theories are usually mutual advantage theories. The two larger classes generally do not fit well together. Yet Rawls has remarkably brought the two classes of theories together in one theory of distributive justice that seems to be reasonably coherent. Barry wishes to do the same under the rubric of reasonable agreement and impartiality.

Let us summarize and highlight the distinctive differences between these two kinds of theory. Fairness theories generally apply to distribution of a fixed sum once we have produced or come upon something, or, conversely, to a fixed burden such as the risks of military service, or to division of something that comes from a fixed production function that is not itself a function of the nature of the division. Fairness therefore applies when one may reasonably suppose production is not at issue. If production is at issue, incentive effects foul ordinary analyses of fairness because they effect what there is to be distributed. Mutual advantage theories are inherently concerned with how we motivate production of whatever we are to distribute. One might think these two simply do not belong together, as traditionally they have not gone together.

Rawls's theory is relatively original in bringing mutual advantage and fairness together. (This is a central thesis of Barry's *Theories of Justice*.)[8] He does not do so as some contemporary pluralists might, first on the one hand and then on the other. Rather he integrates them by placing them at different points in the deduction of his eventual distributive principles or, rather, his principles for the basic structure of a just society. Mutual advantage might be defended purely pragmatically, as it is by Hobbes. But it is a purely co-ordination criterion because, as in a Pareto allocation, there are many ways we could go, all of which would be mutually advantageous to some status quo. Rawls grounds the selection from these mutually advantageous states on their relative fairness. This is one of the few fundamentally original moves in Anglo-Saxon political theory since Hobbes.

Note, however, that in his theory Rawls is concerned with fairness of an odd kind. Fairness in the allocation of the joint social product is an issue just because that product is joint. I might claim to 'deserve' a fair part of it because I contributed to its production. But Rawls does not want a simple desert model in which I get what I deserve as a result of my effort or whatever. If market wages and profits really mirrored contributions, allocations according to desert would reduce to little

---

[8] Brian Barry, *Theories of Justice*, Berkeley, CA, 1989.

more than what markets do. Rawls clearly thinks market wages and profits do not mirror contributions. We cannot causally relate your effort to your share of the social product. Your wages are related to the supply and demand functions for your talents, rather than directly to your output. What you produce may stay constant while your wage changes, or vice versa. Rawls's theory of justice therefore generally entails a distribution other than what the market would produce.

Yet, his theory does not simply correct for the distortions that supply and demand might impose on your wage. Rawls does not tie your desert to what you produce. He ties it *merely to the fact that you produce*. The fact that you produce gives you a claim on a share of the joint product. The capitalist or well-paid professional may think she deserves what she gets from market relations. A Rawlsian and virtually any contemporary economist would reject such desert claims and would say that the capitalist or professional is merely in part very lucky to be in the right place at the right time – as, for example, the child of an immigrant to Silicon Valley might prosper radically better than her cousin back in Bangladesh.[9] As John Stuart Mill noted, 'As civilization advances, every person becomes dependent, for more and more of what most nearly concerns him, not upon his own exertions, but upon the general arrangements of society'.[10] Bill Gates is not in any plausibly meaningful sense worth the four billion dollars a year that he has recently been making, but that is what our (somewhat distorted) market yields him. Still, Rawls's theory retains an odd tie to desert or entitlement. Barry wants to break this tie with his theory of impartiality. Those who like desert talk might say he wants to base desert in simple humanity, not in any specific capacity or accomplishment. But in any standard view, Barry's theory, unlike that of Rawls, is freed of any connection to desert as merit of some kind.

Again, a central insight of Rawls is that fairness cannot stand alone as a theory of the good or the right because it is fully consistent with egalitarian misery. Inequality that produces greater overall welfare trumps pure equality under some circumstances. Those who dislike this assertion sometimes argue against it with an implicit dismissal of the possibility that inequality could have this effect or with claims that all we need is to correct aberrant psychologies to get people to produce for the general good rather than merely for selfish benefit (as in the theory of new Soviet man). Barry has his feet planted in the real world

[9] See, *inter alia*, K. J. Arrow, 'Nozick's Entitlement Theory of Justice', *Philosophia*, 7 (1978), 265–79, esp. pp. 278–9.
[10] J. S. Mill, 'Civilisation', in *Essays on Politics and Society*, ed. J. M. Robson, Toronto, 1977, *Collected Works of John Stuart Mill*, xviii, 129.

where one cannot sustain these claims even for those who are productive but especially not for those who are incapacitated in various ways.

MUTUAL ADVANTAGE

Although he gives specific attention to deontological libertarianism that is grounded in principles of rights, especially in the variant of Robert Nozick (pp. 202–5),[11] Barry's main alternative theories of justice are variants of mutual advantage: justice as reciprocity, which has a contractarian ring, and Hobbesian or Humean justice. The latter could be conceived as straight mutual advantage in a merely sociological and, hence, non-normative sense. Sociological mutual advantage is arguably the best going theory of actual liberal governments historically, because the way a typical democratic society is organized can be characterized as mutual advantage sociologically rather than normatively.[12] In comparison to substantial alternative ways of organizing those societies, it is advantageous for important, which is to say politically efficacious, major groups in the society.

Once this organization of the society is in place, it then is also advantageous for many or even all groups that might prefer a quite different organization. It is advantageous for these groups in the sociological sense that there is no reorganization they could cause that, *taken together with the costs to them of changing to that alternative organization*, would make them better off. This is essentially Hobbes's defence of any extant government for virtually all citizens.[13] As what Barry calls a proto-utilitarian, Hume makes mutual advantage a normative theory, because he supposes government arranged to support mutual advantage will produce good results.

Mutual advantage theories are commonly focused on what Sidgwick derides as justice as 'order'.[14] Some libertarians, Hobbes, Hume and Adam Smith seem to think the main function – or, for the libertarians, the only function – of government is maintaining a system of law and order. Adam Smith asserted that the only appropriate function of justice is 'commutative'.[15] But the sometime reason for this focus, as in the arguments of Hobbes most specifically and of many libertarians, is that justice as order is the institutional guarantor of mutual advan-

---

[11] Nozick, *Anarchy, State and Utopia*.

[12] This is a central argument of Russell Hardin, *Liberalism, Constitutionalism and Democracy*, Oxford, forthcoming.

[13] Russell Hardin, 'Hobbesian Political Order', *Political Theory*, 19 (1991), 156–80.

[14] H. Sidgwick, *Methods of Ethics*, 7th ed., London, 1907. See also Hardin, *Morality Within the Limits of Reason*, pp. 36, 44–7.

[15] Adam Smith, *The Theory of Moral Sentiments*, ed. D. D. Raphael and A. L. Macfie, Oxford, 1976 [1759], 7.2.1.10.

tage. In this sense, justice as order is a second-order theory.[16] Its point is not the achievement of justice in your relationship with me through, for example, forcing you to restore what you have taken from me. Moreover, the proponents of such a theory are generally not concerned with the rightness or wrongness of individual actions (although deontological libertarians generally are). Indeed, Hobbes famously argued that there could be no meaning of right and wrong without a government that has a system to enforce law.

One could, of course, suppose that our only purpose in commutative justice is that of righting or punishing wrongs. And one might want a system of law to accomplish this first-order purpose merely for the pragmatic reason that there is no other plausible way to accomplish it well. But Hobbes, Hume and Smith want a system of law and order for the second-order reason that it structures the kind of society they thought we must want – a society graced with stable expectations and commitments that make for prosperity and, in Hume's and Smith's eighteenth-century vocabulary, contentment.

Let us turn now to the motivational structure of mutual advantage theories. They typically are grounded in motivations of self-interest on the part of citizens and are therefore not normative for citizens in their own personal actions. Note the striking difference with justice as reciprocity, which requires, in addition to calculation of what serves mutual advantage, a motivation beyond merely self-interest: concern not to be unfair (p. 112). Once we settle on justice as reciprocity, either by contract or by convention, we must then act normatively against our own interests to defend the position of those too weak to defend their own interests (pp. 48–51). Barry cites the example of American Indians during the nineteenth century. Whites repeatedly made treaties when peace was advantageous to overcome Indian disruptions and then broke them when Indian capacities faltered (p. 45n). For Hobbesian mutual advantage theory, the weak do better under a regime that largely ignores them than they would do if the regime failed to maintain order. Therefore, they have an interest in being obedient to the regime even though no one else is motivated to defend the interests of the weak.

One might object that the difference between justice as reciprocity and justice as impartiality is not motivationally very significant, that, indeed, it is plainly a matter of philosophical or conceptual interest. The difference is this. Justice as reciprocity requires deduction of what system of rules we should have from the interests of all concerned, from nothing more than what would serve mutual advantage if those rules are instantiated. Justice as impartiality requires deduction of

---

[16] Hardin, *Morality Within the Limits of Reason*, pp. 100–5.

the rules of justice from what reasonable agreement (motivated by fairness) would entail. The latter is an internally consistent theory because the actual backing of the system of justice that it defines would follow adequately from the same motivation, namely fairness, as that from which it was deduced. The former, justice as reciprocity, is internally inconsistent in that it requires for its maintenance a different motivation, fairness, from that, namely interest, from which its structure is determined.

Does this difference in internal consistency of motivations matter substantially? Perhaps the answer is a matter of taste. Of course, philosophical taste is not a concern of much practical significance. This is a fact to be applauded by those who consider very extensively the range of philosophical tastes in vogue historically. It may be especially applauded by those appalled by much of contemporary philosophical taste, with its nihilistic, elitist bent and its vocabulary that oddly defies understanding by anyone other than sycophantic insiders even while it is anti-intellectual. Should those concerned with justice on the ground be bothered by the difference between the two classes of theory? Only if they have significantly different implications for the actual structure of our institutions and the actual content of our policies. Do they? Unfortunately, this question is very hard to answer. Its answer turns heavily on the implications of 'reasonable agreement'. It is a striking omission of the work of Thomas Scanlon, Barry and others who argue for reasonable agreement as an apparent criterion for choosing structures of justice that they do not either define the term or even very much constrain it.

Note, incidentally, that many of us actually even do act from Barry's supposedly incoherent pair of motivations. We support tax and other law changes that would make us pay more to enable welfare transfers. But we also figure our own taxes sharply, striving to pay no more than the law mandates. Is this inconsistent? Well, no. We have many quite different motivations for the actions we take in our lives. Of course, we also have many ends, most of which compete with each other for our time and resources. Any theory that supposes this is inconsistent should give us hard argument for its implausible claim.

Also note that, as part of his defence of the superiority of justice as impartiality over mutual advantage because of the greater coherence of its motivational structure, Barry appeals to the game-theoretic representations of the two theories. He says mutual advantage has the structure of a prisoner's dilemma while justice as impartiality has the structure of an assurance game (p. 51). The best individual outcome for a large-number prisoner's dilemma is to have all others co-operate while the lone individual defects. The best individual outcome for an assurance game is the same as the best outcome for the collective. This discussion is slightly odd, however, because the ordinary game theoretic structure of an assurance game is that, in it, while players act from the usual game-theoretic motivation (self-interest), they produce a generally good overall result. In an assur-ance game, ordinary self-interest produces an optimal outcome; in a prisoner's dilemma, self-interest produces a suboptimal outcome. It is only with a very different, not a standard game-theoretic, motivation that justice as impartiality is an assurance game.

In the end, the coherence of motivations in the theory of justice as impartiality is what we might call sector-coherence. I am not to have coherent motivations across all sectors of my life – this would be perverse, because I should, for a trivial example, play to win at chess or poker if these endeavours are to be worth the effort and, contrariwise, I should probably act with great altruism in familial and other relationships of love (perhaps you with your values should not, but I with my values certainly should). Rather, I am only to have coherent motivations in the sector of my life concerned with social justice, in which my single motivation is 'to behave fairly' (p. 51). Just what is the force of this concern? Why not let motivations be relatively coherent or even incoherent in similar ways across all sectors of my actual behaviour while I plump for institutions that align those motivations with just and otherwise good outcomes? This is, of course, Hume's vision of the roles of government and citizenship.

The main complaint by Hobbes, Hume and many other theorists against a theory such as reciprocity or Barry's impartiality is that it depends on a motivation that is, though perhaps not rare, nevertheless too limited to underwrite government. The pragmatic appeal of Hobbesian and Humean theory is not grounded in a nice philosophical concern with the tastefulness of internal coherence. It is grounded in the deep conviction that such motivations of morality as altruism, fairness or even justice somehow defined simply will not carry the day in real life. Barry, Rawls and others speak of the extent to which a just social structure will lead to different motivations in citizens over time. No doubt, there are many considerations that explain the failure of the theory of the new Soviet man during the seven decades of Communist rule in the Soviet Union. But even the most optimistic backers of such a theory must count that seven-decade experience as fundamentally distressing. It seems unlikely that any contemporary philosopher with a normative theory of justice that depends on richly normative motivations on the part of all or virtually all citizens could genuinely believe the theory would ever work on the ground.

Let us stipulate that an explicitly contractarian version of justice as reciprocity is not a compelling theory for the reason that it seems implausible that contractarian argument works at all, either practically or normatively.[17] The central question for reasonable agreement is therefore whether it would lead to institutions that, in their working, are distinctively different from institutions created by either a theory or a politics of mutual advantage. The crux of this question is arguably whether there would be a difference in the treatment of a stable minority whose interests differ substantially from those of some majority. Given that Barry and other reasonable agreement theorists seem to agree with at least Madisonian mutual advantage theorists that our institutions will be roughly democratic and majoritarian, we have to ask whether we can count on majorities to protect the interests of minorities as defined in an initial mutual advantage or fairness vision.

IMPARTIALITY

Barry's principle of impartiality can be used to argue against three positions that might, in different ways, be called partial: solipsism, the group level analogue of solipsism or group solipsism, and any particular theory of the good. No one supposes a solipsist account of justice is credible, reasonable or compelling. Barry also rejects, virtually by analogy, any group solipsist account (p. 8). In the face of the contemporary onslaught against universalist, impartial theories, this is, of course, a crucial move. As it happens, this move is conceptually related to Barry's claims about neutrality toward variant conceptions of the good. Let me briefly discuss these two matters: group solipsism and commitment to a particular (hence, partial, not in the sense of incomplete but in the sense of biased) theory of the good.

Anti-Solipsism

First, note that justice, unlike a theory of the good, seems to be an inherently social notion. Hence, it is incoherent even to think it could be solipsist, whereas a theory of the good could be (egoism is one of Sidgwick's methods of ethics). But it is not analogously incoherent to think justice could be *group*-specific. To assert impartiality over group specific norms seem *ex cathedra*, just as to assert the specialness of my group seems *ex cathedra*. There may be considerable force to the more general position of those who think abstractly. There may contrariwise be considerable force to the group-specific vision for those who think more concretely and pragmatically. The contemporary communitarian claim that there is no ground on which to stand to weigh the one position against the other is therefore not silly. Reason is the slave of the passions, Hume said. You have a passion for abstract visions; I have a passion for my tribe. My reason, therefore, disagrees with yours

---

[17] Hardin, *Liberalism, Constitutionalism and Democracy*, ch. 4.

and there appears to be no knock-down argument either of us can deploy against the other. Or, at least, no such argument has made it into currency.

Note that I think communitarianism has reprehensible implications that cannot be handled from within the communitarian vision but that must be addressed only from a more universal perspective. The woeful implications of communitarianism are, of course, not a matter of logic and they are not of the essence of communitarianism. Rather, they are in its all too often realized potential to be reinforced with norms of exclusion, often to the point of violence against those outside the community. This goes both ways, of course. As Murray Kempton remarks, a community is where when you leave it you get beat up. That suggests the good side of community. It is unfortunately implicit in Kempton's quip that community is also a place where when you enter it as an outsider you get beat up. On its bad side community has led to the violent persecution and deaths of tens of millions of people in only the twentieth century and to the moral and social suppression of plausibly hundreds of millions.

The usual defence of communitarians to such complaints is that there is also a good side to community, as in good communities. To critics of communitarianism this sounds like the trivially true and uninteresting claim that good community is good. The thesis that good community is good does not merit the extraordinary outpouring of blissful paeans to community that have cluttered journals and bookshelves in the past decade or so, many of those paeans vigorously directed against the universalism of Rawls, Kant and utilitarianism. It does not seem tendentious to read much of this odd literature as holding community good *per se*. But I do not have an argument against this view that should convince anyone who continues to assert the inherent goodness of the communitarian vision even after seeing the evidence of Rwanda, Bosnia, the Ku Klux Klan, the Nazis and various other group-solipsist, communally driven groups and populations. In so far as it presumes that community is inherently good, however, I think that the current vogue of communitarian thinking and argument is morally incomprehensible and pernicious.

Theories of the Good

Now turn to specific theories of the good and their breach of impartiality. With the caveat noted below, reasonable agreement makes some sense as a political theory. It makes much less sense as a moral theory. It makes sense as a political theory for the contingent reason that it seems likely that pushing for a particular theory of the good would often not actually put that theory into political practice and hence would not bring about that good. A utilitarian or an autonomy theorist might readily therefore think it more likely to enhance utility or autonomy to follow something like the Scanlon and Barry reasonable-agreement approach in constructing a constitution for a society. But then, of course, the reasonable-agreement or fairness theory does not trump utilitarianism or autonomy but may merely be a practical means toward instantiating as much as practically possible of either of these.

And this is the caveat on reasonable agreement: what is 'reasonable' to me, with my theory of the good, is how much of that good I can get out of our political arrangements. How could I plausibly say my theory of the good should be trumped by a theory of mere fairness? I might, however, have no option to seeing it trumped by an array of contrary political forces. This is a pragmatic, not a moral matter.

One might suppose that my sticking to my theory of the good come what may is a variant of solipsism. To paraphrase G. K. Chesterton's criticism of patriotism, it is a defence of my theory drunk or sober just because it is, after all, mine. But that is wrong. I back that theory because I think it is compelling and correct, not because it is merely mine. The connection between my thinking it right and its being mine is merely logical, not solipsist or otherwise psychological. My willingness to compromise my theory of the good in political decisions is not a choice grounded in the alternative morality of fairness but is a pragmatic choice grounded in my theory of the good. We could properly rewrite the title of one of Rawls's papers from 'Justice as Fairness: Political not Metaphysical' to the title of this essay 'Reasonable Agreement: Political not Normative'.

A political theory of reasonable agreement is an analogue of Locke's argument for religious toleration. Locke did not assert fairness as a prior or trumping principle against any particular religious value. Rather, he argued for accommodation as a practical antecedent to achieving any religious value. It is the practical consideration of opposing forces that makes agreement to less than one's full theory of the good reasonable. Let us turn to Barry's reasonable agreement.

REASONABLE AGREEMENT

Barry writes that 'A theory of justice which makes it turn on the terms of reasonable agreement I call a theory of justice as impartiality' (p. 7). The terminology is slightly confusing, as virtually all terminology is in political theory, because there are theories other than his, Rawls's and Scanlon's that are also grounded in impartiality (or, in a slight twist in vocabulary, impartialism): Kantian and utilitarian theories (p. 232). What Barry's formulation of his theory of justice urgently demands, then, is an account of reasonable agreement that lets us know how that theory differs from those other impartial theories. The difference is somehow in that term, reasonable agreement, because there must be a normative term somewhere in the account or, by Hume's strictures on deducing values from mere facts, we are cheating ourselves into believing values reside in nature. We cannot reach a normatively grounded principle of reasonable agreement without imposing some normative principles. But agreement is merely a factual matter when it happens. Hence, to paraphrase a quip of William Godwin's that Barry uses, we must unpack the magic in the adjective reasonable (p. 223). In that term lies all the good of justice as impartiality.

The starting point of the account of reasonable agreement is Scanlon's formulation of his contractualist variant of contractarianism. Hume contributed a theory of co-ordination mostly in a series of long footnotes.[18] A pithy statement of Scanlon's central contribution to political theory is one footnote. The full relevant text is: 'On this view [Scanlon's contractualism] what is fundamental to morality is the desire for reasonable agreement, not the pursuit of mutual advantage.'[19]

Merely pragmatic principles will not do for the reasonable-agreement crowd because they sound too much like mutual advantage (p. 193). This is arguably the implicit reason many critics of liberalism assert that the reasonable-agreement programme is inherently not value neutral. In Scanlon's concern for reasonable agreement, the condition is negative: I must accept any arrangement that I cannot reasonably reject. Barry – rightly, I think – rejects this view of the condition as merely negative (pp. 69–70). Either way, the condition is a co-ordination condition of reasonable agreement. As Barry writes, 'the theory of justice as impartiality will rarely prescribe a unique outcome' (p. 197). It was once an aspiration of utilitarians, such as Bentham, to reach definitive conclusions. Those who have understood the complications and difficulties of welfarist value theory in its development over the past two centuries can no longer ground such an aspiration, and utilitarianism, especially in its ordinal mutual advantage form, similarly sets little more than co-ordination conditions.

Reasonable agreement seems to be a matter of judgement. It is not Kantian rationalist deduction from transcendental principles. It is perhaps rather like Aristotelian or Millian judgement that depends on a broad range of experience and analysis. That makes it relatively unsatisfactory for a newcomer to the enterprise. One might even

---

[18] David Hume, *A Treatise of Human Nature*, ed. L. A. Selby-Bigge and P. H. Nidditch, Oxford, 1978, III.ii.3, pp. 504–13 (see also III.ii.10, pp. 553–67). See further, Hardin, *Morality Within the Limits of Reason*, pp. 47–53.

[19] T. M. Scanlon, 'Contractualism and Utilitarianism', in *Utilitarianism and Beyond*, ed. Amartya Sen and Bernard Williams, Cambridge, 1982, p. 115n.

question whether the theory is impartial to theorists (admittedly not a group whose welfare is of great concern), some of whom are evidently qualified to apply the term and some of whom are not qualified. Presumably, for example, Nozick thinks (or once thought) his libertarian principle reasonable. I most certainly think my utilitarian principles to be as reasonable as any other principles in moral or political argument, as Barry (and even Rawls) perhaps once did also. Evidently, Nozick and I lack relevant judgement. Part of what Barry means by reasonable is fair. But both libertarians and utilitarians can make sensible claims for the fairness of their visions, although they would not usually start from fairness as their first principle.

Rawls, perhaps uniquely among major theorists of our time, openly starts from two first principles: mutual advantage and fairness. There is debate over whether the one or the other of these is evidently prior morally, although, since both are necessary, priority is an odd concern. (Both RNA and DNA are necessary for human life. Which is prior?) Utilitarians start from the single value of welfare, although the singularity of this value is problematic if there are multiple contributing factors to welfare, as there must be. Libertarians typically start from a putatively single principle of something like pre-Adamic or natural rights, although the singularity is clouded by the sheer number of these rights, which libertarians toss out with seeming abandon. If there is more than one non-redundant value or right, then there must be the logical possibility of conflict between them, which is a difficult problem for multi-principle theories, a problem that Rawls attempts to avoid. Rawls's attempt conspicuously fails in a way fully analogous to the apparent failure of singularity in utilitarianism because his category of basic goods includes multiple goods and lacks a functional form for combining them.

Barry is less worried to work out this issue of the multiplicity of underlying concerns in his theory, although his accounts of the specific political policies here (and presumably also in the promised third volume of *A Treatise of Social Justice*) suggest that he too has problems of multiplicity in the underlying considerations to which reasonableness leads us. In fact, any theory that does not have such problems is probably derelict and worthy of no attention. More fundamentally, Barry's project is specifically motivated by the multiplicity of extant conceptions of the good and by the concern to erect a system of justice that does not impose one such conception on everyone. But in this aspect, his theory is directed at an *outward* multiplicity of values. The difficult issue, as with utilitarian, libertarian and Rawlsian theories, is the *internal* multiplicity of considerations. Until we have more of a grasp on this issue, we cannot confidently claim to know the magic of the adjective reasonable.

In conclusion, consider two examples of what one might call inferences from reasonableness, two examples that must be contested and that therefore want further discussion from reasonable agreement theorists. The first example is essentially about a conceptual problem. The second is about the content of agreement even among those who share Barry's programme. We would need to know more about the meaning of 'reasonable' if we are to resolve these and related issues.

First, the conceptual problem. Barry argues against what Bentham called the pre-Adamical rights that are assumed in most libertarian theory (p. 125) and he generally rejects at least Nozickean libertarianism as outside the range of reasonable agreement (pp. 200–4). The latter move is perhaps the severest test he offers of the notion of reasonable agreement. Many serious philosophers and others would counter that the libertarian vision is eminently reasonable. They might readily concede that others would not agree with that vision. Mill's claims against entitlement might seem to knock the stilts from under libertarian rights. But one might argue for them on grounds that they are the best way to go rather than that they are 'natural'. They could be the best way to go because they serve mutual advantage or because they serve autonomy. Nozickean libertarians seem to think they serve autonomy or even that they are defined by autonomy. How is autonomy only a specific theory of the good rather than a relational notion comparable to fairness? The point of autonomy seems typically to be to let individuals choose their own good just as Barry's impartiality with respect to conceptions of the good is intended to do.

Second, the content of reasonable agreement. It is a peculiarity of Rawls's theory that the welfare component of his value theory has a remarkable shape. Initial income matters a great deal but after some level further income matters not at all. The curve that relates welfare to income flattens out. (Further income might matter *causally* if it affects other components of the value theory, such as equal political voice. But it does not matter as a contribution to further value.) The implication of this is that the staggering inequalities among, say, the upper eighty per cent of people in American society are of no concern to Rawlsian distributive justice. It is only the inequality of these eighty per cent as a class and the remainder of the population – some of whom suffer lacks of some of Rawls's basic goods – that is unjust. Is this a conclusion on which we can reasonably agree? We do not know from their writings what Scanlon and Barry might say; Rawls evidently has spoken.

CONCLUDING REMARKS

Return for a moment to the brief discussion of the priority of principles when there are more than one. Some readers of Rawls suppose that fairness is morally prior to mutual advantage. Yet many theorists make mutual advantage prior. One can understand why an anarchist or one who is committed to self-interest as the right motivation would elevate mutual advantage above fairness. The move that some contemporary contractarians make is to give concern with coercion moral priority over concern with welfare and other plausible principles. They generally do not face the full implications of this move for priority. Does a government act unjustly if it coercively organizes production and distribution of food and other necessaries in the face of grim poverty and failures of collective action? Or is the only morally correct response for such a government to let the society and its people be destroyed? Such conditions of destitution fall outside the realm of application of Rawls's theory, as he explicitly asserts. This means, of course, that his principles of justice are not prior to all other considerations.

Hume and various writers before him recognized the artificiality of various principles of justice in the sense of their being constructions that apply to particular human circumstances as opposed to a priori or natural principles that apply in all circumstances. In correctly asserting that justice is an artificial virtue in this sense Hume offended his lazier readers, who were offended with the notion that a virtue could be artificial rather than absolute (and perhaps directly apprehended by those benighted souls who know such things). Barry grants that his own theory is artificial in this sense as well and he lays out the circumstances of impartiality that make the theory workable. Is there a prior moral position we can take in judging this theory? For a utilitarian theory of anything, the prior theory is clear enough. Because utilitarianism is a full two-level theory, we can at least rough out the structure of its second-order political theory from its first-order moral theory. For justice as impartiality, we jump into the fray in *medias res* and try to analyze justice under certain circumstances. That makes it a strangely partial theory. This conclusion is, seemingly, a demand of reasonableness.

10

Care, Justice and the Good

DIEMUT BUBECK

One of the main tasks of Brian Barry's *Justice as Impartiality* lies in the vindication of both first- and second-order impartiality against various possible criticisms. Barry engages with two types of 'anti-impartialist' critique in Part III of his book – Bernard Williams's and the feminist critique of impartiality – clarifying, in the course of his argument, how he means to construct the interrelations between first- and second-order impartiality and partiality and/or care. His argument is two-pronged. On the basis of the crucial distinction between first- and second-order impartiality, Barry on one hand exposes universal first-order impartiality, as a moral theory or a theory of justice, for the implausible doctrine it is and suggests that it is this doctrine that provides the easy target of critics of impartiality such as Williams (§§ 36–8) or feminist critics (§ 41). On the other hand, Barry argues that partiality and/or care as well as first-order impartiality have a rightful place in his justice as impartiality. He concludes, given these two strands of argument, that justice as impartiality, unlike universal first-order impartiality, is not really touched by the critics of impartiality: 'the core contentions of the friends and foes of impartiality (as they conventionally represent themselves) are equally valid ... there can be no contradiction between them' (p. 192). Noting his surprise that 'so much passionate invective has been poured on ideas so infrequently advocated' (i.e. first-order impartiality), Barry expresses nevertheless hope that he 'may have been able to convince anyone who approaches the book with a reasonably open mind that the large and growing anti-impartialist literature leaves justice as impartiality unscathed' (p. 256).

It will be the task of this chapter to analyze in detail Barry's section on the feminist critique. I will argue that Barry's conviction that justice as impartiality and care as partiality are easily and nonproblematically compatible derives from two interconnected mistakes. On one hand he misconstrues and thus too easily dismisses feminist criticism of impartiality based on a perspective of care. On the other, he asserts the compatibility of care and justice on the basis of the

154

lexical priority of justice over care – a compatibility claim that no care theorist would be prepared to accept. I will discuss Barry's section on the feminist critique in the first section, and move on to an analysis of (some) compatibility claims in the second.

Barry's response to the feminist critique of impartiality, however, is pertinent not only for those interested in this particular issue, but also more generally because he is more explicit about the interrelations between justice and care than he is about the more general question of the relation between justice as impartiality and what has come to be called 'conceptions of the good'. I focus on this question in the third section where I explore the roots of Barry's categorical separation between justice as impartiality and conceptions of the good and argue that this separation is implausible as well as a mistake in view of the moral presuppositions of his own original position. I hope, therefore, that my discussion will throw a light both on Barry's argument with feminist care theory and on the broader question of the interrelation between conceptions of the good and justice as impartiality. Feminist and care issues thus dominate the first, second and fourth sections, while the broader question of the relation between conceptions of the good and justice as impartiality will be addressed in the third and fourth sections.

BARRY ON CARE AND JUSTICE

Barry starts his section on 'Justice and Caring' with a discussion of the claim, widely debated among feminists, that women tend more towards embracing an ethic of care while men tend to embrace an ethic of justice.[1] His response to the issue of the gendered division of moral labour between caring women and rights-asserting men is to ask '[w]hy ... a division of moral labour [should] necessarily be associated with a differential evaluation of the two stereotypical roles' (p. 248). Barry answers that there is no 'particular reason' to think that one should be evaluated more highly than the other, and that he sees no principled reason to object to such a moral division of labour between

---

[1] Not all care theorists are feminists, nor are all feminists care theorists, but some feminists have found care theory an interesting and productive theoretical perspective in moral and political theory (e.g. S. Ruddick, *Maternal Thinking*, London, 1989; V. Held, *Feminist Morality: Transforming Culture, Society, and Politics*, Chicago, 1993; J. Tronto, *Moral Boundaries: A Political Argument for an Ethic of Care*, London, 1993; D. Bubeck, *Care, Gender and Justice*, Oxford, 1995; V. Held, ed., *Justice and Care: Essential Readings in Feminist Ethics*, Oxford, 1995). It is with this particular strand of feminist care theory that I shall take sides in what follows. Note that there is agreement among these theorists that gender difference is primarily socially constructed, but there is disagreement about exactly what follows from this fact as well as about various versions of the ethic of care.

men and women, given certain 'quite stringent conditions' which he promises to discuss in his Volume III 'in the context of equality of opportunity' (p. 249). It is not clear from this reference what these conditions are, apart from, presumably, the equal opportunity for both men and women to choose whether they want to conform to their respective gendered moral roles or not, since the point of equal opportunities is usually unconstrained choice on the basis of one's interests and preferences. Now I take it as sociologically sound that any society in which systematic distinctions are associated with oppressive conditions – and such distinctions usually are systematic, because oppressive conditions produce, or at the very least reproduce, and reinforce them in the first place – will equally systematically and predictably evaluate the characteristic belonging to the oppressed as less valuable or important than the characteristic belonging to the oppressors. Hence as long as gender distinctions are correlated with oppressive gender relations, and I believe that Barry would agree that current gender relations are oppressive, gender differentiated moral roles will not be thought of as having 'equal value' (p. 249). Nor is it likely, in such societies, that either men or women have much of a free choice about their moral or other gendered roles, since their gendered socialization and identity formation, in combination with material and social pressures, will make it very hard to go 'against the flow' of gender differentiation.[2] Barry's suggestion, then, that there is no reason why women's and men's moral labour should not be equally valued is either sociologically naive or utopian in the sense of only being sound in societies without oppressive gender relations. If it is sociologically naive, however, it should have been ruled out, as he points out elsewhere about another case of bad sociology, by the information condition which, among other conditions, specifies the situation in which principles of justice are chosen (p. 124). If it is utopian, it is not apposite to the very situation Barry wants to apply it to, i.e. gendered social structures.

Furthermore, as I have argued elsewhere, as long as there is a gendered division not just of moral, but also of actual caring labour which puts most of the burden of unpaid care on women's shoulders, women are exploited as carers and therefore unjustly treated.[3] If this is so, the question of gender division raises issues of justice and cannot, as Barry suggests, be relegated to an argument 'in terms of alternative visions of a good society rather than in terms of justice' (p. 249). However, Barry is clear that his suggestion that these issues be treated as

---

[2] For a more detailed description of what channels women into what I call the 'circle of care' and keeps men out of it see Bubeck, *Care, Gender and Justice*, chs 4 and 6.
[3] Ibid.

part of political argument based on differing conceptions of the good is conditional on the above mentioned 'appropriate conditions' concerning justice being met (p. 249), hence he might retort that he has already provided for whatever questions of justice gender divisions raise. Moreover, Barry says elsewhere that the demand for the 'more equitable distribut[ion] ... of the burdens of caring' is not incompatible with justice as impartiality (p. 256). Am I raising a false alarm, therefore, about Barry's treatment of gender issues? It is impossible to tell whether the bell that alarmed my feminist instincts when I read Barry's discussion of the gender division of moral labour rang unnecessarily, since we have to await the discussion of principles of justice in Volume III before we can tell whether his principles of justice can appropriately deal with these kinds of issues and whether the application of these principles to gender issues is sound. For the time being, therefore, I can only note two points of feminist concern deriving from Barry's discussion of the gender division of moral labour: first, Barry's explicit mention of equality of opportunity, which causes concern because of the (either naive or utopian) focus on choice rather than gendered constraints that is often characteristic of such discussions; and secondly, his suggestion that gender divisions be understood as questions of the good life which, although conditional, makes me wonder how seriously Barry takes the claim by feminists that care raises issues of justice. But, as I said, I can offer no conclusive argument either way because it is too early to tell, as it were.

After this initial take on gender divisions in morality, Barry moves on to state his own position before discussing feminist criticism. For Barry both the ethic of care and that of justice are 'valid, and should be incorporated within any satisfactory account of morality' (p. 249). The only version of justice that care is incompatible with, according to Barry, is universal first-order impartiality, which is in any case already suspect on independent grounds. But care is perfectly and unproblematically compatible with both first- and second-order impartiality since care and first-order justice are 'complementary' and as such can be fitted into the overall framework of second-order impartiality. And here lies the nub of Barry's solution to the 'care vs justice' debate: first-order justice is lexically prior to care such that considerations of care only apply when principles of justice are either satisfied but do not decide the case, or do not apply. There is no conflict between justice and care in Barry's construction, nor are there genuine moral dilemmas involving considerations of justice and care. It is worth quoting his explanation at full length:

I believe that, if justice is interpreted on the lines I have advocated, there is no plausible case of a genuine moral dilemma involving a clash between justice and caring. The cases that are put up seem to me to fall into two groups: those where plausible rules of justice do not determine the choice, so it is perfectly legitimate to use a 'care' approach to decide what to do; and those where plausible rules of justice do determine the choice, so that it is a mistake to suppose that it is necessary to make a choice between the deliverances of two rival 'ethics' that both bear on the case. (p. 250)

Barry illustrates this position with two cases exemplifying the two possibilities and adds a third case to illustrate his claim that

[t]he other cases are bogus dilemmas which arise from the fallacy of supposing that some generally admirable trait (loyalty, say) can somehow create a moral counterclaim to what are demonstrably the requirements of justice. (p. 251)

Barry does not use the notion of lexical priority to describe his solution, but it is clear from his explanation of the three kinds of possible cases that care only 'gets a word in' when justice has nothing to say, and that the word of justice is final if and when justice has spoken. It would be a 'mistake' or 'fallacy' to suppose otherwise (pp. 250, 251). Given the lexical priority of justice, then, there *are* no genuine dilemmas between justice and care because there *cannot* be any, since Barry has ruled dilemmas out of court by giving justice a superordinate role to care to begin with: 'principles of justice win', as far as Barry is concerned (p. 251).

More generally, although Barry does not say so explicitly at this point, the ethic of care is subordinate to principles of justice because the ethic of care is a conception of the good by his reckoning (cf. p. 249), and the role of conceptions of the good in general is circumscribed by first- and second-order justice: conceptions of the good are only 'allowed' to determine action in cases where justice is silent. Barry admits at least implicitly that the scope of conceptions of the good may reach into choices of action determined by justice, in which case, however, their validity in guiding action is overruled by justice.[4] Thus even if there may be conflict between conceptions of the good and justice in principle, for any given case of moral choice where such conflict may arise, the conflict is 'solved' by giving justice lexical priority with regard to the choice of action.

Barry's position, however, fails to confront one of the most central questions that feminists and other anti-impartialists have raised, namely why impartial rules or principles – in this case principles of first- and second-order justice – should always overrule other moral considerations. Barry seemingly provides us with an indirect argument for his position by arguing against Noddings's by now notorious version of the ethic of care and critique of impartial principles.[5] Her

---

[4] I discuss this point further in the third section below.
[5] N. Noddings, *Caring: A Feminine Approach to Ethics and Moral Education*, Berkeley, CA, 1984.

ethic is interpreted by Barry as endorsing universal first-order care by all, where care is lexically prior to justice (p. 252).[6] Such an ethic is implausible for two reasons according to Barry. First, a society where such an ethic were realized would be characterized by a kind of 'amoral familism' where care obligations, even if they reached beyond the family, would not be 'subordinated to the demands of justice as impartiality' and might possibly constitute even more of a threat to social order than 'pure egoism' does (p. 253).[7] Secondly, actions in such a society would be thwarted by social co-ordination problems given 'the lack of any authoritative co-ordinating rules' (p. 254). Hence people in such a society would find it in their interest to accept rules of justice and thus leave a society of pure universal first-order care behind (pp. 254–5). Universal first-order care, Barry concludes, like universal first-order impartiality, is a 'pathological overextension of [an] idea that [is] valid within certain limits but become[s] pernicious beyond those limits' (p. 255). Barry concludes, moreover, that universal first-order care illustrates the need for principles of justice perfectly since it is a socially undesirable and unstable ethic if 'implemented' in any society.

Barry's rendition of Noddings is implausible, however, for two reasons. First, it distorts Noddings's ethic as a kind of 'amoral familism' because her account of obligation is misrepresented. Obligation arises for Noddings out of relation to other people, but, as Barry quotes himself, this can be either actual or potential relation ('the existence of *or potential for* present relation' – p. 252, my emphasis), hence obligation can at least in principle cover all of humankind. Noddings restricts moral obligation *in practice* to those relations in which care can be completed, i.e. relations where an actual interaction can take place. Thus while stressing that the obligation to care is general (in virtue of potential relation to everybody), Noddings claims there are actual limits to our following up these obligations: '*We are never free, in the human domain, to abandon our preparedness to care*; but, *practically ... we shall limit* the calls upon our obligation quite naturally' (p. 252, my emphasis). Hence even if her account of obligation is not satisfactory as far as the integration of obligations of justice are concerned,[8] it should be obvious that it does not sanction the kind of 'ruthless[ ] ... pursuit of the interests of their nearest and dearest' that Barry speculates amoral familism does (p. 253), since it does not sanction ruthless interaction with anybody. Noddings's ethic of care may be myopic about

---

[6] I omit Barry's alternative and even more implausible interpretation of Noddings which, in any case, is not his main target (p. 252).

[7] The threat to social order arises because, Barry speculates, people act even more ruthlessly to defend their beloved's interests than their own (p. 253).

[8] Cf. Bubeck, *Care, Gender and Justice*, ch. 4, sec. vii.

justice, but it is not the kind of aggressive extended family egoism
Barry makes it out to be. Secondly, Barry's argument that some social
co-ordination is needed even in a society of carers is not as good as it
seems, for the same reasons for which anarchists resist arguments
that urge the need for a state. Note that I have already countered
Barry's suggestion that a universal first-order care society would find
itself in a quasi-Hobbesian state of war of families by pointing out that
an ethic of care would not sanction any form of aggressive behaviour,
hence that no restraints on behaviour would be needed on the usual
Hobbesian grounds. The only other reason for having rules that Barry
mentions is the social co-ordination problem.[9] The point that is usually
made by anarchists in response to that problem is that, given general
willingness to co-operate (which can be presupposed in our case), rules
can be negotiated 'locally' and spontaneously as and when the need for
them arises.[10] There is no reason to think, in other words, that rules for
social co-operation have to be general and enforced locally, unless
there are *other* good reasons, such as social justice, for wanting
universal rules. Now this may be overly optimistic and demanding
a solution, and it is certainly weak on distributive justice, but it is not
an impossible position to hold, and it can point to a long tradition of
anarchist argument in its favour. It does not convince me for reasons
of social justice, hence I would not want to defend it, but I also think
that Barry is wrong in claiming that the 'internal contradictions [of a
universal care society] would lead to its transcendence' (p. 255), hence
he is also wrong in thinking he has won the argument with Noddings.

Not only is Barry's argument against Noddings inconclusive, however, but also her version of the ethic of care is, for various reasons, an
easy target for criticism and has been criticized by ethic of care
theorists who do consider justice an important moral value and are
thus keen to integrate justice into their theories.[11] The issue that such
theorists have nevertheless wanted to raise, however, is begged by
Barry, to wit, why impartial rules should be lexically prior to other
moral considerations in the first place or, more generally, what the
theoretical relation between considerations of care and considerations
of justice should be. Barry fails to discuss any of the more moderate
versions of the ethic of care that do give a place to considerations of
justice while, however, not necessarily agreeing with him that justice

---

[9] It is worth stressing the difference between the need for social co-ordination and the
need for restraint of anti-social (aggressive, violent) behaviour. Barry does not distinguish between them, hence does not realize that the former, without the latter, does
not provide a conclusive argument for justice as impartiality.

[10] I don't know what Noddings's response would be, since she does not address the
problem, but I assume she would want to resist any hard-and-fast rules for co-operation.

[11] See Tronto, *Moral Boundaries*; Held, *Feminist Morality*; Bubeck, *Care, Gender and
Justice*.

is lexically prior to care.[12] Barry thus goes for the easiest target in an (unsuccessful) *ad feminam* argument, but leaves unaddressed other arguments and challenges which would be harder for him to reject.[13] I shall introduce the most important criticism of impartialism that can be found in the care vs. justice debate by way of looking at compatibility claims regarding care and justice.[14]

CARE AND JUSTICE: COMPATIBILITY, COMPETITION OR BOTH?

Barry's main response to care theorists is that he doesn't see what all the fuss is about since care and justice are perfectly compatible. Compatibility claims have been the main defence strategy by impartialists against care theorists.[15] However, compatibility claims can take many forms. Some are obviously implausible, while some sound more plausible to begin with, but come with presumptions that care theorists would want to reject, while at the same time endorsing some other version of compatibility. Compatibility claims, therefore, come in many versions and have to be distinguished very carefully. All compatibility claims divide up the social or moral realm into different 'domains' for

---

[12] Barry does mention two more theorists whose compatibility claims (between justice and care) he acknowledges, but 'has reservations about' (p. 249, n. e). Susan Moller Okin is critical of ethic of care theorists and shares with Barry the prioritization of justice, although she has a version of justice as impartiality which incorporates some care elements in its reconstruction of the Rawlsian original position (S. Moller Okin, *Justice, Gender and the Family*, New York, 1989). Marilyn Friedman is a 'compatibilist' in the paper Barry refers to. However, she not only argues for the integration of justice into a morality of personal relationships or care, but also urges 'the relevance of care to the public domain' – a claim that Barry must have overlooked since he would probably have had to disagree with it (M. Friedman, 'Beyond Caring: The De-Moralization of Gender', in *Science, Morality and Feminist Theory, Canadian Journal of Philosophy Supplement*, ed. M. Hanen and K. Nielson, Calgary, 1987, p. 103). Friedman has subsequently expanded this paper to discuss the relationship between care and justice, which she now says is 'a *dynamic, although uneasy balance* between abstract commitments to important values and principles ... on one hand, and particularized commitments to the people we care about, on the other' (M. Friedman, 'Gendered Morality', in *What Are Friends For?: Feminist Perspectives on Personal Relationships and Moral Theory*, Ithaca, 1993, pp. 138–9, my emphasis). Her use of 'balance', however, suggests the equal importance of care and justice, rather than the prioritization of justice. In summing up her discussion, she even explicitly rejects the lexical priority of impartial principles: 'To suppose that the abstract commitments to values and principles ... should always prevail in any conflict with our commitments to loved ones would be to cut ourselves off from an invaluable source of inspiration for critical moral rethinking' (Friedman, *What Are Friends For*, p. 140). Thus while Okin is clearly on Barry's side but cannot be construed as a care theorist, Friedman turns out to have moved to the 'other side' from a rather ambivalent position to start with.

[13] Mendus makes a similar point about Barry's discussion of Bernard Williams – see S. Mendus, 'Some Mistakes About Impartiality', this volume, p. 179.

[14] See Bubeck, *Care, Gender and Justice*, ch. 5.

[15] Ibid., ch. 6.

which care and justice, respectively, are responsible, but they do so in very different ways. To start with, I shall present two obviously implausible versions, and then look at two seemingly more plausible ones, before elucidating just why these, too, are unacceptable to care theorists.

First, it has been said that justice and care apply to two different social spheres, i.e. that justice applies to the public sphere and care to the private sphere.[16] Barry agrees with feminists in rejecting this division on the grounds that there is every reason to think that considerations of justice also apply within a family context (p. 15). Feminist care theorists, of course, have also wanted to stress conversely that considerations of care are relevant in the public sphere, a claim which I am not sure Barry would want to endorse.[17] Nevertheless, Barry's agreement with feminists on the relevance of justice in the family is sufficient to reject this compatibility claim.

Secondly, it might be thought that justice applies to impersonal relations while care is appropriate for people's personalized relations with family and friends.[18] However, the same point applies here as above, namely that personal relations are not immune from issues of justice. More strongly, one could argue that considerations of justice form an important part of such personal relations characterized by caring.[19] Moreover, caring does take place between strangers in (often too impersonal) settings such as hospitals, health clinics, or even schools and universities.[20] Hence care and justice cannot be identified with different types of relationships either. There is, therefore, no easy way of dividing up the competence of care and justice by reference to social spheres or types of relationships. It is worth noting that even if such divisions were possible, there would still be a question over which ethic would apply in cases where both spheres or types of relationship are involved. Such cases, depending on their interpretation, can only be *either* genuine dilemmas *or* resolved by giving priority to one of the two 'domains' and/or ethics.[21]

Thirdly, it has often been claimed that care and justice describe two different modes of moral reasoning, care being context-sensitive,

---

[16] This corresponds to the traditional view of the family as a 'haven in the heartless world' which allocates to selfless women the cares of the family and to just men the cares of the world.

[17] Cf. Friedman, 'Beyond Caring'; Tronto, *Moral Boundaries*; Bubeck, *Care, Gender and Justice*, and my 'A Feminist Approach to Citizenship' in *Gender and the Use of Time*, ed. O. Hufton and Y. Kravaritou, The Hague, forthcoming, 1998.

[18] Friedman originally interprets the ethic of care as an ethic of personal relationships, but insists that justice is relevant to these relationships too – see Friedman, 'Beyond Caring'.

[19] Cf. Bubeck, *Care, Gender, and Justice*, ch. 5.

[20] Ibid.

[21] Ibid.

bottom-up and concerned with the particular persons involved in a given situation, finding a solution which is right just then and there, while justice is principled, top-down and concerned with applying general, impartial rules as and when they are relevant, disregarding irrelevant circumstances. This claim has been widely adopted by care theorists,[22] but also, for example, by Habermas.[23] Habermas and care theorists disagree, however, about exactly how these different modes are to be understood and hence about how they are compatible. For Habermas they refer to different moral competences which will be combined in a morally mature person, and are not in conflict.[24] Thus, sensitivity to others and to context is relevant to the application of impartial rules and, in a supportive, empathetic role to their conception, but not their justification,[25] but the care competences clearly play a subordinate role in Habermas's impartialist theory. Thus Habermas's compatibility claim, like Barry's, depends on according priority to impartial rules of justice. It would be inconceivable to both that the care mode could stake a claim to the same moral territory that, for them, is occupied by justice, but it only is thus inconceivable because both presume the priority of justice. Impartialists like Habermas and Barry, then, manage to claim compatibility because they demote care – in different ways – to a subordinate role in their impartial theoretical framework. What care theorists, by contrast, have wanted to claim is that care does represent a genuine new ethical epistemology with which to reconceive the moral realm, including justice.[26] Care is presented by these theorists as a serious contender in the realm of moral theories, and it is as such that neither Habermas nor Barry take it seriously in their representation of care as compatible but subordinate.

A fourth, distinctively liberal, type of compatibility claim is the claim that the ethic of care is one of many (first-order) conceptions of the good life while questions of justice are part of the (second-order) impartial system of morality which is needed to reconcile and arbitrate between the widely disagreeing and incompatible conceptions of the

[22] See C. Gilligan, *In a Different Voice*, Cambridge, MA, 1982; J. Tronto, 'Beyond Gender Difference to a Theory of Care', *Signs*, 12 (1987), 644–63; Held, *Feminist Morality*.

[23] J. Habermas, *Moral Consciousness and Communicative Action*, Cambridge, 1990.

[24] Habermas, *Moral Consciousness*, p. 182. A similar idea can be found in Gilligan's early discussion of the ethic of care – see Gilligan, *In a Different Voice* – but not in her later work where she likens care and justice to two different moral perspectives – see C. Gilligan, 'Moral Orientation and Moral Development', in *Women and Moral Theory*, ed. E. F. Kittay and D. T. Meyers, Savage, MD, 1987.

[25] Habermas, *Moral Consciousness*, p. 179.

[26] For care as a moral perspective see, Gilligan, 'Moral Orientation'; Tronto, 'Beyond Gender Difference'; Bubeck, *Care, Gender and Justice*; for care as a new moral epistemology see Held, *Feminist Morality*, and M. Walker, 'Moral Understandings: Alternative "Epistemology" for a Feminist Ethics', in Held, *Justice and Care*.

good life.[27] As in the third compatibility claim, this strategy involves a theoretical move which subordinates care (first-order) to justice (second-order, which is superordinate to first-order conceptions of the good). I add this fourth claim here for the sake of completeness, but will discuss it in more detail below.

What should be clear from my discussion of all four compatibility claims is that care theorists will not accept a compatibility claim which is successful to the extent that it subordinates care to justice, i.e. posits justice as lexically prior. They will not only insist on the possibility of genuine dilemmas involving considerations of justice and care – dilemmas which can only be generated if justice and care are posited theoretically as on a par, hence preclude the subordination of either to the other (see the first two examples) – but they will also, and more importantly, insist on the ethic of care as a genuine competitor in the field of moral theory. With regard to the latter question, two points are at issue between care theorists and justice theorists: first, which framework or perspective is used to conceive of and define the moral realm: impartial justice or the practice of care? and secondly, which meta-ethical framework is thought to be appropriate? Note that these two questions are distinct: the first question refers to the *content* of morality, i.e. to the values, virtues or principles most central to it, while the second question refers to the *form* a morality takes, e.g. whether it is primarily one of virtue, of duty, of rights or of goals, whether it is principled or particularist.[28] The theorization of the practice of care as a moral practice, as I have argued elsewhere, leads to the questioning of both content and form of impartialist theories.[29] As I have shown above, Barry's argument against the ethic of care begs the question of the lexical priority of justice over care, on the one hand, and, as we can add now, the theoretical priority of second-order impartiality over other forms of moral enquiry and moral framework, on the other. Barry thus asserts the priority of justice both at the level of content – where first-order justice and care may at least in principle lead to conflicting moral conclusions, but where Barry finds there are no genuine dilemmas because 'justice wins' – and at the meta-theoretical level where procedural second-order impartiality determines both the shape and content of moral theory as the main and only method used to arrive at theoretical conclusions, thus excluding other possible forms of moral enquiry and framework. In the following section, I shall

---

[27] Habermas, *Moral Consciousness*, p. 180.

[28] Cf. Bubeck, *Care, Gender and Justice*, ch. 5.

[29] Ibid. Content and form are confused in impartialist theories because form is used to determine content: what justice as impartiality does, like any universalizability test, is to derive content through a formal procedure (the 'reasonable non-rejectability' criterion). If the moral theory is a comprehensive theory, all content will be derived from

discuss Barry's main argument for second-order impartiality, thus querying his grounds for endorsing the priority of justice.

SECOND-ORDER IMPARTIALITY AND CONCEPTIONS OF THE GOOD

Like in any liberal theorist, Barry's version of justice as impartiality trumps any particular conception of the good. Before I discuss his argument for justice as impartiality, I shall elucidate Barry's specific version of the priority of justice. Barry uses a contrast with Rawls's account in *A Theory of Justice* [30] to illustrate what he has in mind: while in Rawls 'justice constrains the *content* of the good', in Barry's version 'justice constrains the *pursuit* of the good' (p. 57, note a; cf. p. 77). Thus while Rawls's constraint is theoretical or conceptual, Barry's is practical. People may hold any conception of the good whatsoever, and may reach conclusions with regard to action on this basis, but if these conclusions contradict first- or second-order impartiality the choice of action has to be determined by justice as impartiality. Justice wins, in other words, not just when in conflict with care, but when in conflict with any other moral (or non-moral) considerations. It wins, however, not because it leads to the right conclusion, but because there is a practical necessity for it to win. Justice has this primarily practical function in Barry because the truth of any one particular conception of the good cannot be established as against other conceptions of the good, hence it is sorely needed for Hobbesian reasons: if people are allowed to pursue their different conceptions of the good without any constraints, they will sooner or later end up attacking each other.

Barry's argument for the practical priority of justice goes as follows:

1. *The sceptical premise*: conceptions of the good 'give rise to conflicting practical implications and these conflicts cannot be resolved by rational argument' (p. 30).
2. *The Hobbesian premise*: 'a society in which people accept no guide to conduct except their own conception of the good ... is one doomed to mutual frustration and conflict' (p. 30).
3. *The contractarian conclusion*: 'some mutually acceptable basis for the

---

some version of the universalizability test; if it is merely a constraining moral framework, like justice as impartiality, it may leave certain questions open, but will determine conclusively the answers to those questions which fall in its remit, hence determine some content. Care theorists do not necessarily object to the impartialist procedure as such – although they may want to modify it (see Okin, *Justice, Gender and the Family*) – but they will object to claims of its necessary exclusivity as a moral epistemology (see Held, *Feminist Morality*; Walker, 'Moral Understandings') and/or lexical priority as a system of rules (see Friedman, 'Gendered Morality'; Bubeck, *Care, Gender and Justice*).

[30] John Rawls, *A Theory of Justice*, Oxford, 1971.

accommodation of different conceptions of the good is thus a matter of the utmost practical importance' (p. 31).

4. *The specific conclusion*: justice as impartiality is the best such 'mutually acceptable basis'.[31]

Before I argue that the Hobbesian premise is wrong, I need to look at Barry's conception of 'conceptions of the good'. Conceptions of the good are nowhere defined in Barry, except possibly obliquely through a positive reference to Rawls's usage of the term in *A Theory of Justice* (pp. 29–30); we are thus left in the dark about what precisely qualifies as a conception of the good and on what grounds. It becomes obvious during his discussion of justice as mutual advantage, however, that Barry treats the pursuit of any good whatsoever, whether religious, secular (moral and/or ethical) or self-interest as functionally equivalent in that it poses an essentially Hobbesian problem of 'finding a *modus vivendi*' (p. 32) between people who 'wish to advance their own conception of the good' (p. 33). A conception of the good, in other words, is any conception of any good whatsoever: given the main problem of finding 'ground rules of social life', Barry states earlier on in the discussion, '[s]ecular conceptions of the good and religious views are to be assimilated ... because they create the same problems for the project' (p. 30), and he later on 'assimilates' self-interest as well (pp. 31ff.). Furthermore, there is an interesting slippage in Barry's discussion, and seemingly no difference, between his usage of 'people's pursuit of their own good' and of 'people's pursuit of their own conceptions of the good'. As I shall argue in what follows, however, there is a considerable difference between the two, and this difference undermines Barry's Hobbesian premise.

While Hobbes's original argument in *Leviathan* states explicitly that there is no 'right' or 'wrong', hence no conception of the good except self-interest, in the state of nature,[32] Barry, as I have pointed out above, allows for conceptions of the good of all sorts in his Hobbesian premise, including self-interest. However, there is an enormous *practical* difference between people's pursuit of their self-interest and people's 'pursuit' of the conception of the good they endorse. Thus imagine, on one hand, somebody's completely unrestrained pursuit of her interest which, as in the Hobbesian state of war, may be as 'ruthless' as we could possibly imagine, and, on the other, somebody living his life according to some moral or ethical

---

[31] I have added the specific conclusion for the sake of completeness: it represents the conclusion of Barry's argument against other contractarian theories of justice. I leave the specific conclusion aside, since the practical priority of justice is already established – if it is – with the contractarian conclusion.

[32] Thomas Hobbes, *Leviathan*, ed. R. Tuck, Cambridge, 1986, ch. xiii.

conception of the good which constrains his behaviour considerably.[33] The difference between the two, of course, is that self-interest does not constrain one's behaviour at all, while any system of religious or moral values does. Thus what I have argued above about the ethic of care holds equally for a 'state of nature' composed, say, of Buddhists or altruists, or even both together: people may need co-ordinating rules in such 'states of nature', but they will not enter into wars with each other because they disagree about, or come to different practical conclusions on the basis of, their conceptions of the good. They will not do so *because the very fact that they try to live – 'pursue' – the conceptions of the good they have actually constrains what means they can and would want to choose to do so.* Hence not everybody's pursuit of the good, even if inconsistent with that of others, leads on to the slippery slope to religious or civil wars which Barry, like Hobbes, threatens us with as the worst but inevitable outcome to motivate agreement to his conclusion.[34] I am not suggesting, of course, that there is no danger of such conflicts. The current world as well as history sadly prove such a claim wrong. Supposing, however, that I am right in resisting Barry's assimilation of moral conceptions of the good to self-interest as causes of inevitable conflict, the cause of such conflicts must lie elsewhere.

My alternative explanation of such conflicts is that it is only if political and power interests are fused with differing (usually religious or anti-religious) conceptions of the good that conflict arises. Thus there is usually some group, holding one conception of the good which oppresses another group (or groups), usually a minority, holding another conception of the good. Given such oppressive contexts, it is not surprising that violent conflicts arise, and that the question of political power gets confused with questions of belief. That different conceptions of the good, and 'pursuers' of conceptions of the good, can peacefully coexist, however, is equally evident, mostly in situations of little or no power differential between them.[35] Now given that we live

[33] Ironically enough and, as I argued above, completely mistakenly, Barry uses the epithet 'ruthless' when discussing Noddings' ethic of care and the supposedly ruthless pursuit of the interests of their 'nearest and dearest' by those holding an ethic of care (p. 253).

[34] Barry's Popper epigraph warns us already at the very beginning of the book of 'ultimately [the use] of violence' (p. vi), and throughout we are reminded of the danger of religious wars, which illustrate how ferocious and devastating can be the conflicts arising from religious differences and of ethnic conflicts.

[35] A good example is the two main Christian religions in Germany, Lutheran Protestant and Catholic, whose status is equal. The status of Islamic believers in Germany compares less favourably for historical and political reasons. Most Moslems are Turkish so-called 'guestworkers' whose access to German citizenship is rendered more or less impossible. Hence political conflict could be expected with regard to Germany's Turkish minority, and this conflict would be genuinely political not religious. The recent granting of German citizenship to second-generation immigrants, however, may have reduced the risk of such conflict.

in a world of established states, all of which rule people with differing conceptions of the good, power structures are inescapable and, where they are not impartial between such different conceptions of the good, they are therefore even on my explanation of conflict bound to lead to conflict. Hence supposing a structure of states as there is in the real world, I agree with Barry that only actual impartiality by political regimes between conceptions of the good can avoid such conflict. I arrive at this practical conclusion – which may also be derived from the specific conclusion 4, but should not be confused with it – by a different route, however, and this different route matters since it establishes the falsehood of the Hobbesian premise for all conceptions of the good but self-interest. I conclude, then, that the Hobbesian premise is wrong and does not establish the need for a common system of rules *on Barry's quasi-Hobbesian grounds.*[36]

Now my ultimate interest in rejecting Barry's Hobbesian premise does not so much lie in resisting the contractarian conclusion, but in a corollary of my disagreement with Barry about the role of conceptions of the good. Note that this disagreement is empirical, not conceptual, since Barry's Hobbesian premise, like Hobbes's own, is based on what we might call a theory of conflict – which is what we disagree about. A corollary of these differing theories of conflict is that we evaluate conceptions of the good very differently: according to me they are socially beneficial in restraining people's conduct to the extent that they are followed, while according to Barry they are recipes for disaster.[37] Therefore any search for the sorely needed social ground rules, it seems, would have to steer well clear of them so as not to get infected by their volatile and explosive nature: conceptions of the good are to be constrained and contained by justice as impartiality, but have nothing to contribute to it. On my theory, by contrast, there is little reason to be wary of conceptions of the good and every reason to try to integrate a conception of justice with them, since they already have a beneficial motivational and practical effect on people's actions. (Remember that the necessity for justice is presented as exclusively

[36] Barry's envisaged state of nature – as a state without common ground rules – is thus more comparable to a pluralized Lockean one than to Hobbes's own, although Barry wants to tell a Hobbesian story about it. The Lockean state of nature, however, precisely because it allows for moral constraints on people's behaviour, has a crucial weakness as far as contractarian conclusions are concerned: it makes some (i.e. anarchists) doubt whether it needs to be left behind at all.

[37] My claim holds true especially in contrast to self-interest. In order to avoid having to state this exception every time, I shall henceforth mean 'conception of the good' to refer to any conception of the good excluding self-interest, thus departing from Barry's usage of 'conception of the good'. This departure also signals the importance of one of my disagreements with Barry, i.e. that the pursuit of self-interest poses a very different social and theoretical problem compared to the 'pursuit' of differing conceptions of the good.

practical according to Barry.) Conceptions of the good, however, are not only practically important and thus essentially misjudged by Barry, but his theory does not even get off the ground without them.

There are at least three respects in which Barry's Scanlonian original position presupposes that people hold and act according to prior conceptions of the good, and in two of these respects their holding the conceptions of the good they do is in fact necessary if common rules of justice are to be found. First, consider the agreement motive. Barry claims that people have 'a desire to reach agreement with others on terms that nobody could reasonably reject' – i.e. that people have the 'agreement motive' (p. 168). The agreement motive in its turn, however, presupposes that people have a basic commitment to equality in the minimal sense of taking others seriously enough as their equals so as to feel the need to justify their choices to them.[38] Now those who are already in the habit of restraining and justifying their behaviour on the basis of moral, ethical or religious considerations are much more likely to conform to this precondition since they would think at least of those sharing the same conception of the good with them, if not of all human beings, as their moral equals and feel some kind of moral obligation towards them. The argument with those holding a less than universal conception of the good would therefore only have to convince them that others are their moral equals even if they do not hold the same conception of the good. This argument may be difficult, but it can build on an already existing basis of moral equality: it simply has to widen its scope (if necessary). By contrast, as Barry points out himself, the most consistent threat to this fundamental commitment to equality which underlies the conception and implementation of any system of rules of justice is the self-interested free-rider, who will be perfectly consistent in her rejection of any obligation of justice if it is against her self-interest (pp. 36–7).[39] The real threat, in other words, to any minimally moral or ethical community – which is what the original position is, given Barry's stipulation of the agreement motive – is that person who does not accept any moral commitment whatsoever except as and when it suits her purposes. Barry rightly points out that such persons simply have to be forced to conform to the rules (cf. pp. 168–9), but he fails to realize that he helps himself to a prior commitment to equality which, I have argued, can only derive from the very conceptions of the good that he otherwise so insistently distances himself from or even vilifies as the causes of civil and religious wars.

[38] Cf. also section 16, where Barry claims that the circumstances of impartiality necessitate 'a disposition to see fellow citizens as equals in a fundamental sense' (p. 102).

[39] Barry subsequently asserts that 'strictly analogous problems arise if we replace self-interest by the pursuit of any conception of the good' (p. 37).

Secondly, Barry's original position presupposes 'reasonable' behaviour by those who participate in it.[40] People in this position have a veto right against any particular proposal to allow them to express their objections and to force others to take their objections seriously. As Barry notes when discussing procedural rules, however, a veto right can be misused to block any solution, whether reasonable or not (pp. 106–7), and there is 'no procedural alchemy whereby a majority bent on injustice can be made to pursue justice instead' (p. 101). Procedural rules by themselves, therefore, will not produce the right outcomes unless they have been followed in the right spirit, or by people motivated in the right way (cf. p. 100). What people in the original position need, therefore, much as in any other procedurally structured situation, is an already existing commitment to behave 'reasonably', which is, we have to suspect, nothing other than an already existing moral commitment to follow the rules, especially a basic commitment to equality. While Barry notes candidly that 'what you get out [of the original position] is what you put in' (p. 113), he is not as candid about the fact that it can only be already existing conceptions of the good that can give people an idea of what it is to behave 'reasonably' and not urge unfair demands on others. What Barry is forced to 'put into' the original position, then, is a presumption of moral ideas, motivation and behaviour which can only derive from the very conceptions of the good people bring to it.

Thirdly, there is one respect in which Barry makes positive reference to people's already existing values, that is when he points to the likely agreement of people that harm is 'deleterious from the point of view of a very wide range of conceptions of the good' (p. 88). Harm plays a central role in Barry's argument in that it constrains the possible content of rules of justice, although not in the shape of Mill's harm principle (sec. 14). If it is possible for people with different conceptions of the good to agree on their evaluation of harm, however, why would it be impossible for them to find further areas of agreement? In other words, why should conceptions of the good – barring in this one respect – be considered antagonistic to rather than a moral resource for justice?

Barry's treatment of conceptions of the good thus raises a more general question: how can we conceive of the relation between conceptions of the good and second-order impartiality, given a diversity of incompatible conceptions of the good to start with? It seems to me

---

[40] We are never told by Barry exactly what is 'reasonable', except that '"reason" means reasoned argument, from premises that are in principle open to everyone to accept'. Barry adds 'a contemporary gloss' to this rather vague formulation by specifying, question-beggingly, that 'these are premises which reasonable people, seeking to reach free, uncoerced agreement with others, would accept' (p. 7).

there are at least three possible strategies.[41] The first, *independent* strategy consists of a complete disregard of the conceptions of the good, while attempting to devise a theory of justice 'from scratch', without any recourse to these conceptions of the good. The second, *consensus* strategy looks for possible points of consensus between the varying conceptions of the good, building a theory of justice on already held moral or ethical convictions, but without requiring any change to these convictions. The third, *transformative* strategy would seek, through an ideal type of discussion situation, to achieve enough common ground between the various participants with their differing conceptions of the good and interests so as to arrive at a conception of justice. This discussion would induce the participants to modify their originally held conceptions of the good so as to at least accommodate, if not support, the agreed upon principles of justice.

All of these strategies have their strengths and weaknesses, but they are not all equally plausible. The independent strategy, which is, of course, Barry's, is not only implausible because, as I have argued above, it does not succeed without recourse to the moral motivation, commitment and values that conceptions of the good typically provide, hence it does not succeed as an independent strategy full stop. It is furthermore implausible because it duplicates, as it were, the moral realm into a realm of justice and a realm of conceptions of the good, the former completely separate from and constraining the latter. There is such a duplication because there is no reason to assume that conceptions of the good do not contain any conception of justice, or of common ground rules. In fact, one of the functions of conceptions of the good is exactly to provide a conception of social ground rules, values or virtues, among other things.[42] This duplication, however, not only offends against Occam's razor, it also offends against moral and psychological common sense: why should people separate out second-order justice from the rest of their moral values, principles and virtues, rather than integrate it with those, and why should people's motivation to accept and follow rules of justice be completely separate and unrelated to their general motivation to act morally? Thus note that the point I made above about the moral motivation presumed for the original position can be generalized to include people's motivation to

---

[41] A fourth strategy would be to posit one particular conception of the good as the correct one and to develop a conception of justice from within this framework – see A. MacIntyre, *Whose Justice? Which Rationality?*, Notre Dame, 1988. This would not represent a *second-order* conception of justice.

[42] Even the most spiritual of conceptions of the good usually contain rules, values and virtues regarding social interaction, and less exclusively spiritual conceptions of the good do so at much greater length. Hence the devising of a contractarian conception of justice, if done without taking into account people's already existing intuitions or conceptions of justice, is literally a duplication of the moral realm.

follow the rules of justice, once they are ascertained. It does not make psychological sense to assume that this motivation is completely unrelated to people's more general ethical or moral motivation. On the contrary, the strongest possible motivation for justice surely is one that is fuelled by, and an organic part of, an already existing motivation to act according to the conception of the good one holds, given that this is, as Barry agrees, what people believe most strongly in and feel most strongly about.[43] The independent strategy, therefore, is simply implausible.

The other two strategies avoid the implausibility of duplication and bifurcation of the moral realm by exploring possible connections between conceptions of the good and second-order justice. The consensus strategy, however, is limited by the extent of diversity of conceptions of the good that it attempts to bring together: the more diverse the conceptions of the good, the less likely is consensus, and the less substantive it will be. Alternatively, some conceptions of the good can be excluded from consideration on some prior grounds, but the consensus then ceases to be general and can only hold 'locally' and conditionally.[44] Barry wants to resist such rescue attempts, but it is worth noting that his strategy already excludes at least two types of conceptions of the good (as embodied in people's behaviour in the original position), i.e. that of pure self-interest and any type of ethical theory, such as Nietzsche's, that is not universal in scope (cf. pp. 193–4). Thus the difference between Barry's independent strategy and a potentially successful consensus strategy is only one of degree, and not as categorical as he seems to suggest when discussing Rawls's political conception of justice. The main disadvantage of the consensus strategy thus is that it is either impossible or, to the extent that it is possible, it will either be completely insubstantive or will have to renounce universal aspirations.

The transformative strategy, by contrast, has the advantage of being at least potentially, and plausibly, all-embracing, but the disadvantage of being rather unpredictable with regard to its possible outcome, depending on how much weight and importance the process of discussion is given, and how different the conceptions of the good of the participants are. Most importantly, the relationship between conceptions of the good and justice in this strategy is dynamic, not static as in the consensus strategy, hence participants may have to recon-

---

[43] We can speculate that the ultimate reason for Barry's failure to explore the relation between justice and general moral motivation must lie in his quasi-Hobbesian distinction between conceptions of the good as the supposed 'causes' of social conflict and justice as the solution to such conflict.

[44] See Rawls's notion of an 'overlapping consensus' between reasonable comprehensive doctrines, in John Rawls, *Political Liberalism*, New York, 1993.

struct some aspects of their conceptions of the good on the basis of the rules of justice they have come to agree to.[45] The main advantage of this strategy is that, because it envisages a dynamic integration of rules of justice with people's differing conceptions of the good, it can make full use of conceptions of the good as a kind of moral resource which, on one hand, will shape and possibly prejudice people's notions of justice, but, on the other, will also support their attempts in coming to an agreement about, and living according to, rules of justice. The main disadvantage, as I have mentioned above, is its unpredictability (but maybe I simply lack imagination). As compared to Barry's independent strategy, however, it seems to me preferable because it does not require us to go beyond theoretical, psychological and moral good sense.

In conclusion, Barry's quasi-Hobbesian characterization of conceptions of the good as causes of social conflict in his argument for justice as impartiality causes him not only to hold an entirely implausible view of the theoretical and practical relations between conceptions of the good and second-order impartiality, but it also leads him to be less than candid about the presumptions of his own theory regarding the necessary role of conceptions of the good in his original position. I have argued, by contrasting Barry's 'independent' conception of these relations with two other possible positions (the consensus and dynamic strategy), that other positions are more plausible, but cannot in this context provide more substantive argument for the dynamic conception which I think is preferable. In the last section I will return to care theory and the possible reconceptualization of justice that would be suggested from this perspective.

JUSTICE AND CARE: FROM COLONIZATION TO CO-OPERATION

If the relationship between justice and conceptions of the good is not as independent as Barry posits it, and if, as I have argued, compatibility claims between justice and care which hinge on the priority of justice are contested by care theorists, how are we to reconceptualize the relationship between justice and care? Are they compatible, and if so, how? Can they form part of an overarching moral theory without one being subordinate to the other, or are they necessarily antagonistic?

With regard to first-order impartiality, I have argued elsewhere

---

[45] Rawls's 'reflective equilibrium' in his *Theory of Justice* may be seen as a version of such a more dynamic relationship, but the dynamics could, of course, be much more transformative than the kind of slight conceptual adjustments that Rawls has in mind.

that considerations of justice form an organic and important part of the ethical perspective of care and are thus far from incompatible or antagonistic with considerations of care, but I have also argued that this integration has its limits and that it is modified by the public/ private divide.[46] Other care theorists have been more insistent in stressing the need for justice to 'keep in check' certain moral dangers inherent in the ethic of care, thus insisting on first-order impartiality as a necessary corrective to the partiality thought to be inherent in care. The question of organic vs antagonistic integration is thus at the moment contested and far from being fully explored, but care theorists certainly agree in their rejection of the lexical priority of first-order justice over care, even if they conceive of the relation between care and justice differently. As a result of this rejection, and *contra* Barry, genuine dilemmas are conceivable involving considerations of care and justice, where it is not obvious at all that 'justice wins'.[47] Much more work needs to be done from a care perspective to work out and discuss details and problems, so the challenge at the moment is still in its infancy. But the challenge is there, and should have been taken more seriously by Barry.

With respect to second-order impartiality, my main argument in the last section was that Barry artificially and inconsistently separates his theory of justice from conceptions of the good. If conceptions of the good are a moral 'resource' that Barry needs to use to get his original position going, however, can he continue to insist on the priority of second-order justice? If, on the other hand, conceptions of the good are given a more prominent role, how could we conceive of their informing the original position and its outcome? Okin has argued that the virtues and moral knowledge crucial in care are presupposed in Rawls's original position, properly conceived.[48] In a parallel move, it might be argued about Barry's Scanlonian position that the virtues of openness and receptivity, combined with a principle of consensual decision-making, are functionally equivalent to the veto principle, which ensures that everybody's reasonable concerns and interests are taken into account.[49] Given that, as I have argued above, the procedural constraints are not sufficient to guarantee the right outcome in the original position in any case, if the participants in Barry's original

---

[46] Bubeck, *Care, Gender and Justice*. I am more optimistic now regarding the possibility of a more overarching perspective of care in which justice could be incorporated in all relevant aspects than I was before (cf. Bubeck, *Care, Gender and Justice*, pp. 249–54).

[47] Ibid., p. 234.

[48] Okin, *Justice, Gender and the Family*.

[49] The functional equivalence is comparable to that in Rawls's original position between the limited self-interest stipulation and universal altruism – see Rawls, *A Theory of Justice*.

position had the virtues of carers, they would be sure to arrive at the right outcome, even without those procedures, because their behaviour would be functionally equivalent to behaviour constrained by the veto principle: if they were thus virtuous, they would listen openly and with a view to accommodating everybody's needs and interests equally.[50] The rather individualist and somewhat antagonistic Scanlonian version, in other words, could be mimicked and at the same time improved in its workings by requiring people to enter with more substantial moral endowments. Having the virtues and values of carers, however, might at the same time change the perspective of the participants in the original position, thus possibly influencing the rules of justice they would agree upon. Moreover, if the arguments of care theorists are correct, participants with caring virtues would be a lot less sure than Barry's Scanlonian ones that second-order impartiality can uncontestedly and in all possible circumstances constrain and override whatever conclusions may be derived from the conceptions of the good people may hold. They might also insist, with Aristotle, that general rules can only ever be approximations or rules of thumb, hence that good solutions are not necessarily always those derived from principles of justice without also taking equally into account specific circumstances and other values, principles or virtues. Their morally pluralist world may thus be morally less predictable than one where justice always wins, but it may be a morally richer, livelier and more challenging world for that.

[50] Cf. Bubeck, *Care, Gender and Justice*, ch. 5.

11

Some Mistakes About Impartiality*

SUSAN MENDUS

The cover of Brian Barry's book shows a detail from Goya's *Fight with Cudgels*, and its motto is taken from Karl Popper's *The Open Society and Its Enemies*:

> If a dispute arises, then this means that those more constructive emotions and passions which might in principle help to get over it, reverence, love, devotion to a common cause etc., have shown themselves incapable of solving the problem ... There are only two solutions; one is the use of emotion, and ultimately of violence, and the other is the use of reason, of impartiality, of reasonable compromise.

Auden's injunction to love one, another or die is supplemented by a third possibility: reasonable compromise or impartiality. But reasonableness has fallen on philosophical hard times: the Enlightenment project has been subjected to unrelenting criticism by those who claim that we can do no more than articulate the shared beliefs of members of our own society, and that reason is what is shared by those who already agree, not something which can transcend disagreement. Similarly, the voice of impartiality has been almost silenced by the clamourings of anti-Kantians and feminists, who urge the priority of context and commitment to specific others and are suspicious of injunctions to treat everyone impartially.

Brian Barry is dismayed. If we deny the power of reason to arbitrate between discordant groups, we become impotent in the face of regimes which deal in wholesale violations of human rights; and if we deny the importance of impartiality, we condone capriciousness and render ourselves a danger in political life. Since we know that love fails, and since we should be reluctant to engage in fights with cudgels, hope must lie in the possibility, after all, of defending impartiality against its many critics. It is this task which forms the focus of the third and final section of *Justice as Impartiality*. Having despatched justice as mutual advantage in Part I, and articulated his own conception of justice as

* I am grateful to my colleague, Matt Matravers, for helpful discussions on these questions.

impartiality in Part II, Barry turns his attention in Part III to the opponents of impartiality, and in particular to their claim that any commitment to impartiality must entail the 'crazy view' that we should not favour our children over other people's children, or our spouse over a complete stranger. This view, he concedes, is indeed crazy, but fortunately it is not entailed by a theory of justice as impartiality properly understood. Justice as impartiality requires impartiality only at the second-order level (as a test to be applied to the moral and legal rules of society). It does not entail, and indeed is inconsistent with, a commitment to universal first-order impartiality (impartiality as a maxim of behaviour in everyday life). Since this is so, his theory of justice as impartiality can escape unscathed by the attacks of anti-impartialists, which rest either upon a failure to distinguish between the first-order and the second-order, or upon a commitment to the already discredited conception of justice as mutual advantage. In brief, then, the battle between impartialists and anti-impartialists is mislocated or 'ill-joined', and sensible anti-impartialists can concur with the basic tenets of Barry's defence of justice as impartiality.

In discussing the mistakes which Barry attributes to anti-impartialists my main aim will be to suggest that, at least sometimes, it is he who mislocates the problem. Certainly, his theory would be mortally damaged if it entailed universal first-order impartiality, but even if Barry can demonstrate that such entailment does not hold, there are still problems about the scope of the theory and about the personal and political costs exacted by it. Anti-impartialists are concerned about these implications and, I shall argue, Barry ought to share their concerns. Indeed, in many instances he *does* share their concerns, but he does not fully acknowledge their importance for the status and working out of his own theory of justice as impartiality.

WILLIAMS AND THE COSTS OF IMPARTIALITY

The central question informing the whole of Part III is, Barry tells us, whether second-order impartiality entails universal first-order impartiality. Since he agrees that there would indeed be something crazy about a world in which people acted on the injunction to treat everybody with complete impartiality (a world which enjoined universal first-order impartiality), it is crucial to his defence of justice as impartiality to demonstrate that it does not entail this crazy conclusion. His argument involves a series of criticisms of the opponents of impartiality, specifically of Bernard Williams's attacks on Kantianism and utilitarianism, and of feminist defences of an ethic of care.

Barry claims that Williams's attacks on Kantianism and utilitarianism depend very heavily on his adopting eccentric and implausible variants of both doctrines: variants which do indeed suppose a commitment to universal first-order impartiality, 'but this is a cheap victory that gains nothing because the "utilitarianism" thus destroyed is not that of Bentham or Mill, and the "Kantianism" would have been repudiated by Kant' (p. 217). There is, however, a *tu quoque* response to be made here, for Barry's discussion of Williams itself distorts the real force of his (Williams's) arguments and ignores aspects of it which have important implications for justice as impartiality.

The discussion of Williams centres around two famous examples: Godwin's 'famous fire cause' and Williams's preferred variant, the case of the man faced with a choice between saving his wife and saving a complete stranger. Godwin's insistence that Archbishop Fénélon should be rescued in preference to his own mother was found shocking by his contemporaries but, Barry concludes, any second-order impartialist theory would have to reach the same conclusion as Godwin in a truly exceptional case. 'It is an unavoidable implication of any set of moral norms that can be squared with second-order impartiality in any of its forms that people may be unlucky enough to find themselves in situations where doing the right thing entails a great sacrifice' (p. 223). The real problem with Godwin's discussion is not that it arrives at that conclusion, but rather that 'there is nothing in it to restrict the imperative to sacrifice your parent to a case as extreme as that. In principle, even a slight advantage in total future utility on the side of rescuing one person rather than the other should determine where your duty lies' (p. 224). And he concludes that since both sophisticated forms of utilitarianism and his own theory of justice as impartiality *can* restrict the imperative to truly exceptional circumstances, Williams's objection counts as an objection only to extreme and implausible variants on the impartialist theme.

Throughout the discussion of Godwin, and indeed of anti-impartialism generally, Barry's main concern is with whether or not a theory delivers the right answer. His concluding flourish in the 'famous fire cause' takes the form of a pronouncement that second-order impartiality will require that the Archbishop be saved, and second-order impartiality is right so to do. But Williams is much less interested in whether the answer delivered is right and much more interested in the implications of requiring that the agent pose the question. In part, this difference of focus is consequent upon the fact that whereas Barry is primarily concerned with the attainment of social justice, Williams is concerned with the nature and limits of morality. And while it might be appropriate to eschew formulation in the area of the ethical, it surely cannot be a promising strategy in the discussion of social justice. To this extent, Barry is right. A Williams-type rejection of formulation in the political world would deteriorate into a licence for all kinds of capriciousness and inconsistency.

Nevertheless, moral and political considerations cannot hang completely free of one another, and a wider part of Williams's concern is to draw attention to the personal costs which may be exacted by impartialist political theories. On these, Barry is largely silent except to express the hope that most of us are never put in positions in which we are forced to make such dramatic choices as that envisaged in the 'famous fire cause'.

But what are these personal costs, and how do they affect the theory which Barry wishes to advance? In the second part of his attack on Williams's anti-impartialism, he turns his attention to anti-Kantianism and to the 'well-worn' example of the man faced with a choice between saving his wife and saving a complete stranger. Of this case, Williams famously remarks:

The two-level approach provides the agent with one thought too many: it might have been hoped by some (for instance by his wife) that his motivating thought, fully spelt out, would be the thought that it was his wife, not that it was his wife and in situations of this kind it is permissible to save one's wife.[1]

Barry is dismissive of this line of thought, responding acidly:

I am inclined to doubt whether anything very informative is to be gained by asking what is the optimal number of thoughts for a person to have in any give situation. Perhaps in general it is better to have only the number necessary for the purpose in hand but I do not think much follows from that. (p. 231)

But it may be that something does follow from that, and that what follows is important, not merely for opponents of impartiality, but for Barry himself. However, before suggesting what that might be, it is worth noting that the example is not, in any case, one which Williams deploys in order to reject second-order impartiality, or to support the contention that second-order impartiality entails universal first-order impartiality. And after much discussion Barry concedes this (p. 231). However, since it is conceded that Williams's complaint is not that Kantianism must entail universal first-order impartiality, and since Barry's targets are those who *do* claim that second-order impartiality entails universal first-order impartiality, we may wonder what the point of the whole discussion is. Whatever is wrong with Kantianism on Williams's account it is not that it must entail universal first-order impartiality. So what is wrong with it, and how might the identification of what is wrong be helpful (and important) to Barry himself?

In the opening sections of the book, Barry discusses the 'common

---

[1] B. Williams, 'Persons, Character and Morality', in *Moral Luck: Philosophical Papers 1973–1980*, Cambridge, 1981, p. 18.

sense' idea of impartiality, and argues persuasively that although common sense does involve some appeal to impartiality (often more than is acknowledged by its philosophical opponents), it is nevertheless true that impartiality 'does not play a central role' in commonsense moral thinking. Crucially for his purposes 'it would be possible for anyone to satisfy all the requirements of impartiality, as they are understood in common-sense morality, and still be left with a lot of discretion' (p. 190). This claim is important to his thesis, since he concedes the undesirability, and indeed the sinister implications, of advocating a world in which the scope of impartiality was unduly wide. Justice as impartiality is not, he insists, a complete guide to the art of living. Nor should it be. He then expands on this point by citing the example of our choice of friends. Commonsense morality does not require us to choose our friends because 'they score higher on some list of objective characteristics than other people' (p. 15). We choose our friends simply because 'for some reason or other' we like their company and want to be associated with them. Of course, this is not to say that there can be no moral judgement about one's choice of friends: people may be said to fall into bad company, or be led astray. To that extent, there can be criticism of the use people make of their choice of friends, but the criticism is not one which alleges a defect of impartiality. The choice of friends thus serves as one, very important, example of an area where discretion is permissible and is compatible with justice as impartiality.

More importantly, however, Barry's expression 'for some reason or other' suggests (to me at least) a slightly different point, which is that there are no fully justificatory reasons which can be given in the case of a choice of friends, and that a willingness and ability to provide such reasons implies that the relationship is not, after all, a relationship of genuine friendship. To put the point strongly, impartiality in the choice of friends is not merely not required, it represents a misunderstanding of friendship. And this much is at least implicit in Barry's own expressed reservations about the person who chooses his friends on the basis of social usefulness. To the extent that we are prepared to 'cash out' our friends either in terms of their objectively admirable qualities or their more general 'worth', we indicate that we have a distorted understanding of what friendship is. Again, it does not follow, and it is not true, that *nothing* can be said by way of explaining why someone is my friend, but that explanation need not and must not take the form of a completely justificatory account. Part of Williams's argument, in the example of the man who saves his wife, is to emphasize precisely this point, and it is, I shall suggest, a point which Barry not only concedes, but needs to concede in order to maintain the distinction between first-order and second-order impartiality while at the same time allowing room for individual discretion.

It has already been pointed out that Barry is anxious to limit the scope of justice as impartiality and to insist that it does not provide a complete guide to the art of living. The point of this insistence is to note that, if it did provide a complete guide to the art of living, the burdens of compliance would be intolerably great, and the dangers of corruption omnipresent: in a society in which universal impartiality was the norm, 'a huge number of decisions that are now left to private judgement would have to be turned over to public officials; and all decisions left in private hands would be open to scrutiny and censure on the basis of the hypertrophied positive morality of the society' (p. 205). Here, Barry emphasizes the temptations to disobedience and corruption which would be attendant upon such a state of affairs, but there is a further difficulty, which is that the relevant private relationships and decisions are not ones which lend themselves to such scrutiny. An acknowledgement of this fact is implicit in Barry's comment:

There is a natural inclination to make special efforts on one's own behalf and on behalf of those one cares about. It is the role of rules of justice to set bounds to the working of this inclination, by ruling out actions that injure others and prohibiting such violations of impartiality as nepotism. But it is one thing to channel people's attempts to advance the welfare of themselves and those to whom they are closely attached and altogether another to seek to extirpate any tendency in this direction. The burden of compliance that this would give rise to would be insupportable (p. 205).

The force of Williams's argument, however, is to suggest that it is not merely impractical and politically inexpedient to force this extension of the scope of impartiality: it is also, and crucially, a deformation of concepts such as love and friendship, which are what they are precisely because they are not underpinned by completely justificatory explanations. In the example of the man saving his wife, willingness to pose the justificatory question is, in part, an acceptance of this deformed model.

In discussing these examples Barry implies that the only costs exacted by an impartialist theory will be those which are consequent upon the need to make difficult choices in disastrous situations. It would be a dreadful thing to have to choose between one's wife and the President of the United States, and we must all hope never to be in the position where such a choice is demanded of us. Indeed we must. But the real cost lies in the fact that the example forces us to consider whether justification is necessary or available. It is the cost of asking the question, not the cost of answering it in a particular way, which troubles Williams, and it should also trouble Barry given his own account of friendship and his insistence that justice as impartiality leaves a large area for individual discretion. For the justificatory question, however it is answered in the disastrous case, jeopardizes the area of individual discretion and simultaneously threatens a quite general transformation in our understanding of relationships of friendship and of love.

A further point of importance arises from Barry's discussion of the inconveniences associated with relocating private judgements in the public sphere and thus extending the scope of impartiality. To recall:

> In an attempt to secure strict impartiality in all areas of life a huge number of decisions that are now left to private judgement would have to be handed over to public officials; and all decisions left in private hands would be open to scrutiny and censure ... the opportunities for corruption would be enormous. Nor would the sphere of public morality be immune to its own form of corruption. There is ample record of what happens in societies where censoriousness about private conduct is rampant, and from this it is clear that the system of informal sanctions can very easily be hijacked by people who are pursuing grudges and vendettas of their own. (pp. 205–6)

This insistence on limiting the scope of impartiality has consequences for his discussion of feminism, and his criticisms of an ethic of care. In fact, and as with the criticisms of Williams, his discussion has implications beyond those which he himself acknowledges and serves not only to highlight important conflicts within feminist theory but also to suggest ways in which Barry himself makes implicit appeal to some of the tenets of feminism which he explicitly rejects.

FEMINISM AND THE SCOPE OF IMPARTIALITY

Barry's discussion of feminist anti-impartialism concentrates upon what has come to be known as 'care theory', and his criticisms of one version of it are important and telling. He is surely right to denounce those who, wittingly or not, eschew all considerations of impartiality in favour of contextualization and attention to particular others. Such accounts have precious little to recommend them in any area of life, and in the political world their implications are potentially corrupting. It should, however, be noted that such people are few and far between, and the vast majority of feminist care theorists simply do not subscribe to the extreme Noddings view which Barry concentrates on to the exclusion of all others. To that extent, his criticisms are not, in the end, criticisms of care theory; they are criticisms of Noddings, and of Noddings uniquely.

What is more interesting and, in the end, more important is his sympathetic response to those feminists who accept the importance of second-order impartiality, but argue that it has been worked out in a way which puts women at a disadvantage. He writes:

Rawls has been criticized for treating as unproblematic the justice of the family as that institution is currently constituted in western societies and for building patriarchalist assumptions into his theory of intergenerational relations. I have no quarrel with this line of analysis ... There is no question that the liberal conception of a 'private sphere' where the writ of public values such as justice does not run, is a damaging myth. However, my subject in this section is not impartialist views about women, but rather certain feminist views about impartiality. (p. 246)

However, impartialist views about women and feminist views about impartiality are connected in ways which are unacknowledged, yet which have important implications for Barry's theory.

In the first place, it is not clear that it is open to him simply to declare the liberal conception of a private sphere a 'damaging myth' for, as we have seen, he too wishes to demarcate an area in which impartiality is not central (even though it may not be wholly absent), and the force of his claim that justice as impartiality does not purport to provide a 'complete guide to the art of living' depends, in part, on there being a tenable distinction between the public and the private. Of course, that distinction need not be the one traditionally delimited by liberal theory, much less the one identified by Rawls, but some version of it is implied both by the denial that impartiality provides a complete guide to the art of living, and by the examples which Barry invokes in order to support that contention.

Additionally, by allying himself with those feminists who have complained about the way in which impartialist theories work to women's disadvantage, Barry concedes a considerable hostage to fortune, for part of the force of those complaints is precisely to object to the injustice which is licensed by the privatization of, for example, marital relationships. This, however, generates a difficulty, for how can it be the case both that the myth of a private sphere is damaging and that we should be reluctant to extend impartiality in a way which would leave currently private judgements open to scrutiny and censure? To give a specific example, feminists who object to the myth of the private sphere do so because they are seized of the problems of domestic violence and marital rape, and concerned that traditional liberal theory, including Rawlsian theory, has nothing to say about the injustice of those practices. If they are right to be concerned about this, and if Barry agrees that they are right, then presumably the solution will be to bring those practices within the scope of a theory of justice as impartiality. But if that happens, what is to block the move to the kind of society which Barry fears – one in which very little is left to private judgement and almost everything to public scrutiny and censure?

Of course, the options are less stark than here described, and a decision to reject Rawls's own distinction between public and private need not degenerate into advocacy of a society in which all private judgements are handed over to public scrutiny. Nevertheless, there is at least a tension between Barry's desire to concede that the myth of the private sphere is damaging, and his insistence that the burdens of compliance would be intolerable in a society which licensed extensive transfer of private judgement into public hands. For the latter complaint presupposes precisely what the former questions – namely that there is an acceptable and stable distinction between public and private, or a clear answer to questions about the legitimate extent of state power.

In his article 'Theoretical Foundations of Liberalism'[2] Jeremy Waldron draws attention to the more general form of this point, noting that liberals are characteristically concerned both that society should be 'a transparent order, in the sense that its workings and principles should be well-known and available for public apprehension and scrutiny' and that it is 'important to establish a distinction between the public and private aspects of a person's life – between those activities for which he is accountable to society (those which are open to evaluation and criticism by others) and those that are not'.[3] But there is, as he indicates, a dilemma here, for the private area which liberals identify is, typically, not an area of solitude, but the area of the family. The family, however, is an area in which questions of power regularly arise and therefore to the extent that liberals prefer to keep this area outside the public gaze, they raise doubts about their own commitment to the need for legitimation of *all* structures of power in modern society. Yet at the same time, a refusal to include the family within the area of legitimation and transparency sits ill with liberal commitment to an area of life free from the public gaze. Again, there is no straightforward contradiction in all this, but equally there is no easy solution to what is a deep difficulty in liberal theory. Barry's acknowledgement of the importance of feminist concerns about the working out of second-order impartiality sits ill with his acknowledgement of the intolerable burdens of compliance which would be evident in a society which advocated universal impartiality. And it is not good enough simply to insist that this problem will be solved by regulating the society in accordance with rules of justice (p. 206), since the disagreement is precisely a disagreement about which areas of society should be so regulated – and why. Put bluntly, appeal to the rules will be at best unhelpful and at worst disingenuous in those (many) cases where it is the legitimate scope of justice which is in dispute.

[2] J. Waldron, 'Theoretical Foundations of Liberalism', *The Philosophical Quarterly*, 37 (1987), 127–50.
[3] Ibid., pp. 146–7.

CONCLUSION

Justice as Impartiality is a powerful and timely defence of the importance of impartiality and particularly of the distinction between first- and second-order impartiality. It is a warning against the very real dangers which may lurk in a world which renounces or marginalizes justice: care for particular others can license capriciousness, favouritism and, at the limit, nepotism. But capriciousness and favouritism are the dark sides of qualities which, in some contexts, we cannot and should not aim to eliminate.

There can be too much first-order impartiality and Barry appears to acknowledge this in his account of friendship and his rejection of a society which seeks to extirpate all tendencies to advance the welfare of one's nearest and dearest. But in his acceptance of feminist reservations about the working out of impartiality, he acknowledges that there can also be too little first-order impartiality and that, where there is too little, injustice results. His response is to propose that we aim for 'just enough', but what counts as 'just enough' depends in part on what we take the scope of justice to be. Feminist criticisms of Rawls suggest that the scope must be wider than it is at present, and Barry appears to agree with them. But Williams's arguments suggest that if the scope becomes wider it will deform our understanding of relationships of love and friendship. And Barry needs to agree to at least some version of this in order to sustain his claim that justice as impartiality leaves a large area for individual discretion.

The crucial question therefore is not, or not simply, whether second-order impartiality entails first-order impartiality, but what the scope of justice as impartiality should be, and what pressure it exerts on the area of discretion which is important to liberal theory generally, and to Barry in particular. On the final page of his book Barry writes:

> The concrete demands of the moderate partisans of an ethic of care are for caring to be given greater social recognition and more financial and logistical support. They also call for the burdens of caring to be more equitably distributed. There is nothing in either of these demands that is incompatible with justice as impartiality. On the contrary, I believe (though showing it will have to await a later volume of this Treatise), that the principles of justice that flow from the conception of justice as impartiality will endorse both demands. (p. 256)

My own hunch is that they will also exact a price. A price which is, perhaps, worth paying and which is certainly preferable to fighting with cudgels, but one which is nevertheless high. We must await the third volume of the *Treatise* to find out just how high.

12

Something in the Disputation not Unpleasant*

BRIAN BARRY

My odde opinions are bayted. but I am content wth it, as beleeuing I still have the better, when a new man is sett vpon me; that knows not my paradoxes, but is full of his owne doctrine, there is something in the disputation not vnpleasant.

Thomas Hobbes.[1]

I. THE BASIS OF AGREEMENT

1. Introduction

It is, needless to say, highly gratifying to be the subject of so much shrewd and penetrating critical attention. In the course of reflecting upon these commentaries, I have been led to see where the argument in *Justice in Impartiality*[2] needs to be restated more perspicuously. I have also been forced to amplify it, extend it, and in at least one case reformulate it.[3] In framing my response, I have tried to give it a certain coherence by focusing on some themes that cluster round the contrac-

* About a quarter of the material in the first four sections bears some resemblance to parts of my contribution to the *Utilitas* symposium in which four of the pieces here were first published. (See 'Contractual Justice: A Modest Defence', *Utilitas*, 8 (1996), 350–80.) About half of the material that appears here in section V is drawn from my contribution to a symposium in *Political Studies*: 'A Commitment to Impartiality: Some Comments on the Comments', *Political Studies*, 44 (1996), 328–42. The *Utilitas* symposium originated in an all-day meeting at University College, London, in 1996; the *Political Studies* symposium began life as a round-table discussion at the annual conference of the Political Studies Association at the University of York in 1995. In addition, Russell Hardin's contribution was first presented at a session of the American Political Science Association meeting in San Francisco in 1996, and Richard Arneson was a participant in a round-table discussion at the annual meeting of the Conference for the Study of Political Thought at Yale University in 1995. I should like to express my thanks to the organizers of each of these meetings, to Simon Caney for helpful written comments on Jonathan Wolff's contribution, and to Jerry Cohen, Richard Noble, Richard Arneson and (especially) Paul Kelly for comments on the draft of this reply.
[1] *The Correspondence of Thomas Hobbes*, ed. Noel Malcolm, Oxford, 1994, 2 vols. Letter 39, quoted on p. 308 of the review in *Political Theory*, 25 (1997), 305–17 by Arlene W. Saxenhouse.
[2] B. Barry, *Justice as Impartiality*, Oxford, 1995.
[3] See section IV, subsection 2 (hereafter IV.2).

tual device that I associate with the notion of justice as impartiality. Is it necessary? If it is not necessary is it nevertheless useful? Within an overall contractual framework is the form of contract that I propose uniquely justifiable? And does the form of contract that I defend generate the implications that I claim for it?

I shall devote the remainder of this section to the nature of the contract and its implications for utilitarianism. In the next section, I begin by explaining what I take a theory of justice to be about, and then go on to suggest that some criticisms of the theory of justice as impartiality rest on a misapprehension as to its objectives. Section III addresses the relations between justice as impartiality and two rival versions of contractualism, focusing especially on the argument against justice as mutual advantage. These first three sections relate for the most part to the first four chapters (which make up Part I) of *Justice as Impartiality*. The fourth section takes up a central idea developed in Part II (Chapters 5–7), that a theory of justice should be in a certain sense neutral between conceptions of the good. The fifth section relates to Part III of the book (Chapters 8–10), defending the kind of impartiality that is, I maintain, required by justice.

2. *Why Contractualism?*

As Albert Weale mentions, I said in my reply to critics in *Utilitas* that I did not see myself as a fundamentalist contractarian.[4] What I meant by this is that, as far as I am concerned, the contractual device is helpful but not essential. In early drafts of *Theories of Justice*, the volume that preceded *Justice as Impartiality*, all I had to say about contractualism was the criticism in Part II of the Rawlsian original position.[5] I thought (and still think) that this obscures the real moral foundation of Rawls's principles of justice in *A Theory of Justice*.[6] What changed my mind about the potential of contractualism was the publication in 1982 of T. M. Scanlon's 'Contractualism and Utilitarianism'.[7] In common with a number of other political philosophers of a liberal egalitarian persuasion, I became convinced that I could best say what I wanted to say within the framework of Scanlonian contractarianism.[8] At the minimum, it constituted an attractive way of setting out a conception of justice of a broadly egalitarian nature. At the maximum, it

---

[4] Albert Weale, 'From Contracts to Pluralism', p. 13, citing Barry, 'Contractual Justice', p. 357.

[5] Brian Barry, *Theories of Justice*, vol. 1 of *A Treatise on Social Justice*, Hemel Hempstead, 1989.

[6] John Rawls, *A Theory of Justice*, Cambridge, Mass., 1971.

[7] T. M. Scanlon, 'Contractualism and Utilitarianism', in *Utilitarianism and Beyond*, ed. Amartya Sen and Bernard Williams, Cambridge, 1982, pp. 103–28.

[8] A good example is Charles Beitz, *Political Equality*, Princeton, NJ, 1989.

held out the promise of imparting a degree of deductive rigour to the argument for this conception, by showing how it might arise out of a hypothetical situation in which rules and principles for living together were to be chosen by those to whom they would apply.

One way of approaching Scanlonian contractualism which seems to me illuminating is to think of it as a way of embodying the ideas underlying Rawls's theory of justice more effectively than his own original position succeeded in doing. Thus, let me suggest that Rawls's theory has three main building blocks. The first is a notion of the fundamental equality of human beings. This establishes a presumption in favour of equality in the sense that any departure from equal treatment requires specific justification. The second is the demand that inequalities in the distribution of rights and resources must be capable of being justified to those who stand to get the least of whatever is being distributed. The third is the idea encapsulated in the Rawlsian slogan of the 'separateness of persons'. The operational significance of this is that we cannot justify a policy to those who do badly under it *simply* by saying that others are doing very well under it, and that (in comparison with some alternative) the aggregate gains exceed the aggregate losses.

The premise of fundamental equality says that inequalities of rights and opportunities will have to be justified. Surely then, they must in particular have a justification that is in principle available to those who do least well under them, since the burden of justification must be greater in their case. (There is no trick in justifying an inequality to those who do well from it.)[9] As far as the 'separateness of persons' is concerned, the point is that the choosing situation contains a multiplicity of people with divergent interests, and any proposal has to be minimally acceptable to all of them. (This is what is meant by saying that it cannot be capable of being reasonably rejected by any of them.) The assumption is that nobody can reasonably be expected to accept the sacrifice of his vital interests (including perhaps his life) on no better ground than that his loss is outweighed by an overall gain which might be a tiny amount for each of a large number of people.

The thesis of the 'separateness of persons' is quite often understood in a way that makes it hopelessly implausible. In its most extreme form, it is taken to entail that 'numbers do not count'.[10] But I do not

---

[9] See Scanlon, p. 123: 'Under contractualism, when we consider a principle our attention is naturally directed first to those who do worst under it. This is because if anyone has reasonable grounds for objecting to the principle it is *likely* to be them' (emphasis in original).

[10] A well-known argument to the effect that they should not is John Taurek, 'Should the Numbers Count?', *Philosophy and Public Affairs*, 6 (1977), 293–316. See *Justice as Impartiality*, pp. 225–6.

intend to suggest that it is never a valid justification for some policy that it serves a greater rather than a smaller sum of interests. I understand the 'separateness of persons' as stating a negative: that a greater sum of interests does not automatically amount to a justification. Some additional story of an appropriate kind is always required.

Here is an example of a case in which the numbers count.[11] Suppose that an aircraft's engines have failed and it cannot reach an airport before coming down. If the pilot's only choice is between making for a densely populated area and making for a sparsely populated area, nobody could reasonably reject a standing rule instructing him to choose the latter. It might be said that this is an easy case: the pilot cannot avoid taking a decision that may kill some people, so the choice concerns only the number at risk. Let me make it plain, therefore, that I do not intend the 'separateness of persons' thesis to correspond to some readings of Kant's precept of 'not using people as ends' that give a central place to the distinction between killing and letting die. Suppose, again, that the engines had failed but that this time the plane is a Boeing 747 full of passengers and the pilot has the following choice: he can either land in a sparsely populated area, thereby saving the lives of those aboard at the expense of a small number of people on the ground, or he can head into a mountain, with the consequence that the crew and passengers will die but nobody else will.

Some moralists in the Kantian tradition maintain that in this case the pilot should choose the second course of action, even though more lives will be lost as a result.[12] The rationale for saying this is that, if the pilot adopts the first course, he will be deliberately killing the people on the ground, whereas the cause of the ensuing deaths if he heads for the mountain is the failure of the engines – in conjunction, of course, with the implications of the injunction not to take life intentionally. It can be suggested, to back up this conclusion, that in boarding the aircraft the passengers are to be understood as having accepted that they must die in such a contingency. But this can be no more than a convention. The question remains: is it one that a society should adopt? I believe that it is not and that a rule providing for the pilot to take the death-minimizing choice is the one that people with an appropriate concern for their individual interests would agree on in advance of the contingency's actually arising. Some people are going to

---

[11] Sophia Reibetanz has argued that the Scanlonian construction runs into difficulties in endorsing the commonsense answer in such cases. See her 'Contractualism and Aggregation', presented at the ISUS conference, 'Utilitarianism Reconsidered' (held in New Orleans, March 1997), and forthcoming in *Ethics*. Although I was not aware of the paper when I wrote this paragraph and the following one in the *Utilitas* symposium, what I say here may be taken as my response to it.

[12] See, for example, Alan Donagan, *The Theory of Morality*, Chicago, 1977.

die as a result of the bad luck of the failure of the plane's engines, and it could not reasonably be denied that as few people as possible should die as a result of that bad luck.

Rawls's own original position has no difficulty in incorporating the building block of fundamental equality because everybody in his original position stands on an equal footing. But his original position notoriously runs into problems in trying to accommodate the second and third building blocks. The special concern for the worst off can be worked in only by ascribing to the people in the original position an implausible criterion for choice under uncertainty (maximin). Even worse, Rawls's specification of the original position cannot represent the 'separateness of persons' because all the people in it are interchangeable: they are all pursuing identical objectives on the basis of identical information. We can thus think of the choice of principles as being made by a single representative person who is trying to do the best for whomever he or she turns out to be.

Now compare the Scanlonian construction. This shares with Rawls's original position the virtue that it automatically incorporates the building block of fundamental equality by putting the participants on an equal footing.[13] Where it scores is in its ability to provide a representation of the other two ideas: the requirement that inequalities must be justifiable to those who do worst under them and the demand that the 'separateness of persons' should be respected. In contrast to Rawls's original position, the Scanlonian contractors retain their own identities. They know that they will be differently affected by any given proposal, and they can protect their interests because they can refuse to accept any proposal that could reasonably be rejected as a basis for agreement. That one will do very badly under some proposal is a strong prima facie ground for reasonable rejection of it.

In his commentary, Jonathan Wolff appears to accept the idea that principles should have to be agreed upon by all while finding difficulties with the idea of a veto.[14] Yet it seems to me that the two are simply different ways of saying the same thing, so if there are problems with one there must be the same problems with the other. That is, however, a minor point. The major one is the difficulty that Wolff claims to find in the operationalization of the notion of reasonable rejectability.

I concede that, if this were to be done in the way that Wolff envisages, the theory would be in trouble. But I wish to deny that it should be done in this way. As I understand it, Wolff imagines that the people in a Scanlonian original position might disagree about whether

---

[13] The sense in which the participants in a Scanlonian contract have an 'equal footing' is discussed more extensively below in III.3.

[14] Jonathan Wolff, 'Rational, Fair and Reasonable', pp. 37–8.

or not some proposed principle could reasonably be rejected, and asks what should happen to resolve the dispute. He suggests that there should be some procedure for reaching a collective decision on the question of reasonableness which would have the effect that those who were in the minority would lose.[15] But this proposal is completely foreign to the construction. A vote on the reasonableness of rejecting a proposal is tantamount to a vote on the proposal itself: if the majority can vote to declare the minority's objections unreasonable, that presumably legitimizes the conclusion that the proposal itself cannot reasonably be rejected. Thus, the veto is to all intents and proposes replaced by majority voting.

My answer to the conundrum set by Wolff is that it could never arise. If there were disagreement about whether or not some proposed principle could reasonably be rejected, the construction would have broken down. I therefore stipulate that it cannot happen. That is to say, it is part of the specification of the way in which the choosing situation works that the following propositions are true. First, if one person could reasonably reject a proposal then anybody else affected by it in the same way could also do so. And, second, if a proposal could reasonably be rejected by somebody adversely affected by it, nobody else (however favourably affected by the proposal) can deny that the rejection would be reasonable.[16]

Let me emphasize that these propositions have the status of stipulations about the way in which the theory is to be interpreted. They are not intended as (inherently dodgy) predictions about the course that actual negotiations might take. We are talking here about figments of the imagination – 'agents of construction' in Rawls's terms. The essence of the theory lies in creating a productive tension between the 'separateness of persons' – the distinct interests of the different parties – and their search for agreement on reasonable terms. Their search can be successful only if they have a common standard of reasonableness, so the theory imputes this to them.

A good reason for scepticism about the workability of a choosing situation with a built-in veto for everybody would be its having the implication that 'any sacrifice which it is not in an individual's considered interest to accept would be ruled out.'[17] What is the baseline against which a 'sacrifice' is to be measured? Obviously, if we say that

---

[15] Ibid., p. 38.

[16] For the converse of this proposition, see Scanlon, p. 121: 'If I believe that a certain principle, *P*, could not reasonably be rejected as a basis for informed, unforced general agreement, then I must believe not only that it is something which it would be reasonable for me to accept but something which it would be reasonable for others to accept as well, insofar as we are all seeking a ground for general agreement.'

[17] Paul Kelly, 'Taking Utilitarianism Seriously', p. 57.

it is contrary to your interest to settle for less than you would get under the most favourable alternative proposal that can be conceived, any proposed rule or principle is liable to impose 'sacrifices' on most people, because each of them can compare it unfavourably with some alternative. These alternatives will, of course, be different (and diametrically opposed), so there will be no chance of reaching an agreement. Indeed, we may anticipate that any particular proposal will not merely fail to gain unanimous consent but will not even be able to garner the support of a significant minority.

Albert Weale seems to have in mind something not too unlike this notion of a sacrifice when he canvasses the notion that the contracting parties might be able to veto a 'large concession', understood as one 'taking them a long way from their ideal point.'[18] Thus, he says, if the status quo is close to the ideal point of 'adherents of conceptions of the good that have been given historically privileged status', they 'may have to give up much in order to implement principles of justice'.[19] And, leaving aside any reference to the status quo, Weale adds that 'fundamentalist members of certain religions, to whom it may seem very important that their religion receives special privileges, will be disallowed from claiming any special privileges.' This, as he says, follows from the way in which 'no one is allowed to assert the superiority of their own conception of the good in defining the basic structure of political and social organization.'[20]

If the reasonable rejectability criterion really implied 'that the agreement that is negotiated will only involve modest compromises of their interests by the parties from within their conceptions of the good', it would certainly be in trouble. However, there is nothing in *Justice as Impartiality* to suggest that the status quo can be invoked by the parties in the contractual situation to provide a baseline against which deprivation can be assessed.[21] This is not to deny that established expectations have a part to play in a theory of justice. But they come in when we have already determined independently what justice requires, and then move to the subsidiary question of the way in which the transition from the status quo to a more just order might be made. It is for the theory of justice to say what justice actually calls for, and

---

[18] Weale, p. 24.

[19] Ibid.

[20] Ibid., p. 23.

[21] See Steven Luper-Foy, 'International Justice and the Environment', in David E. Cooper and Joy A. Palmer, *Just Environments: Intergenerational, International and Interspecies Issues*, London, 1996: 'We cannot assume that ways of life are acceptable just because they are established. We need principles of justice to tell us which sorts of consumption patterns and hence which cultures are permissible' (p. 96). For example, a culture dependent on extensive use of private cars is incompatible with justice to people in the future.

I plan to be more forthcoming about that in the next volume of the *Treatise*, to be entitled *Principles of Justice*.

As far as Weale's second and more general point is concerned, I say explicitly in *Justice as Impartiality* that 'it is no part of the case for justice as impartiality that all positions are equally well accommodated by it. Those who start by making the most oppressive demands must naturally expect to have them cut back the furthest' (p. 77). Taking an example of precisely what Weale has in mind – people 'to whom it may seem very important that their religion receives special privileges' – I point out that 'before a Thomist could assent to the claims of impartial justice, he would have to abandon the demand that all other conceptions of the good must give way before the Thomistic one. And this would represent a pretty profound reconstruction of Thomism as MacIntyre presents it' (p. 123). Thus, I do not deny that justice will be far from the ideal points of some people. But, given how far apart the ideal points of different people are, this will inevitably be true of any conception of justice. The only special problem that justice as impartiality faces, in comparison with other theories of justice, is the expectation in some quarters that its claim of neutrality between conceptions of the good commits it to somehow squaring the circle and pleasing everybody equally. But that is simply a misconception of what 'neutrality' means. The concept of fairness incorporated in neutrality is indeed one of equal treatment in a certain sense; but it is not a sense that makes any reference to equal satisfaction with outcomes.[22]

3. Great Expectations

I fear that Albert Weale is looking for something rather more exciting than I have to offer. All I can really do is disclaim any intention of being very exciting and apologise if I inadvertently raised false expectations in *Justice as Impartiality*. What he says he wants is 'an element of surprise, rather as though you were getting a colour signal from a black and white broadcast'.[23] This would certainly be surprising, since it would presumably require a suspension of the laws of physics. And in asking that 'what comes out at the end should not have been deliberately put in at the beginning', he seems to be asking for a suspension of the laws of logic, which give us the boring news that whatever is in the conclusion must already have been contained in the premises.[24]

I imagine that the kind of thing Weale has in mind is Arrow's theorem, which shows that several seemingly innocuous conditions for a social welfare function (a collective ranking of all possible states of

[22] For a discussion of neutrality, see below, IV.5.
[23] Weale, p. 29.
[24] Ibid., p. 29.

the world) cannot all be satisfied. But Arrow's theorem is surprising only because it is extremely hard to grasp intuitively how remarkably strong the conditions actually are.[25] When we are dealing with fundamental questions in moral and political philosophy this sort of legerdemain is liable to be self-defeating. Unless everything is done in plain sight nobody is going to be convinced. It may be possible to construct a philosophical black box that by some inscrutable means cranks out conclusions, but why should we accept them? If we have any inclination to dissent, we are far more likely to suspect some hocus-pocus in the specification of the premises than go along with the conclusions.[26]

The reference that Weale himself makes to 'Rawlsian contraptions' illustrates this point. As he says, once we put Rawls's veil of ignorance in place, 'the irrelevance of social circumstances and personal qualities had an obvious rationale'.[27] It is very obvious indeed, since the theory specifies that the people behind the veil do not know anything about their social circumstances and personal qualities. We can then derive some conclusions about what they would choose, but the reasons for accepting that these choices tell us anything about justice can be no stronger than the reasons that there are for accepting that the Rawlsian original position is the appropriate way in which to frame questions about social justice. Justifying the characteristics ascribed to the original position can be done only by presenting substantive arguments for the proposition that social circumstances and personal qualities ought to be irrelevant to social justice. If that can be done, we can move directly to the implications without the 'contraption' of the original position – and a lot more perspicuously.

Weale complains that the people in my Scanlonian original position 'would have exactly the same conversation that we could have outside the original position in our own societies'.[28] Of course we could. If that were not so, how would we be able to talk about what they could agree upon? The Scanlonian construction is, as far as I am concerned, no more than a device for focusing our thoughts. It depicts, in Habermasian terms, an 'ideal speech situation'. Habermas, however, says that all we can do is strive to make our society one in which an 'ideal speech situation' obtains. If we ever achieved that, we would see what

---

[25] This includes the initial demand that we must be able to produce a single ranking of all possible states of the world – a task that no person or institution ever faces or has any reason for facing.

[26] As Scanlon puts it, 'the standing of any judgement or principle, however theoretical or concrete, rests simply on its power to convince us, in the light of everything else we are inclined to believe, that it represents part of the truth about morality.' T. M. Scanlon, 'The Aims and Authority of Moral Theory', *Oxford Journal of Legal Studies*, 12 (1992), 1–23, p. 14.

[27] Weale, p. 28.

[28] Ibid.

we would see. But in the meantime, speculation about what would happen is to be condemned as 'monological' instead of 'dialogical'. I am prepared to accept that burden, and ask what might be agreed in a hypothetical situation, because it seems to me absurd to suggest that we should have to wait for an 'ideal speech situation' to exist before we can make arguments about what justice requires.[29]

I also want to be a bit bolder than Scanlon himself – but not to the extent anticipated by Weale. In 'Contractualism and Utilitarianism', two conceptions of contractualism are contrasted. One approach would be 'to give a technical definition of the relevant notion of agreement, e.g. by specifying the conditions under which agreement is to be reached, the parties to this agreement and the criteria of reasonableness to be employed.' Alternatively, contractualism might be 'understood as an informal description of the subject matter of morality on the basis of which ordinary forms of moral reasoning can be understood and appraised without proceeding via a technical notion of agreement.'[30] Scanlon clearly inclines to the second way of understanding contractualism. What I have already said earlier in this section indicates that I have some ambitions in the first direction. Ideally, I would like to develop, as constitutive of the choosing situation, a repertory of moves that are to count as valid. But the rationale for stipulating any such moves must be that we can recognize them for ourselves as moves whose validity people concerned to reach agreement on reasonable terms would accept among the ground rules for their deliberations.

Perhaps I can best put my point by saying that I do not see why we have to regard the two approaches outlined by Scanlon as mutually exclusive. Suppose we seek to tighten up the specification of the construction so that it will constrain the kinds of argument that can be made. There is no reason for that to lead us to lose sight of the point that it is not a substitute for thinking for ourselves, but merely a way of thinking for ourselves in a more structured way. We must always keep in mind that there is not really any original position: whatever use we make of the idea, we have to do it in our own persons. We cannot actually turn the job over to surrogates.

4. Contractualism and Utilitarianism

So far, I have claimed for the Scanlonian construction only that it instantiates the three Rawlsian building blocks more satisfactorily than does Rawls's own original position. If I were to leave it there, I

[29] See below (III.4) for a discussion of empirical approximations to this ideal and their role in the theory of justice as impartiality.

[30] Scanlon, pp. 112 and 113. (The distinction is elaborated and refined in 'The Aims and Authority of Moral Theory'.)

would be doing no more than making a move internal to the post-Rawlsian debate within political philosophy. But I wish to claim a far wider significance for the conclusion I have reached. For there are relatively few avowed racists or sexists around in public life in the western liberal democracies, and none that I know of in the ranks of Anglophone political philosophers. That is to say, it is common ground that human beings should not have different rights and privileges as a consequence of their membership of ascriptive groups. When we ask for the justification of principles and rules to govern our relations with one another, we cannot discount the interests and claims of some people simply in virtue of their identities. This is the premise of fundamental equality.

I do not wish to suggest that the premise of fundamental equality entails either of the other Rawlsian building blocks: the relation is not as close as that. The possibility of taking the first and leaving the other two is classically illustrated by utilitarianism. For it conforms to the premise of fundamental equality in virtue of 'Bentham's dictum "everybody to count for one, nobody for more than one"',[31] which, as Mill explained, means that 'equal amounts of happiness are equally desirable, whether felt by the same or by different persons.'[32] But the implication is that an increment of utility is equally important regardless of the amount the recipient has already. This denies the demand that we should pay special attention to the position of the worst off. And by throwing all utilities into one pot and simply asking about the total amount, it violates the maxim that the 'separateness of persons' must be respected.

If we ask why utilitarianism is so generally repudiated, I believe that we shall find that a major reason is precisely its failure to accommodate the second and third Rawlsian building blocks. If I am right about this, the capacity of the Scanlonian framework to incorporate them must surely constitute a strong point in its favour. Thus, I have no difficulty in accepting Arneson's claim that the special concern with the position of those who do worst from an inequality is 'not an implication of the reasonable rejectability test itself, but of a purportedly reasonable supplement to it'.[33] However, I do not merely offer the opinion (as Arneson suggests) that the test should be formulated so that utilitarianism fails it. I offer reasons, which seem to me powerful ones, for adding to the bare specification of the choosing

---

[31] J. S. Mill, *Utilitarianism*, in *Utilitarianism, Liberty, Representative Government*, ed. H. B. Acton, London, 1972, p. 58.

[32] Ibid., footnote.

[33] Richard Arneson, 'The Priority of the Right Over the Good Rides Again', p. 62.

situation some stipulations about the forms of argument that the parties are to accept as valid.[34]

I should perhaps make it clear, however, that saying all inequalities must be capable of being justified to those who fare least well under them does not amount to a 'dictatorship of the worst off'.[35] That is to say, it is not sufficient for somebody to be able reasonably to reject a proposal that he is liable to be worse off as a result than anybody need be with some alternative proposal. One reason is that the contracting parties would, I contend, endorse a principle of personal responsibility from which it follows that those whose voluntary choices turn out badly might under certain circumstances do worse than anybody has to.[36] Hence, the Scanlonian construction does not reproduce the maximin decision rule that Rawls attributes to the people in his original position, and which he needs if he is to show that they would choose the difference principle.[37]

Paul Kelly claims that my argument in favour of contractualism and against utilitarianism 'begs the question in favour of contractualism' by reflecting 'an understanding of utilitarian theory as primarily an answer to questions about the nature of the good rather than about what ought to be done'.[38] I deny this. It is true that I talk about conceptions of the good in *Justice as Impartiality*, especially in the first chapter. But I am careful there to refer to anthropocentric and zoocentric conceptions of the good as those corresponding to forms of utilitarianism that are concerned with human beings and sentient creatures respectively. I do not identify utilitarianism with any such conception of the good. Rather, I treat utilitarianism as a theory of what is right for people to do. (Even in the zoocentric form, utilitarianism is still a theory about what human beings should do: Peter Singer does not address injunctions to even the great apes. Non-human animals can be the objects of morality but not its subjects.)[39]

So far from failing to treat utilitarianism as a rival to justice as impartiality, I specifically discuss utilitarianism in Chapter 9 of *Justice*

---

[34] See I.2 above.

[35] See Stephen Strasnick, 'Social Choice and the Derivation of Rawls's Difference Principle', *The Journal of Philosophy*, 73 (1976), 85–99.

[36] Jonathan Wolff alludes to the point that the worst off may in certain circumstances bear some responsibility for this position as a basis for an exception to his own version of maximin. See Wolff, p. 43. I return to the principle of personal responsibility in the next section (II.3).

[37] See Scanlon, p. 123.

[38] Kelly, p. 45.

[39] See Joel Feinberg, 'The Rights of Animals and Unborn Generations', *Philosophy and Environmental Crisis*, ed. William T. Blackstone, Athens, GA, 1974, pp. 43–68, who says that animals are 'incapable of being moral subjects, or acting rightly or wrongly in the moral sense, of having, discharging or breeching [sic] duties and obligations'.

as *Impartiality* as an alternative kind of impartialist theory. Moreover, I devote much of that chapter to a defence of utilitarianism against the half-baked criticisms still to be found in philosophical discourse. The version of utilitarianism that emerges from this is, I believe, congenial to the recent revaluation of Bentham to which Kelly himself has made a distinguished contribution.[40] The device that is central to my exposition of justice as impartiality, the distinction between first-order and second-order impartiality, was originally worked out within utilitarianism, and I acknowledge my debt to this body of utilitarian literature (p. 219).[41] Far from playing down the parallels between justice as impartiality and utilitarianism, I actually draw attention to them.

Kelly suggests, specifically, that utilitarianism should be regarded as a rival solution to the problem of dealing fairly with the phenomenon of conflicting values in a society.[42] I agree. In fact, I opened Chapter 6 of *Justice as Impartiality* by saying so and drawing out the way in which utilitarianism can be presented as an alternative candidate for a basis on which people might 'agree to disagree' (pp. 139–40). In retrospect, I think my only mistake here was to neglect to mention that utilitarianism could be thought of not as an alternative theory of justice but rather as an alternative proposal to mine about the implications to be drawn from the framework of justice as impartiality. In 'Contractualism and Utilitarianism', Scanlon remarked that utilitarianism could be a theorem of his kind of contractualism, though there were good reasons for thinking it was not.[43] I should have said the same.

Kelly would, on the evidence of his chapter, object that treating utilitarianism as a possible form of contractual justice rigs the issue by bestowing a built-in advantage on principles that pay attention to distribution and thus disadvantaging the purely aggregative utilitarian principle. However, he is happy to take over from me the idea of the 'agreement motive', and he proposes utilitarianism as a principle capable of appealing to it. I think, therefore, that his objection can stem only from the belief that the Scanlonian construction rules out any balancing of interests.[44] I have argued that balancing cannot always be rejected even by those on the losing end.[45] Utilitarianism goes to the opposite extreme in holding that balancing can never

[40] Paul Kelly, *Utilitarianism and Distributive Justice: Jeremy Bentham and the Civil Law*, Oxford, 1990.

[41] See V.2 below for a discussion of two-level moral theory.

[42] Kelly, 'Taking Utilitarianism Seriously', p. 48.

[43] Scanlon, p. 115.

[44] See Kelly, pp. 56–7.

[45] See I.2 above.

reasonably be rejected. The Scanlonian framework may be said to emphasize the burden that the advocate of any rule faces in justifying it to the prospective losers. But that is the burden that utilitarians face too, once we accept that the problem is correctly set up as one of finding principles capable of attracting general agreement.

Now Kelly will, of course, immediately wish to point out that we are to consider standing rules and policies that can feasibly be implemented in the real world of imperfect information and unreliable agents.[46] I am happy to accept this and on the strength of it throw out the usual gimmicky examples involving sheriffs and mobs, organtransplanting press-gangs, and the like. But we are still left with serious suggestions made in a utilitarian spirit which suggest that societies should operate with principles that explicitly violate the 'separateness of persons'. Consider the Kaldor-Hicks criterion for a social improvement. Suppose our society is in condition S1, and the question is whether or not to enact some reform that would result in a shift to S2. (The only constituents of S1 and S2 are individual utilities.) Then, 'S2 is Kaldor-Hicks efficient with respect to S1 if and only if in moving from S1 to S2, those whose welfare [i.e. utility] increases could fully compensate those whose welfare diminishes so that at least one individual has an increase in welfare'.[47]

The point to grasp is that 'Kaldor-Hicks efficiency requires only hypothetical, not actual, compensation'.[48] This ideal of efficiency lies at the foundation of two significant programmes: cost-benefit analysis and the so-called 'economic analysis of law' associated especially with Richard Posner.[49] Cost-benefit analysis asks if the aggregate gains of some proposed development outweigh the aggregate losses, while the cornerstone of the 'economic analysis of law' is the idea that a right should be assigned to the party that can benefit most from its exercise. Thus, a high-speed rail link from London to the Channel Tunnel should be built so long as the gainers could more than compensate the losers, regardless of whether or not the losers are actually compensated; and a factory should be allowed to pollute if it could afford to pay the victims and still gain from doing so, even if there is no suggestion that it should actually be made to do so. Now it may, of course, be that the knowledge that such policies could be put into effect would make

---

[46] Kelly, p. 47.

[47] Stephen R. Munzer, *A Theory of Property*, Cambridge, 1990, p. 200. The criterion is named for Nicholas Kaldor and J. R. Hicks who both proposed the criterion in 1939 (see ibid., p. 200, n. 13 for references).

[48] Ibid.

[49] Richard A. Posner, *The Economics of Justice*, Cambridge, Mass., 1981. Although I discuss cost-benefit analysis in *Justice as Impartiality* (pp. 152–9), the focus is not on its aggregative characteristics but on the way in which it turns beliefs about the right policy into a species of want. (See IV.4 below.)

people so miserable that the criterion could not be endorsed by a sophisticated utilitarian. But I think that anybody could reasonably reject the proposition that the acceptability of such a policy should turn on the results of fine-drawn computations by adepts of the utilitarian calculus.

II. THE LIMITS OF CONTRACTARIAN JUSTICE

1. What Kind of Theory?

To be well-aimed, criticism of *Justice as Impartiality* needs to start from a recognition of its objectives. Otherwise it can easily be criticized for not doing what it does not set out to do. The book is intended as a work of political philosophy, but that is as it stands too vague to be useful as a characterization. In a loose sense, political philosophy may be thought to include any normative analysis of issues in public policy. This is the typical subject-matter of the journal *Philosophy and Public Affairs*. Is abortion like disconnecting yourself from the life-support system of a dying violinist? Should drunk driving that leads to death be treated as manslaughter? Asking questions such as these is a legitimate and valuable form of academic activity. What I must emphasize, however, is that *Justice as Impartiality* is offered as a work of political philosophy in a narrower, more classical sense.

We have all learned not to assume that the history of political philosophy consists of a series of different answers to the same set of questions. Nevertheless, it seems fair to say that the social contract tradition has especially focused on the location, scope and content of legitimate political authority. Eschewing appeals to God or Nature as the underpinnings of political authority, it has had to find a basis in convention, represented within the tradition in the form of consent to a contract. *A Theory of Justice* shows Rawls to be the heir to this tradition. Thus, in Part II of *A Theory of Justice* he locates the source of legitimate political authority in a polity whose decision-making apparatus respects certain kinds of political equality. The question of the scope of legitimate authority is addressed by the first principle of justice, which sets out limits to what can be decided collectively: for example, it demands that some matters (e.g. religious worship) are to be left to individual discretion. Finally, the content of legitimate collective decision-making is specified by the second principle of justice, which constrains legislation and policy in socio-economic matters by setting out the criteria for the justice of the 'basic structure of society'.

It is widely believed that this third element is a departure from the social contract tradition, but it seems to me that we can find all three elements in Locke's corpus. Thus, the *Second Treatise* lays down the way in which polities are to be constituted; the *Essay on Toleration* lays out the claim that the salvation of souls is not within the legitimate scope of government; and the theory of property developed in the *Treatise* is taken to have the implication that, while governments can regulate property and impose taxes on it for public purposes, they cannot seize the property of citizens (or even defeated enemies).

It is worth noting that Locke did not propose that religious toleration (to the extent that his doctrine of the state's limited remit supported it) or property rights should be inscribed in a written constitution to be interpreted by judges whose decisions would take precedence over those of the executive or legislative branches of government. (It is perhaps doubtful if he would have found the idea intelligible.) Nevertheless, saying that some piece of legislation or some public policy is illegitimate – an abuse of state power – is a distinctive move within political discourse. It is qualitatively different from expressing disagreement or disapproval. This needs emphasizing because an aspect of the coarsening of American political discourse due to the dominance of 'rights talk'[50] is a tendency to equate justice with those rights that would in an ideal world be protected constitutionally. (Ronald Dworkin appears to believe something like this, and he is in this respect a representative figure.) Against this, I wish to insist that what should go in a constitution and what should be left to ordinary legislative processes is a practical question, and that how it is answered has no direct bearing on the content or scope of justice.

In *A Theory of Justice*, Rawls proposed that his first principle of justice should form the basis of constitutional protection of civil and political liberties. However, he did not propose that the second principle, which concerned the distribution of socio-economic benefits and burdens, should be turned over to the courts. Rather, he saw it as a touchstone for assessing the working of institutions. In a Rawlsian society, then, arguments about public policy issues would turn on the prospect of alternative policies realizing equal opportunity and making the position of those at the bottom as advantageous as possible (the 'difference principle'). Subsequently, I believe that it is possible to detect the malign influence of 'rights talk' on the thinking of Rawls and his followers. Although he remains officially committed to the difference principle, he now tends to equate justice with 'constitutional essentials', leaving the justice of the 'basic structure of society' to figure as an afterthought at best. Here, as in many other matters, my view is that Rawls got it right the first time in *A Theory of Justice*. In some cases, justice is best secured by constitutional protection,

[50] Mary Ann Glendon, *Rights Talk: The Impoverishment of Political Discourse*, New York, 1991.

whereas in others this is not an appropriate device.[51] But justice is equally important in both kinds of case.

In *Justice as Impartiality*, I define 'rules of justice' as 'the kind of rules that every society needs if it is to avoid conflict – on any scale from mutual frustration up to civil war' (p. 72). This is the Hobbesian strain in the theory that Diemut Bubeck correctly identifies.[52] For what I have defined might more properly be described, in the absence of further qualification, as 'rules of order'. My answer to the natural objection that 'rules of justice' so defined might be substantively unjust is that my definition of rules of justice is intended simply to specify the general subject-matter of the concept of justice. As far as the substantive content of justice is concerned, I depart from Hobbes in denying that order and justice amount to the same thing. Although justice as impartiality has built into it the assumption that civil peace is valuable, it is not a theory of 'peace at any price'. A system of apartheid, for example, would supply 'rules of justice' in that it would in principle settle all disputes by allocating rights and duties un-ambiguously in a way that makes them fit together. But these rules would obviously be unjust, since there is no question that they could reasonably be rejected by the victims of racial discrimination. This provides a reason for fighting apartheid.[53] I also allow, as Hobbes would not, that conflict can be avoided by the general observance of social norms: thus 'rules of justice' do not necessarily have to be backed by the strong arm of the state to be effective.

Since the scope of 'rules of justice' encompasses social norms (rules that define what is right and wrong) as well as laws and public policies, *Justice as Impartiality* is not solely a work of political philosophy. In as far as it is one, it is devoted to the pursuit of political philosophy in what I have called the classical sense. It will be recalled that I attributed to political philosophy within the social contract tradition a tripartite structure. In its political aspect, *Justice as Impartiality* conforms to this tripartite structure. The first element is the way in which collective decisions are to be taken. Although it is not central to the book, Chapter 4 contains a discussion of the way in which alterna-tive decision-making mechanisms are more or less likely to result in just outcomes. The second element is the limits of legitimate collective

---

[51] See *Justice as Impartiality*, pp. 93–9, for a discussion which broadly supports the position taken by Rawls in *A Theory of Justice*.

[52] Diemut Bubeck, 'Care, Justice and the Good', pp. 165–6.

[53] How far the sense of justice can be expected to be causally efficacious is discussed briefly on p. 114 of *Justice as Impartiality*. A point worth emphasizing is that the sense of injustice may not only strengthen the resolve of the victims but also weaken that of those who gain from the injustice. In addition, it may be possible for those who are not directly involved to make a difference at relatively low cost to themselves by throwing their weight on one side. (See III.2 below for an application of this idea.)

decision-making. This question is given much attention in the same chapter and elsewhere.

Thus, I argue in *Justice as Impartiality* that justice demands freedom of religious worship and go on to suggest that, by following the same line of argument, we arrive at the conclusion that homosexual relationships cannot be prohibited by law (esp. pp. 83–4). In both cases, what is at stake is the expression of a core element in the personal identity of many people. Within the theory of justice as impartiality, the argument is articulated by saying (in the words of Albert Weale) that 'given the role that religious and sexual expression play in the way that people give meaning to their lives, parties to a hypothetical contract could reasonably assert that their lives will be blighted if freedom is not allowed.'[54] Some people will, of course, claim that they are in possession of the true faith and that all spurious faiths should be suppressed, or that homosexual acts are unnatural, wicked, or forbidden by God (maybe all three). But such beliefs can, I claim, reasonably be rejected. (The basis for this is the sceptical thesis advanced in *Justice as Impartiality*, esp. pp. 168–73.[55]) Therefore, those whose lives would be blighted by repressive legislation can reasonably reject the proposal that such legislation can legitimately be enacted, and those who support repressive legislation cannot reasonably object to such a veto, because it would be unreasonable of them to deny that their views could reasonably be rejected by others.

As Weale correctly observes, my argument is that 'religious and sexual freedom are to be built into constitutional arrangements.'[56] The context within which the question of religious and sexual freedom is raised in *Justice as Impartiality* is that of the role of constitutions in justice as impartiality, and that explains why I discuss it in those terms. I am now inclined to regret that this may have tended to conceal the larger point, which is about justice rather than about constitutions. The basic argument is that it would be unjust for these freedoms to be abridged, regardless of the constitutional position. In practice, the constitutions of western democracies tend to protect freedom of worship but not freedom of sexual expression. I believe it would be better if both had constitutional protection. But whatever their constitutional status is (or ought ideally to be), my main claim is that it would be equally unjust for states to limit either. The primary question we have to ask is what is required by justice. After that we can ask essentially pragmatic questions about the most appropriate ways of securing justice, and the answer may in some cases differ from

---

[54] Weale, p. 21.
[55] The sceptical thesis is defended below in IV.1.
[56] Weale, p. 21.

one country to another, depending on its ethos and the details of its political structure.

As far as the third leg of the tripartite structure is concerned, I have a good deal to say in *Justice as Impartiality* about the way in which justice constrains the system of collective decision-making. Thus, in Chapter 4 I discuss a variety of forms of discriminatory treatment that are proscribed by justice (pp. 98–9). Again, the context is what courts can do to secure justice. But the whole discussion is premised on the presupposition that we can identify some policies as unjust (because discriminatory) and that the question of the best way of preventing such injustice is subordinate. Chapter 5 is largely devoted to the proposition that collective decision-making systems should not, if they are to be just, have built into them the attempt to promote any particular conception of the good. As Weale puts it in his admirable exposition of the theory, 'the impartial rules that are supposed to emerge from the Scanlonian contract are ... intended to provide a way in which citizens with competing conceptions of the good can nevertheless live together in society.'[57] I should, however, make it clear that the 'impartial rules' referred to here are the rules that set out the way in which laws and policies are to be brought into being. I do not suggest that laws and policies should themselves be neutral between different conceptions of the good. In fact, I deny that this makes sense as an ideal (esp. pp. 160–1).[58]

Weale correctly identifies a 'shift of focus' between *Theories of Justice* and *Justice as Impartiality* in that the latter is 'more focused on issues to do with civil and political liberties', and less with socio-economic issues than the former. This, however, is simply a reflection (as Weale recognizes) of the priority of the question of how it is possible for people with conflicting conceptions of the good to live together. *Principles of Justice* will redress the balance by focusing primarily on socioeconomic issues.

2. Two Examples: Paternalism and Abortion

If I have laboured the point that *Justice as Impartiality* is not intended as a contribution to the literature of 'philosophy and public affairs', my reason will now become apparent. For I wish to suggest that much of Richard Arneson's criticism of the book is premised on inappropriate expectations. As a utilitarian (of sorts) he approaches it with a certain model in mind that conditions his idea of what a theory should look like. According to this, a theory should in principle furnish a determinate answer to any question of public policy by the operation of

---

[57] Weale, p. 20.
[58] For further discussion, see IV.4 below.

some sort of calculus. Utilitarianism fits this model but justice as impartiality is very far from fitting it.

In practice (as against principle), utilitarianism is an empty vessel, and the prescriptions that come out at one end are a function of the assumptions that are fed in at the other. Utilitarians can be egalitarian or anti-redistributive, democrats or autocrats, libertarians or authoritarians, depending on their views on psychology, economics, politics and society. Where we find a band of relatively single-minded utilitarians, such as the Philosophical Radicals, the explanation is not their shared utilitarianism but their common auxiliary assumptions. In contrast, justice as impartiality does not even purport to offer answers to most issues of the day. Its normal answer will be that, while there would be unjust (e.g. discriminatory) ways of doing something, the theory cannot say whether it should be done or not. All it can prescribe óver and above that is that the procedures by which the decision is taken should meet certain conditions of fairness and rationality. However, where justice does come into play, the theory is more determinate than utilitarianism is in practice, because it is less at the mercy of speculation about the way things will turn out. Thus, many policies that could be endorsed on utilitarian grounds if the numbers came out right would be condemned out of hand by justice as impartiality as treating differently people who have a claim to be treated in the same way.

Let me illustrate the greater determinacy of justice as impartiality by returning to the case of freedom of religious worship. In contrast to the argument from principle in *Justice as Impartiality*, all that Arneson can come up with from a utilitarian standpoint is the conclusion that 'all things considered the gains from persecution look to be far outweighed by the gains from across the board toleration.'[59] The premises on which this conclusion rests are the potential for strife inherent in the imposition of an orthodoxy, the 'general case for freedom of expression' (not further specified) and the alleged fact that 'the practical advice given by religious faiths tends to be uncontroversially social useful'.[60] How far these premises hold in any given case is always going to be a contingent matter, and I see no reason for supposing that they hold very widely. Religious orthodoxy can be imposed without creating 'strife' so long as the victims are a small enough minority, as Iran illustrates today. And if religions are to be tolerated only in as far as their 'practical advice' is uncontroversially socially useful, that would rule out most, including the mainstream forms of Hinduism, Islam and Christianity. Between them, they have offered mankind a

---

[59] Arneson, p. 73.
[60] Ibid., p. 72.

toxic brew of fundamental inequality on the basis of birth, pervasive gender inequality, raging homophobia, autocracy, denial of freedom of thought and inappropriate attitudes to our fellow creatures and the natural world.

Arneson says that I hear only 'faint guidance' from the Scanlonian construction.[61] But this makes sense only against a background assumption that the strength of guidance is to be measured quantitatively, by the number of problems 'solved' by a theory. What I would rather say is that the theory of justice as impartiality gives unequivocal answers where things are unequivocally mandated or prohibited by justice; that where this is arguable, it sets out the terms of the argument; and that where justice definitely leaves an issue open it definitely says so. What Arneson does not appreciate is that, on my interpretation of justice, an argument that invokes justice is different in kind from an argument on the merits. If an argument from justice is accepted, it is a conversation stopper: there is nothing more to be said, whatever the merits may be. Of course, an argument from justice may not be accepted, and even if accepted it may not be acted on. But that does not affect its distinctive role in normative discourse. Let me illustrate this by showing why Arneson's thirst for definite answers leads him astray in two cases, those of paternalism and abortion.

The important thing to notice about paternalistic legislation is how pervasive it is in all contemporary western societies. There is a tendency to focus on legislation requiring people to wear crash helmets or seat belts. But we should recognize that, in addition to such laws, virtually all product safety and consumer protection legislation is paternalistic. As my ex-colleagues at Chicago, George Stigler, Gary Becker and Richard Posner were fond of pointing out, people who would prefer to buy products that require special care to operate safely are prevented from doing so by rules designed to protect those who are not prepared to take such precautions. The argument for such rules is twofold. First, many people either cannot or do not want to have to read and interpret the small print to find out if a product is safe before buying it. And second, even those who are prepared to do so may well prefer not to be tempted to buy power tools that are safe only when the user is standing on a thick rubber mat or lawn-mowers that are liable to take off toes unless operated while wearing steel-capped boots. For they realize that some day, due to haste, stress or inattention, they may well fail to take the necessary precautions.

Now if we were to take the line that paternalism is ruled out by justice, we would be saying that no proposal of a paternalistic nature could be argued about on its merits. But this seems to me simply

[61] Ibid., pp. 63–4.

absurd, and I make no apology for dismissing it with a speed that Arneson claims to find 'breathtaking'.[62] Arneson does not attempt to deny my claim that 'it is not plausible for people to say that their lives are going to be blighted – in relation to their own conception of the good – if they cannot travel in a car without wearing a seat belt or ride a motorcycle without protective headgear' (p. 87). A fortiori nobody can make such a claim in relation to the extra cost of double-insulated electrical appliances, machinery with safety guards and so on.

To be put in the scales against the paternalistic limits on free choice is the saving of life and prevention of serious injury that paternalistic legislation without any question brings about. Anybody who wishes to follow Arneson in telling about lives being 'slightly worsened' by the violation of autonomy should pay a visit to the neurological ward of a hospital in a jurisdiction with no crash helmet laws and ask how wearing a helmet compares with life as a paraplegic. (Even with compulsory wearing of crash helmets, motor cycles are so dangerous that there is a good case for prohibiting them altogether.)

As I emphasized in *Justice as Impartiality*, 'there is nothing to prevent those who place a very high value on individual liberty from making their argument based on that and trying to prevent legislation contrary to Mill's harm principle from being enacted' (p. 87). But how high a value can be set on autonomy short of coming up with proposals that can reasonably be rejected? In *Justice as Impartiality*, I argued for what I called the positive harm principle. This says that a just society must have laws preventing the infliction of harm on people against their will. 'Harm' for this purpose is construed quite narrowly so that the pursuit of virtually any conception of the good would be set back by suffering harm without one's consent (pp. 87–8). It would, I suggest, be reasonable for anyone to insist on protection from harm in drawing up a set of rules and principles for a society. But this is already to set a limit to autonomy. For, as Bentham correctly insisted, all laws limit liberty. A fanatical enthusiast for the value of autonomy should be against having any laws at all, and some are. Of course, that is liable to threaten many welfare interests that people have, but if autonomy trumps everything that is an inconvenience to be borne stoically.

If we accept that harm must be prevented, this still leaves it open to those who place a very high priority on autonomy to insist that autonomy should not be infringed any further. Thus, if the positive harm principle covers only physical harm, this will leave all kinds of nuisance and offence to be regulated according to the outcome of ordinary political processes, and justice will not mandate either pre-

---

[62] Ibid., p. 64.

venting them or permitting them. The libertarians are entitled to press for restrictive legislation not to extend beyond that required by the positive harm principle. Similarly, they are free to campaign against any regulation whose justification is to prevent people from harming themselves. But what they cannot do, I wish to argue, is pre-empt the public debate by insisting that any outcome other than the one they favour is unjust.

Of course, some people may well believe in some theory of justice (e.g. one involving a notion of self-ownership) from which the injustice of paternalistic intervention follows directly. But I stipulate that people cannot bring rival theories of justice into the choosing situation and ask for them to be considered. So, they can argue from an idea about the enormous importance of autonomy for human flourishing, but they cannot assert a right to (some interpretation of) autonomy. This may perhaps seem rather high-handed, but I must insist that this is after all *my* theory, and I am therefore entitled to say what goes on in it. I wish to be accommodating, but I have no intention of being a patsy.

There is a methodological point at issue here which is worth making clear. Rights will be endorsed by justice as impartiality. But they have to come out of the theory: they cannot simply be brought in by the people in the Scanlonian original position. Perhaps some complaints of triviality stem from the notion that the participants in the choosing situation might simply agree that some metaphysical theory of justice (e.g. some sort of natural rights theory) was so plausible that nobody could reasonably reject it. That certainly would make the theory of justice as impartiality utterly trivial, so I stipulate that rival theories of justice can reasonably be rejected. This, of course, presupposes that alternative theories of justice are wrong. That is to be established not within the theory but as an independent exercise outside it. (Justice as mutual advantage and justice as reciprocity are two rival theories of justice that will be discussed in the next section.) This kind of move is to be distinguished from a possible move within the theory of justice as impartiality. This consists of asking if people concerned for their own interests but desirous of reaching an agreement on reasonable terms with others might accept some general formula for adjudicating their conflicting demands. I have already considered and dismissed the possibility that utilitarianism might be a theorem of justice as impartiality. I shall argue below that justice as mutual advantage also cannot be such a theorem, and nor can an historical entitlement theory of justice *à la* Nozick.[63]

[63] See for utilitarianism I.4 and for justice as mutual advantage/Nozickean entitlement III.3.

I now want to move on to the second example that I promised to take up, that of abortion. What makes this an especially difficult question is that there is an argument of the right kind for holding that justice demands its prohibition and another argument, also of the right kind, for holding that justice requires it to be permitted. The first argument goes as follows. The positive harm principle demands that any just society must prohibit the shedding of innocent human blood. Since a foetus is presumably innocent and undeniably human, its protection is prima facie a high priority of any set of just laws. The argument on the other side is that, especially in contemporary western societies, an unwanted pregnancy may change a woman's life in a way that runs completely counter to her conception of the good for her. Prima facie this means that a woman could reasonably reject any legislation restricting the right to an abortion, the implication being that any such legislation would be unjust. In the face of these two arguments, my suggestion in *Justice as Impartiality* was that justice had better abandon the field. The issue cannot legitimately be pre-empted in either direction. The opposing parties must lay out their cases as persuasively as they can, and a decision will have to be taken in the ordinary way with the decision-makers voting in accordance with their conclusions about which side has made the best case. I made it plain in passing which side I supported (p. 90, n. c), but I must repeat that that is of no significance for the argument about justice.

Arneson's contribution to this question is so spectacularly inapposite that I am not surprised that he claims to be 'left puzzled'.[64] For it shows that he has failed to grasp the key idea that there are two different kinds of discourse. (It may be relevant that utilitarianism has no room for any such distinction.) Thus, he says: 'One has to look at the arguments.'[65] But looking at the arguments is what is appropriate only once it has been settled that the issue cannot be pre-empted by an appeal to justice. The argument that Arneson advances at this point, that 'it is incorrect to regard the foetus as a person endowed with the rights of persons', is exactly the sort of thing that will be put forward by those in favour of legalizing abortion in public debate on the merits.[66] But it is an argument that everybody who believes abortion should be prohibited must already have thought about, and I do not think they can be said to be unreasonable in failing to find it convincing. This simply reinforces my point that the 'right to choose' cannot be identified with the cause of justice. By parity of reasoning, though, it must be added that the denial of that right cannot be iden-

---

[64] Arneson, p. 69.
[65] Ibid., p. 68.
[66] Ibid., p. 68.

tified with the cause of justice either, because it is not unreasonable to think that the argument put forward by Arneson is a good one.

Arneson complains that I spend less time on what he calls 'the moral issue' (i.e. the first-order question of the morality of abortion) than on what he calls 'the pragmatic political issue, whether trying to settle the abortion issue in the courts, as a matter of constitutional essentials, is more likely to provoke widespread popular resistance to abortion rights than a strategic decision to leave the issue to the legislative sphere.'[67] He is obviously assuming that all we have to do is decide what we think about the 'moral issue' and then equate the answer with justice. (Or perhaps we are to take the second step only if we feel especially inclined to thump the table.) For me, however, the sequence runs in the other direction. The prior question is what the status of 'the moral question' is: does justice settle it one way or the other, or does justice leave it open?

I have already said that we cannot simply identify justice with constitutionality.[68] There are some matters (e.g. the voting system) that are suitable material for a constitution but that (within broad limits) can take a wide variety of forms compatible with justice. Conversely, I have already said that not every question on which justice gives an answer is appropriately removed from ordinary political decision-making processes. Whether or not it is a good idea to entrench some provision in a constitution is, indeed, in Arneson's words, a 'pragmatic' question. But that does not mean that the question about justice is a pragmatic one. Nevertheless, what can be said is that *if* some issue (e.g. abortion) is settled one way or the other within a constitution, that represents a sort of authoritative determination of its status as an issue that falls within the remit of justice. We can thus hope to learn about the effects of treating an issue as one covered by justice by looking at what happens in such a case.

My appeal to evidence about the divisive effect of constitutionalizing what Arneson calls 'abortion rights' in the USA was intended to support one negative point, and I believe that it was relevant in that context. Let me explain how the point arose. In *Justice as Impartiality*, I attacked a principle, the 'preclusion principle', that is quite commonly used to derive the conclusion that justice mandates the preemption of the abortion issue on the 'abortion rights' side. Roughly, the preclusion principle says that, where the morality of some kind of action is controversial, justice requires the decision to be left to the individual's discretion. This is a genuine candidate for a principle of justice in that it rests on the argument that we need not get to the

---

[67] Ibid., p. 69.
[68] See II.1 above.

merits of the case to settle the question of what the law should be. But I argued in *Justice as Impartiality* that it is a flawed principle (pp. 88–93).

One of the arguments made in favour of the preclusion principle is that leaving people to do what they like is somehow less controversial than stopping some people doing what they want to. I pointed out that there is no reason for supposing this to be true, and cited American experience with abortion as a case in point (pp. 92–3). In the United States, opponents of abortion who had acquiesced in legislative moves to liberalize abortion laws were mobilized by the Supreme Court decision that made abortion a constitutionally guaranteed right. There is no reason for thinking that the (first-order) issue does not divide people in western Europe too; but legislation has proved more acceptable.[69] This strongly suggests that, to the extent that the 'preclusion principle' appeals to an argument about conflict, it rests on bad sociology.

3. No Magic Bullet

Simon Caney, Albert Weale and Matt Matravers all express additional doubts about the possibility of contractarian justice. I should like to say something in response to each of them. Let me begin with Simon Caney's suggestion that, even if justice as impartiality cannot generate conclusions about the substantive content of justice, this does not matter too much because the 'terms of agreement' might be accepted as fair simply in virtue of their being the product of a procedure which reasonable people could endorse.[70] Up to a point this is so. But fairly soon people who perceive the outcomes of a decision-making procedure as unjust will reject the legitimacy of the procedure – and will be right to do so. As I pointed out in Chapter 4 of *Justice as Impartiality*, democratic forms of decision-making (which may be said to be fair a priori) are quite compatible with systematic discrimination against some group distinguished by ethnicity, religion, language and so on. As the case of Northern Ireland illustrates, it is no use the majority pointing to its ability to win referenda and elections. This will never convince a minority whose daily experience is one of discrimination that the system is fair. Almost all the democratic constitutions left behind

---

[69] For example, in Britain attempts by American-based organizations to foment direct action against places in which abortions are carried out have conspicuously failed to take off. Also, in the general election of 1997, a political party specifically dedicated to repealing the 1967 Abortion Act achieved substantially less than one per cent of the vote in the constituencies in which it had candidates, and ran behind the Official Monster Raving Loony Party in every constituency in which both stood. This does not show that the abortion issue does not matter, but it shows that it does not have the political salience that it has in the USA.

[70] Simon Caney, 'Impartiality and Liberal Neutrality', p. 102, n. 21.

by departing colonial powers have in fact collapsed because they were exploited by majorities to oppress minorities. It is, I suggest, hopelessly naive to imagine that a consensual society can be created out of an agreement on nothing but a decision-making procedure. What is essential is that the demands of substantive justice are not breached in a systematic way that creates cumulative unjust disadvantage for some communal group.

All this implies, of course, that the demands of substantive justice are not so esoteric as to be beyond the scope of reasonable agreement. I believe that so long as we start from the premise of fundamental equality, the range of reasonable disagreement is far smaller than might be supposed from casual remarks by Caney. The European Court of Justice has shown that some rather simple ideas about equal treatment can go a surprisingly long way to limit the scope of government to behave unjustly. This is, for the most part, a matter of the way in which a policy is to be pursued. For example, it does not say that there must be free prescriptions for people over some age but what it says is that, if there are to be, the age must be the same for men and women. Similarly, the American Supreme Court could not require a local authority in the South to keep its swimming pool open, but it could say that the only alternative to closing it was to open it to blacks and whites alike. These achievements for an interstitial conception of justice are not to be underestimated.

What about policies themselves, as against their mode of execution? I have been at pains to emphasize that justice as impartiality will very seldom pick out a unique policy as the only one compatible with the demands of justice. Most often it will be able only to set bounds to the range of policy outcomes that are consistent with justice. But that does not mean the theory is toothless. The world is full of laws and policies that could reasonably be rejected. Most countries contain inequalities between men and women and between more or less favoured communal groups – in civil rights, political rights, educational and employment opportunities, treatment by the police and public authorities, and so on – that cannot possibly be justified. They exist because those who benefit from them have the power to maintain them, but it is quite clear that they cannot stand the test of reasonable rejectability.

To repeat: where it is clear what justice demands or prohibits, the theory of justice as impartiality gives clear answers; and where it is arguable what justice demands or prohibits, the theory sets out the terms of argument. Albert Weale regards it as a defect of the theory that it does not deliver determinate pronouncement on all questions of justice, citing in particular the problems raised by the principle of personal responsibility that I have already mooted. 'Even if we say that those who suffer misfortune have a claim in justice to some compensation', he writes, 'the precise import of this claim is not easy to determine.'[71] I agree. But if something is not easy to determine then it is not easy to determine, and any theory that makes it look easy must be some sort of fraud.

I anticipated Weale's objection in the course of my reply in *Utilitas* to Caney's doubts about the usefulness of the theory in delivering hard and fast results, volunteering the thought that there would most often be room for legitimate argument about the precise implications of a principle of justice. As it happens, I took as my illustration precisely the case picked by Weale (or more precisely its obverse), the principle of personal responsibility, according to which people cannot legitimately complain about the outcome of their voluntary choices. I went on to observe that this principle opened the way to reasonable disagreement about the criteria of voluntariness. 'Depending on the range of actions one holds people responsible for, the principle will underwrite a greater or lesser amount of inequality in outcomes. Thus, a realistic hope about the role of principles of justice is that they will give a shape to public debate. It is unreasonable to imagine that they can be cranked by the theorist to produce conclusions by a process of strict deduction. The theorist can, of course, offer his own contribution to that public debate, and in the next volume of the *Treatise* I plan to do that. But only someone suffering from advanced megalomania would suppose that once he had spoken everybody would agree that there was nothing more to be said.'[72] All I should like to add here about the principle of personal responsibility is that its interpretation will inevitably turn on one's answer to the so-called 'problem of free will'. Since this has been controverted for a couple of thousand years with no sign of a resolution in sight, it is scarcely surprising if the principle creates a framework for argument rather than settling all the issues itself. I shall be content if it is accepted that it does succeed in that.

More generally, I am not unhappy with Weale's title 'From Contracts to Pluralism'. I dissent only from the suggestion that, to the extent we finish up with pluralism, we must have left contract behind. Why should we assume that any contractual theory must give rise to monistic conclusions, or at least to a Rawlsian lexicographic ordering of principles? I accept that, as Russell Hardin says, conflict between principles is 'a difficult problem for multi-principle theories'. But I also endorse his subsequent remark that 'any theory that does not have such problems is probably derelict and worthy of no attention.'[73]

---

[71] Weale, p. 27. See I.4 for the principle of personal responsibility.
[72] 'Contractual Justice', p. 378.
[73] Russell Hardin, 'Reasonable Agreement: Political not Normative', p. 151.

4. Why are Wrong Acts Unjust?

Finally, I come to Matt Matravers's questions about the relation between justice, wrongness and harm.[74] I accept most of what he has to
say and I find his conjectures about what I would say on matters I have
not addressed in public unfailingly accurate. Indeed, I am reminded in
reading his comments of Henry James's reaction to Max Beerbohm's
parody 'The Mote in the Middle Distance'.[75] When 'an admirer asked
[him] his opinion on some question', he pointed to Max and said 'Ask
that young man, he is in full possession of my innermost thoughts.'[76]
Where I part company from Matravers is at the 'So what?' stage. I
simply cannot share his generous anxieties about the impact of what
he says on the coherence of the theory of justice as impartiality.

As a number of the contributors have pointed out, Scanlon claimed
in 'Contractualism and Utilitarianism' to be offering a contractarian
definition of what it was for an act to be wrong. Thus, for example, 'the
property of being an act of killing for the pleasure of doing so' is a
'wrong-making property', and this is to be cashed out by saying that 'it
would be reasonable to reject any set of principles which permitted
[it]'.[77] So long as the contracting parties have a healthy dislike of the
prospect of dying a violent death (a dislike that strongly outweighs the
desire to be free to kill other people at will), they cannot reasonably
reject a rule outlawing murder. There is no need to say that they are
simply implementing pre-contractual convictions about the wrongness
of murder. This is the reply to the objection cited by Simon Caney that
the Scanlonian analysis 'gets things back to front' by saying that 'torturing babies is immoral *because* reasonable persons would reject it.'[78]
As Caney himself points out, the 'equivalence thesis' does not say this.
Rather, it offers a proposal for what it means to say that something is
wrong.

A person with Scanlonian motivation will not wish to perform acts
that cannot be justified to himself or others, and hence will not do acts
that are wrong, as wrongness is defined by Scanlon. Hence he will not
(among other things) murder. But why should he, as Matravers
suggests, have to think that the wrongness of murder lies in its being
unfair to the other members of his society? The hypothetical contract
has established that it is wrong to murder. But there is no actual

---

[74] Matt Matravers, 'What's "Wrong" in Contractualism?'.

[75] Max Beerbohm, 'The Mote in the Middle Distance', in *A Christmas Garland*, London, 1950 ed., pp. 1–9.

[76] David Cecil, *Max*, London, 1983, p. 317.

[77] Scanlon, p. 118.

[78] Caney, p. 95. This is, obviously, a retail version of the notion discussed earlier (II.2)
that the people in a Scanlonian original position might import wholesale an entire
alternative theory of justice and agree that nobody could reasonably reject it.

contract to which he is a party, so it makes no sense to say that his motive is really a Rawlsian 'duty of fair play'. All our agent needs to hang on to outside the contractual situation is the idea that murder is wrong.

As I pointed out near the beginning of this section, the conception of justice with which I am working is a broad one which includes everything that Scanlon would include in the sphere of wrongness and a lot more besides, including laws and major political institutions. Many of the things covered by justice in my wide sense might more naturally be described as questions of right and wrong. But if one theory can encompass a certain range of phenomena, there is much to be said for having a single word to refer to that range, and the word I am using is 'justice'. The implication is that wrongness is a subset of injustice. Some acts are primarily wrong and hence unjust. Other acts are primarily unfair and hence unjust. (These are also secondarily wrong in that it is wrong to behave unfairly.) Not paying your fair share or in some other way contributing your fair share towards the provision of some collectively beneficial good is the paradigm of an act that is unfair and hence unjust. It is surely pretty clear why such behaviour will be condemned by justice as impartiality. For it means that somebody who (*ex hypothesi*) has no valid special claim to be let off contributing his fair share is stealing an advantage at the expense of others. This is clearly an inequality to which the losers can reasonably object, and the gainer has no reasonable basis on which to rebut their objection. There may, of course, be disagreements about whether or not an act of a certain type is wrong or unfair. The theory of justice as impartiality can accommodate the phenomenon of disagreement. It construes a disagreement as a dispute about whether prohibition of an act of that kind could or could not reasonably be rejected in an appropriately constructed choosing situation.[79]

What I fail to see is why Matravers thinks I should be worried about the existence of more than one source of injustice. Life is complicated: why should we expect that there will be a single way in which all unjust things are unjust? As far as the integrity of the theory of justice as impartiality is concerned, it seems to me that all I have to be concerned about is that we can fit each variety of injustice into the overall framework. I believe that I have succeeded in doing this for the two kinds of injustice analyzed here. If there are others that cannot be fitted in, that will be a limitation of the theory. But I await a convincing argument to that effect.

---

[79] See Scanlon, 'The Aims and Authority of Moral Theory', p. 17, n. 22, for the claim that his account of what it is for something to be morally wrong is consistent with 'a certain amount of persistent disagreement' about what actually is wrong.

III. JUSTICE AND BARGAINING

1. Three Versions of Contractualism

I have said something about the kind of theory justice as impartiality is. I now want to explain why I believe it to be superior to two alternative contractual conceptions. As Jonathan Wolff correctly observes, the opening chapters of *Justice as Impartiality* set up a sort of beauty contest between three rivals for the name of justice: justice as mutual advantage, justice as reciprocity and justice as impartiality. Wolff has several criticisms of the way in which this contest is conducted. One is that I introduce a redundant criterion for success: the requirement that a theory of justice must include in it a congruent story about the motivation for behaving justly. I believe that this requirement can be defended. However, to keep this commentary within tolerable bounds, let me confine myself to saying that I think Wolff underestimates the force of my argument to the effect that the motivation problem makes justice as mutual advantage an incoherent theory.

Wolff says that 'it is far from obvious that the answer "these institutions are to everyone's advantage" will never do as a justification [of social and political institutions]'. Let me accept for the sake of argument that this can function as a justification for a set of institutions. The critical problem that then arises is not the one identified by Wolff. He writes: 'Even if, on this basis, someone, sometimes, finds that the institutions lack justification (i.e. they do not further their long-term interest, all things considered), this is only threatening if the failure is widespread and accumulating.'[80] But this is not the point at issue, which is not the justification of institutions but rather the justification of individual conduct conforming to the demands made by institutions.

Suppose every single person agrees that some set of institutions furthers their long-run interest, all things considered. I take this to mean that they all acknowledge that they would gain (compared to some implicit non-cooperative baseline) if they all did what these institutions require them to do. The trouble is that each of them can quite consistently go on to say: 'But that doesn't entail that it is always in my interest to do what the institutions require me to do.' In fact, a self-interested person will comply with the terms of the agreement to co-operate only when the probability of being found out and penalized is high enough to make cheating a bad bet. The claim that I now add is that no system of penalties can be set up among people motivated purely by self-interest that can ensure a degree of compliance sufficient to prevent the scheme of co-operation from collapsing. (Bear in mind that the police and the judges will always take bribes if it is in

---

[80] Wolff, p. 41.

their interests to do so.) If this claim is correct, justice as mutual advantage is incoherent in the following sense. The only reason anybody has ever been offered for embracing it is that self-interest is the only motive to be relied on. But if justice as mutual advantage has to rely on self-interest all the way down (not only before the contract is struck but afterwards as well) then the contract is in vain, because the motive that led people to assent to it is also a motive that leads them to renege on it.

Suppose that we add some different sort of motivation at the post-contract stage, so that people have a disposition to keep contracts in virtue of a sense of moral obligation to do so. This solves the problem but creates a new one. For nobody but a moral imbecile would imagine that contracts are worthy of moral respect regardless of their content or the fairness of the circumstances that gave rise to them. In Rawls's famous words, 'to each according to his threat advantage' is not a basis for just agreements. People who recognize this will therefore demand the renegotiation of the contract drawn up under conditions of justice as mutual advantage, so the theory will now unravel from the other end.

As far as justice as reciprocity is concerned, I accept that the criterion of justice embodied in justice as reciprocity is not no-holds-barred mutual advantage, and that justice as reciprocity is genuinely a part of justice (p. 50). But Wolff himself points out that it 'shares with justice as mutual advantage the (quite unattractive) feature that those with nothing to contribute, such as the handicapped, are excluded from the concerns of justice.'[81] This unattractive feature is, however, unavoidable if Wolff is right in claiming that 'considerations of justice only emerge under conditions of co-operation'.[82] This is an idea that unites John Rawls with David Gauthier, who quotes with approval 'Rawls's ever-useful phrase that a society is "a co-operative venture for mutual advantage"'.[83] Both are wrong.

Gauthier illustrates the implications of this as follows. Suppose two societies do not have any co-operative relations and the people in one society live upstream of those of the other along the banks of a river. If those who live upstream dump pollutants in the river, simply because it suits them to do so, there is nothing unjust about this even if it has

[81] Wolff, p. 39.

[82] Ibid., p. 41.

[83] David Gauthier, 'Mutual Advantage and Impartiality', p. 121. It is the dependence of justice on relations of mutual advantage that explains Rawls's inability to incorporate the congenitally disabled within his theory of justice, though congenital disability might plausibly be regarded as the paradigm of a 'morally arbitrary' disadvantage – far clearer than the lack of intelligence or drive that Rawls treats as the product of a genetic or social lottery. See *Theories of Justice*, pp. 244–5, for a more extended discussion of this point.

severe effects on the prosperity or the health of those living down-stream.[84] Of course, if the people upstream were ignorant of the exist-ence of the people downstream, or ignorant of the deleterious effects on them of their waste disposal practices, the worst they might be accused of was reckless disregard for the possible impact of their actions. But nothing in Gauthier's conclusion that their behaviour is not unjust turns on either of these conditions. An appeal from the people down-stream, accompanied by detailed evidence of the devastation caused them by the practices of the people upstream, can be turned down without any injustice being committed, given that there are no co-operative relations between them. Starting from the baseline created when they do whatever suits them best, the upstream people are being asked to make a unilateral sacrifice of their interests to benefit others.

I wish to maintain that the conclusion that there is nothing wrong about the behaviour of the upstream group violates a fundamental idea about justice that is prior to any theory. It is, I suggest, wrong to ignore the interests of others in pursuit of your own. If you cause harm to others by your actions, there is a strong prima facie case for saying that you should either desist or at the very least compensate the injured parties. Any theory of justice that is incapable of accommo-dating this idea can be dismissed out of hand. There is no trick in stipulating premises and drawing out implications. Anybody can do that. What is difficult, but is the only thing worth attempting, is to produce theories that are at once systematic and plausible. And a minimum condition of plausibility in a theory is its not having impli-cations so manifestly outrageous that they provide a decisive reason for rejecting it.

To sum up the discussion so far, I do not see that Wolff has given any good reason for abandoning my claim that we should start from the axiom of fundamental equality, and that that generates justice as impartiality rather than justice as reciprocity. But this is quite com-patible with people engaged in co-operative relations having rights and obligations with respect to one another that they do not have to other people. We do not need a special theory of justice to tell us that: it is a direct implication of justice as impartiality properly under-stood.[85]

2. *Justice as Mutual Advantage*

I have already addressed some of the defects of justice as mutual advantage. I now take up David Gauthier's response to my attack on

---

[84] David Gauthier, *Morals by Agreement*, Oxford, 1986, pp. 211–12. See III.2 below for further discussion of this case.

[85] See V.1 and V.2 below.

the theory in *Justice as Impartiality*. He begins by maintaining that both he and Hobbes define a just man as one whose will is formed by the desire to act justly. However, he concedes that his own theory requires us to ask if it is rational to have such a disposition, and that Hobbes regards it as necessary to establish that the precept to keep covenants (which is what justice for him consists in) is a law of nature, and hence commanded by 'reason'. For rationality or reason to endorse the disposition to be just we have to establish in Gauthier's case its tendency to maximize an individual's long-run utility and for Hobbes its tendency to promote self-preservation. Thus, the essential point is that compliance with the rules of justice can be recommended only if it is advantageous to the agent.[86]

I can thus restate in the following way the argument made earlier that there is a mismatch between motivation and rules in the theory of justice as mutual advantage.[87] As before, I begin with the definition of justice: according to the theory, just rules are those that would be mutually advantageous provided they were generally adhered to. The problem then is, I maintain, that having a disposition to behave justly cannot be recommended as rational (for Gauthier) or as commanded by reason (for Hobbes). For adherence to rules that would be generally advantageous if universally adhered to is advantageous to any given individual only under quite specific conditions: those in which monitoring and the application of sanctions are cheap and easy.

Gauthier goes on to reply to my charge that his version of the theory of mutual advantage is incoherent. Gauthier begins his comments by quoting me as describing him as 'the contemporary champion' of the theory, and I of course stand by that – which is why I am delighted to have the opportunity of engaging with him here. However, he also quotes me as saying that Hobbes was 'its greatest expositor', and I stand by that too.[88] My suggestion is that every time Gauthier departs from Hobbes's own formulation of the theory he opens up an inconsistency between the content of justice and the rationale of justice. Thus, Hobbes's 'state of nature' is a nasty place where people can and will use all the helps and advantages of force and fraud. In contrast, Gauthier correctly says that 'in *Morals by Agreement* [he] suggest[s] that just principles of interaction require a non-coercive baseline'.[89] In fact, his 'state of nature' is far more reminiscent of Locke's conception of a pre-political 'society' than it is akin to the Hobbesian 'state of warre'. My question is, by what alchemy does Gauthier conjure up these constraints on the pursuit of advantage, when he also maintains

[86] Gauthier, pp. 120–22.
[87] See III.1 above.
[88] Gauthier, p. 120.
[89] Ibid., p. 123.

that the only rational basis for action is the pursuit of advantage? The secret of transmuting gross self-interest into pure moral self-restraint would indeed be a philosopher's stone. Alas, I do not believe that Gauthier has succeeded in getting the brazen head to speak, though he does get fairly brazen himself later on in his remarks, as I shall seek to show.

Gauthier acknowledges that he is departing from Hobbes, who 'claims ... that a covenant between conquered and conqueror is valid' and that justice demands its observance.[90] But he does not offer any good reason for thinking that he is entitled to clean up the Hobbesian state of nature on the drastic lines he proposes. At one point, he appears to suggest that his theory of justice can haul itself up by its own bootstraps: if everybody believed in it, the only kind of society that could be stable would be one that conformed to it. Suppose a society does start from a coercive non-agreement point. Then, Gauthier says, 'those who believe, correctly, in justice as mutual advantage, will recognize that the practices and institutions of their society do not satisfy the criterion it proposes' and 'will not take themselves to have any reason to conform to the rules of their society ... save that afforded by their coercive imposition'.[91] No doubt a society of dedicated Gauthierians would be unstable if it failed to satisfy the requirements of Gauthier's theory. But the same could be said with equal validity of any other theory. Imagine a society in which it was generally believed that the first-born should be ritually sacrificed. Then it would be stable only if that belief were acted on. For people would refuse to accept the legitimacy of any other. The question is why, if we accept Gauthier's definition of rationality as utility-maximization, rational people should accept the limits he imposes on their freedom to engage in strategic behaviour in order to improve their position. Would they, in other words, be 'correct' to accept Gauthier's theory?

If we reject Gauthier's own transparently circular line of argument, I can see no rationale for saying that utility-maximizers must eschew coercion. Over the course of history, slavery and the systematic oppression of one racial or ethnic group by another have proved stable over long periods of time. Slavery in the United States did not collapse because it could not be maintained coercively. It fell because the South lost a war that was (indirectly, via the 'free soil' issue) precipitated by a distaste for the 'peculiar institution' in the rest of the Union. How can we account for that opposition? Gauthier would like to say that slavery could be opposed on his own premises. But unless slave owners

[90] Ibid.
[91] Ibid., p. 124.

were making a mistake about where their interests lay, there is no room for criticism.

The possibility has, of course, been mooted that, provided the slave-holders continued to own the land, market exploitation might have been more profitable than slavery. But what are we to say about a theory that would make the injustice of slavery turn on the results of counterfactual econometric analysis? The plain answer is that slavery obviously violated the premise of fundamental equality set out in the Declaration of Independence. Justice as impartiality, founded on that premise, can explain what is wrong with slavery in a straightforward way. *Mutatis mutandis*, the same analysis can be applied to Gauthier's own example of South African apartheid.[92]

There are times when Gauthier gives the impression of wishing to make the non-coercive baseline (the 'extended Lockean proviso') into a free-standing principle of fair dealing. That would, in my terms, turn his theory into one of justice as reciprocity.[93] For it would entail the admission of a sense of fair play as a motive not reducible to utility-maximization, however indirect and long-term we conceive it to be. But then it would be subject to my criticism of justice as reciprocity: that its notion of fairness is too eccentric to make an appeal to sensible people. Once we abandon the idea of deducing everything from utility-maximizing, there is no satisfactory stopping place short of justice as impartiality.

The extreme unattractiveness of Gauthier's non-agreement point as a conception of fair dealing can be seen by returning to the case of the two riparian societies:

If you, living upstream from me, merely use the river for the disposal of your wastes, then even though you thereby kill many of the fish in my part of the stream, you do not violate the [Lockean] proviso. For although you worsen my situation in relation to what I should expect in your absence, you do not better your own situation through interaction with me.[94]

Gauthier says that 'the cost [to the downstreamers] is occasioned solely by [their] presence, which from [the upstreamers'] point of view may be simply unwanted.'[95] It is worth dwelling on the implications of this for a moment. From the point of view of most European settlers in the New World, the indigenous inhabitants were 'simply unwanted'. The settlers did not want to gain by interacting with them: all they

---

[92] Ibid.

[93] More precisely, it is an extension of justice as reciprocity 'so that it has built into it a stipulation that the baseline from which advantage is to be reckoned must not be established by coercion' (*Justice as Impartiality*, p. 50).

[94] Gauthier, *Morals by Agreement*, pp. 211–12, quoted and discussed in *Theories of Justice*, pp. 301–2.

[95] Ibid., included in the quotation in *Theories of Justice*, pp. 301–2.

wanted was the land to mine, graze or raise crops on. Can Gauthier's theory of justice, even with its 'proviso', offer any reason that might have been given to the settlers for not systematically hunting down and killing the entire native population, as actually happened in some parts of Australia and the United States? I do not see that it can, and Gauthier does not appear to see that it can, either. All he has to offer is the observation that 'the Europeans who overcame the native Americans had little doubt about the justice of their cause' and that this idea of justice 'had little to do ... with mutual advantage or impartiality ...'.[96] But the question is not what actually motivated the settlers but whether or not Gauthier's theory can provide any basis on which to condemn what they did. I take his response to be an admission of failure on that score.

Gauthier has recently summed up the implications of taking as fundamental the idea of society as 'a co-operative venture for mutual advantage'.[97] These are twofold.

> Someone who did not find a value in society would have no reason to agree to its conditions of interaction. Someone who did not contribute value to others would give them no reason to accept her within the scope of society's conditions of interaction. Each then must be able to draw from society some of what she seeks but could not gain on her own, and each must contribute to society some of what others seek but would lack without her.[98]

For individuals, the first is a version of Hobbes's point that God, being omnipotent, has no need to make covenants. If we think of the 'someone' as a group, we have the case of the settlers and the natives: they can get everything they want on their own, since all they want is the land. Hence, they have 'no reason to agree to [the] conditions of interaction' with the indigenous population.

That is one side of giving a 'deep role' in the 'account of justice' to 'the idea of society as a co-operative venture for mutual advantage'.[99] The other side is, as Gauthier candidly concedes, that he has 'no choice but to accept' the criticism that 'justice as mutual advantage fails to afford any moral basis to the claims of those who lack the capacity to be productive participants in society.' For 'a person is eligible to be a beneficiary if and only if she is a contributor.' Hence, 'those who make no net contribution ... are entitled to no net benefit.'[100] Justice as impartiality, in contrast, makes the basis of justice reside in our common humanity. Human beings can make a claim to fundamental equality of

[96] Gauthier, p. 125.

[97] See III.1 above for the invocation of this Rawlsian expression.

[98] David Gauthier, 'Political Contractarianism', *The Journal of Political Philosophy*, 5 (1997), 132–48, at p. 135.

[99] Gauthier, 'Mutual Advantage and Impartiality', p. 125.

[100] All three quotations from ibid.

moral status, and that notion is instantiated in a situation for choosing principles of justice that embodies the values of freedom and equality. It does this by giving all the participants a veto on proposals that they cannot reasonably be expected to accept. On this basis, I suggest that the principle that 'those who can make no net contribution ... are entitled to no net benefit' could reasonably be rejected and is therefore contrary to the demands of justice.

Gauthier wishes to deny this, since he vehemently rejects my claim that justice as mutual advantage is incompatible with the requirement 'that constraints should be accepted freely as reasonable'.[101] This appears to imply that the congenitally disabled should freely accept as reasonable the prospect of starving on the streets. But surely this cannot be so on any natural interpretation of the words 'freely accept'. Gauthier's response is, as I understand it, that the able-bodied could reasonably reject, 'as a basis for informed, unforced general agreement', the proposal that they must accept an obligation to support the congenitally disabled. His argument for this remarkable claim is that 'a deep violation [of the extended Lockean proviso] unilaterally sacrifices the interests of the violated party'.[102] This, however, presupposes that the notion of a 'sacrifice' is to be interpreted in relation to a certain stipulated baseline: Gauthier's 'Lockean' non-agreement point. But this comprehensively begs the question. For people in a Scanlonian choosing situation would not accept that way of defining a sacrifice. They would take a 'unilateral sacrifice' in this context to be the gratuitous acceptance by the congenitally disabled of the proposal that they should have no claim of right to support by the able-bodied.

What is the sense in which this concession by the congenitally disabled would constitute a 'unilateral sacrifice'? In the Scanlonian context, a unilateral sacrifice is an unnecessary concession: it is a ceding of one's interests that others cannot reasonably demand as the price of agreement. Gauthier accurately quotes me as saying 'that nobody should accept a rule that would require a unilateral sacrifice of their interests'.[103] On the basis of this, he claims that I must agree with him that it is the able-bodied who would be making a unilateral sacrifice by agreeing to support the congenitally disabled. But this would be true only if I understood 'unilateral' to be contrasted with 'reciprocal'. In fact, the briefest glance at the relevant passage in *Justice as Impartiality* should suffice to indicate that a 'unilateral sacrifice' is to be taken as a piece of uncalled-for generosity. 'It is unfair for the generous to be exploited by the hard-hearted at the point at

---

[101] Ibid., p. 131.
[102] Both quotations from ibid., p. 126.
[103] Ibid.

which general rules are being laid down' (p. 70). What I am arguing here is that generosity is a virtue in real life; but it can be acknowledged as generosity (i.e. as not required by justice) only if, under the conditions in which the rules of justice themselves are drawn up, people do not give away too much. I would regard the voluntary agreement of the congenitally disabled to Gauthier's proposal as an act of stupendously quixotic generosity.

There is an alternative to admitting the congenitally disabled to the choosing situation and demanding that they go along with the prospect of starving on the streets. That is to keep them out in the first place. The basis for doing this would be that, since 'society is a co-operative venture for mutual advantage' and they cannot be part of such a venture, they must be excluded from its benefits. This would seem to me to fit in with a good deal of what Gauthier says, including the invocation of Hobbes on equality.[104] For the point of Hobbes's claim that people must be acknowledged as equals is that they are actually sufficiently equal in mind or body that they can disturb any settlement that does not count them as equal. But obviously this does not include the mentally or physically disabled, who are not as a matter of fact equal in mind and body to others. Expelling those who cannot provide benefits for others from the hypothetical choosing situation is in effect to expel them from the membership of the human race. Justice is consistent, Gauthier tells us, with the total disregard of their interests by others, so why should their views be heard?

David Gauthier is personally a nice man. It would not surprise me at all to discover that (like Hobbes, who explained that it maximized his utility) he gives money to beggars.[105] However, I am convinced that the general acceptance of his ideas would constitute a moral degeneration in the human race of incalculable magnitude. For thousands of years, secular and religious moralists have insisted that a society may be judged by the way in which it treats its most powerless members. Their efforts have, I would be the first to confess, met with only indifferent success. But I am persuaded that they have made some difference. Take that idea away and what except inertia stands in the way of a programme for the elimination of the 'unfit' of the kind pioneered by Adolf Hitler? If Paris was worth a mass, surely the preservation of a sense of common humanity is worth the sacrifice of a theory.

---

[104] Gauthier, p. 132.

[105] 'Because, sayd he, I was in paine to consider the miserable condition of the old man [to whom he had just given sixpence]; and now my almes, giving him some reliefe, doth also ease me' ('Thomas Hobbes', pp. 226–38 in Oliver Lawson Dick, *Aubrey's Brief Lives*, Harmondsworth, 1972, p. 236).

3. *Bargaining and Impartiality*

The contrast between justice as impartiality and its rivals can be pursued further by taking up Matt Matravers's point that appealing solely to the 'agreement motive' will not suffice to pick out justice as impartiality uniquely. As he says, if we do not set limits on the conditions under which agreement is to be reached, we cannot distinguish it from justice as mutual advantage. But I wish to argue that Matravers is wrong to suggest that all we have to add to the specification of the situation in which rules and principles are to be chosen is 'a position of equal bargaining power.'[106] The reason is that there are two conditions for the outcome of an agreement to be presumptively fair. One is that 'the parties must be well informed and well matched', but this is not enough. In addition, 'the baseline must itself be fair' (p. 50). Your offering to sell me back the property you stole from me cannot be the basis of a fair agreement. Bargaining towards mutually advantageous agreements has to take place within a 'basic structure' (in Rawls's terms) that will provide the baseline from which the parties count advantage. We cannot expect the outcome of mutually advantageous deals to be just unless the rights and resources that are deployed in making those deals are just. We therefore need rules and principles of justice to tell us what a just distribution of rights and resources looks like.

How do we establish those rules and principles? Matravers, as we have seen, takes the theory of justice as impartiality to stipulate 'equal bargaining power'. But I wish to deny that bargaining is appropriate at all in this context. The essence of bargaining is that the parties seek to gain an advantage over some non-agreement point. This entails that the situation from which rules and principles are to emerge must have built into it a just non-agreement point. But where does this come from? If we say that it in turn arises from bargaining, we are embarked on an infinite regress. For that bargaining position must include the specification of a non-agreement point and so on *ad infinitum*. The only alternative is to come up with a way of specifying a baseline which is pre-contractual. This sets the stage for the standard contractarian move that makes the non-agreement point what people could get in the absence of a social contract. This 'state of nature' may permit force and fraud, as with Hobbes, or set constraints on the manipulation of the non-agreement point, as with Locke and (inconsistently, as I have argued) Gauthier. Either way, it gives moral significance to what people can obtain for themselves in the absence of an agreement.

The whole basis of justice as impartiality is that such a non-agree-

---

[106] Matravers, p. 110.

ment point has no moral significance whatsoever. Whether or not those with superior natural endowments can legitimately claim to reap advantages in a just society is something that is to be thrashed out in the Scanlonian choosing situation. But there is one argument that the parties cannot appeal to, and that is the argument that they would do relatively well in the absence of an agreement. For the theory supplies no basis for saying that the non-agreement point is itself a just starting place.

We must thus be careful to distinguish contexts in which bargaining is appropriate from those in which it is not. I have no quarrel with Weale's argument that 'there are some ways of preserving initial advantages in agreements that seem fair to many people'.[107] Indeed, I have just quoted from *Justice as Impartiality* to the effect that mutually advantageous deals reflecting a fair status quo point and a fair process of bargaining are presumptively fair. But what I am saying in claiming that proposition to be a conclusion of the theory of justice as impartiality is that it could not reasonably be rejected in a situation that did not itself allow for bargaining from a pre-contractual baseline to have any effect on the decisions reached.

Of course, it would be possible to maintain that justice as mutual advantage is a theorem of the Scanlonian construction, in the same way as utilitarianism could conceivably be a theorem.[108] However, the features of justice as mutual advantage to which I have drawn attention earlier in this section seem to me to make this prospect a vanishingly remote one. I wish to say the same, and for roughly the same reasons, about the objection raised by more than one symposiast that I have not demonstrated what is wrong with the suggestion that a Nozickian historical entitlement theory might be a theorem of the Scanlonian construction.[109] Many people (the congenitally disabled for a start) would have to be mad to sign up for such a way of distributing benefits and burdens in a society, and nobody could reasonably deny that they were behaving reasonably in vetoing it.

The key objection to the treatment of the congenitally disabled within the theory of justice as mutual advantage is not that they have unequal bargaining power but that bargaining is out of place altogether in establishing rules and principles of justice. In particular, the question of what people could get for themselves in the absence of an agreement should be thrown out of court. I am not sure what it would mean operationally to give the congenitally disabled equal

    [107] Weale, p. 27.
    [108] See I.4 above.
    [109] See, for example, Hardin, p. 152. This is to be distinguished from the argument that justice as mutual advantage is simply a superior theory of justice *ab initio*. (See II.2 above for the two different ways of arguing in favour of the same theory of justice.)

bargaining power. Let us say, however, that a sign of equal bargaining power is equal gain from bargaining. Then the congenitally disabled, because they start from zero, will always finish up behind the rest. Yet from the viewpoint of justice as impartiality that notional starting point is irrelevant. On the assumption that brute bad luck should attract compensation, there is no reason for the congenitally disabled to be less well treated than those who became disabled later in life. Since they can have no earnings, they should in effect have their social insurance premiums paid for them. This is clearly an approach that is worlds apart from one according to which what is crucial for justice is how well people could get on by themselves.

In any bargaining situation, there must be a non-agreement point, and it must play a critical role in determining the outcome. For it is only the hope of gain in relation to the non-agreement point that induces the parties to bargain at all; and it is only the fear that unless agreement is reached they will all be stuck with the non-agreement point that leads them to moderate their demands so that (with luck) an agreement is reached. Take away the non-agreement point while leaving the motivations of the parties unchanged and there is no reason for anybody to agree on anything. The sky is the limit as far as demands are concerned, and there is no force to press the parties towards agreement. This explains why it is essential to the Scanlonian construction for the motivations of the parties to be different from those that characterize a bargaining situation. It is stipulated that they are driven by the desire to reach agreement on reasonable terms. This gives them a reason for engaging in dialogue, but it also gives them a reason for moderating their demands. They wish to advance their interests, but they are not prepared to press them to unreasonable lengths and will accept the reasonable claims of others. Thus, as I said in *Justice as Impartiality*, the conception of fairness we need will 'make fairness what can freely be agreed on by equally well-placed parties' (p. 51). But 'equally well-placed' cannot be construed as 'having equal bargaining power'. It must be understood in the way set out here.

4. The Circumstances of Impartiality

In *Justice as Impartiality*, I suggested that there are empirical conditions under which laws, policies and social norms are more likely to approximate those demanded by justice than those arising in other conditions (pp. 99–100 and 195–9). Albert Weale has a discussion of the circumstances of impartiality in his contribution that again seems to me to give equal bargaining power an altogether too prominent place. He suggests that we can draw a contrast between on one hand the hypothetical contractual situation, which (contrary to Matravers) he says 'dispenses with any notion of power except the power of argument', and on the other hand the specification of the circumstances of impartiality, which 'requires a positive conception of what rough equality of political power might involve, especially in regard to its organizational and institutional bases.'[110] But I do not see how anybody reading the section in *Justice as Impartiality* on 'Procedures and Social Justice' without preconceptions could conclude that I regard equal power as the critical feature of the circumstances of impartiality (pp. 99–111).

In fact, I quite agree with Weale that, if we had any expectation of equal power generating just outcomes, we would be 'in danger of circularity' because we would have to start by defining a just outcome and then say that an equal distribution of power is one that tends to bring about such outcomes.[111] I completely reject the kind of ideas peddled in the 1950s by some American 'pluralists' that, so long as all groups are equally well-organized, some mechanical process of equilibration will ensure that they all obtain equal success in achieving their goals.

If two groups have equal power, this means only that they are strategically symmetrical. That is to say, the support of either will add the same amount to any given coalition's chance of winning. But this is a measure that tells us nothing about the probability of any group's being on the winning side: that depends on the actual alignment of forces. Assume that every group has power exactly in proportion to the size of membership. On any issue, there will still be winners and losers. All that the assumption of equal power tells us is that victory will go to the side with the biggest battalions. If some group is perpetually in a minority, it will always lose. There is nothing in this that is inconsistent with equal power. The notion (which, however absurd, seems to infect some people's ideas of equal power) that each person, or each group, can be equally often on the winning side, regardless of how many others agree with it, is simply preposterous.

It was for this reason that I emphasized right at the beginning of my discussion of the circumstances of impartiality that 'the most important ... is a motivational one: the willingness to accept reasonable objections to a proposal regardless of the quarter from which they come' (p. 100). I added specifically that, even if minorities are fully represented (e.g. by 'racial gerrymandering' as in the USA), this 'cannot avert a situation in which a majority of politicians gets elected on a platform of neglecting or repressing the minority' (pp. 100–1). I allowed that a stand-off based on equal power between two large

[110] Weale, p. 33.
[111] Weale, p. 33.

groups within a society might with luck create an approximation to just outcomes but even then I added that I was inclined to think this would in the long run be 'stable only if the practice of working together peacefully creates the conditions for justice as impartiality to stand independently of support from justice as mutual advantage' (p. 102).

Thus, I do not believe that the circumstances of impartiality differ from the Scanlonian original position in the way that Weale suggests. Both depend on a general willingness to accept the claim by a group that its members cannot reasonably be expected to accept some proposal, so long as their claim is well-founded. And in both cases what is a reasonable expectation cannot be founded on bargaining considerations. For, as we have just seen, minority groups can be outvoted even if they have power proportional to their size. Hence, the bulk of my discussion in *Justice as Impartiality* is devoted to asking what are the institutional arrangements most conducive to making outcomes depend on reasoned argument rather than on the alignment of political forces.

IV. THE RIGHT AND THE GOOD

1. Reasonable Agreement and the Good

Justice as impartiality is (as the title of Richard Arneson's contribution indicates) a theory in which the right has priority over the good. All that this rather portentous expression means is that the theory starts by taking as problematic the existence of incompatible conceptions of the good and looks for a fair way of adjudicating between the conflicting demands that arise from the pursuit of those conceptions of the good. My argument for the priority of the right over the good turns on the existence of reasonable disagreement over conceptions of the good. Simon Caney, Richard Arneson and Diemut Bubeck all raise objections to this. However, even if they are correct about the possibility of some agreement on conceptions of the good, this does not suffice to show that a society does not need a superordinate set of rules to adjudicate between them.

Here I must confess that I did not make it clear enough in *Justice as Impartiality* what precisely is the problem about conceptions of the good. What we are looking for are rules of justice – rules that allocate rights and duties in an internally consistent way.[112] First of all, then, universal agreement that the good should be maximized cannot be a foundation for such rules unless there is also universal agreement on what the good consists in. Richard Arneson maintains that I have not

---

[112] See II.1 above for a discussion of the concept of rules of justice.

refuted act-consequentialism (the notion that everybody has an obligation to pursue the best consequences overall), but I can draw the refutation from his own mouth. He says that 'this doctrine leaves it entirely open how to evaluate the goodness of consequences'.[113] For precisely that reason, agreement on act-consequentialism would not begin to do the job of avoiding conflicts. The problem that justice as impartiality sets out to solve would exist in an extreme form in a society whose members were devoted single-mindedly to the pursuit of good consequences if they had widely divergent ideas as to what would constitute a good state of the world.[114]

Alternatively, suppose that people did all agree on a number of things being good. This would still not get us very far unless they also agreed on the relative priority to be attached to these good things (pp. 20–2). In the absence of this kind of agreement, nothing of an action-guiding kind can be said to follow from propositions such as those advanced by my critics to the effect that everybody could reasonably agree such-and-such is a good thing. For there is no reason for expecting agreement to follow on the necessity of promoting any particular good to a certain specified degree, so long as there are competing goods at whose expense the promotion of that good will occur.

Moreover, we might all agree that something is good but quite properly doubt that it is fair for public policy to privilege it over other conceptions of the good that are not shared. We might instead think that justice requires giving everybody a fair opportunity to pursue their own conception of the good, whether everyone agrees on its goodness or not. Suppose the most significant element in one person's conception of the good is one that is shared with everybody else, while the most significant element in another person's is one that is more idiosyncratic. Is it fair, we might ask, for us all to have to pitch in and help the first achieve his ends while doing nothing for the second – or perhaps even putting obstacles in his way?

Again, we might well think that in a just society people should be able to make their own trade-offs between goods and bads. Even if mind-numbing work is an indisputable bad (to take one of Caney's examples), we should recognize that somebody whose life is dominated by an idiosyncratic conception of the good that is expensive and time-consuming (Himalayan mountaineering, say) might be willing to do well-paid, mind-numbing work in preference to less well-paid, more interesting work. Should this be prevented, or even discouraged? I do not see how it can be maintained that a just society must take a stand against mind-numbing work. Rather, I persist in the belief that what

[113] Arneson, p. 85.
[114] This point is made explicitly on p. 26 of *Justice as Impartiality*.

a just society should concentrate on is ensuring fair opportunities in education and work – a requirement that in my view has very extensive ramifications. Indeed, Caney himself says of this example only that 'those with boring meaningless jobs would be compensated (financially, say) for this'.[115] But I do not believe, as he suggests, that we would need 'a perfectionist theory of distributive justice' in order to arrive at that conclusion.[116] A fair labour market will have to pay people extra to do unpleasant jobs (in comparison with jobs that require the same abilities but are more intrinsically rewarding), and justice as impartiality will endorse that outcome.

I have already put forward as a principle of justice the principle that laws and policies should be directed at the prevention of harm.[117] Here, then, we do have a principle for the collective suppression of a bad. But can a plausible case be made out for any further principles of justice of an analogous kind? These will have to be principles that specify a collective duty to ensure that some good is promoted. The peculiarity of harm is that being harmed against one's will represents a serious setback for the pursuit of virtually any conception of the good. (Even those who wish to inflict harm on themselves, in pursuit perhaps of a religious vocation, normally regard the voluntary aspect of it as essential to its conferring merit.) If the contractors had merely agreed that harm was bad, they might have concluded only that each person has a good reason for avoiding it. I did not simply move straight from agreement on the proposition that harm is bad to a claim that the contracting parties would agree on prohibiting the infliction of it. Rather, I made an argument that everybody would have a rational interest in being saved (as far as rules can do it) from being a victim of harm inflicted by others. Perhaps there are other examples, but nothing said by my critics persuades me of their existence.

Thus, I maintain that nothing would follow about justice even if the contracting parties were disposed to accept all the propositions listed by Simon Caney about what is good.[118] Suppose that we could not reasonably deny that 'community and love are valuable' and that Scrooge was a better man after his ghostly visits.[119] Can we get from these propositions any rules and principles that a society would have to adhere to if it was to be just? I doubt it. As far as Caney's examples of alcoholism and drug abuse are concerned, let us suppose that we could not reasonably deny that they are bad. What rules or principles could not reasonably be rejected on the strength of that? It will be seen

[115] Caney, p. 93.
[116] Ibid.
[117] See II.2 above.
[118] Caney, pp. 91–2.
[119] Ibid., p. 92.

immediately that we are back with the issue of paternalism raised earlier.[120] Suppose the proposed rule to be that alcohol and hard drugs must be made difficult to obtain or prohibited by law (though this does not necessarily make them difficult to obtain!). It is clear that Arneson for one would cite the competing value of autonomy in opposition to any such proposal. A real fanatic for autonomy might be prepared to say that even the person whose life is ruined is still better off than living under a 'nanny state'. But it is not necessary to be a fanatic of any stripe to recognize that banning everything that can cause trouble if misused or overindulged in is going to eliminate many of life's pleasures. This leads to the conclusion that it is a matter for a case-by-case balancing of pros and cons, with different risks being met by different kinds and degrees of regulation.[121] If this is correct, no conclusions about justice can be drawn from these examples.

As far as astrology is concerned, I am at a loss to know what proposed rule Caney thinks could not reasonably be rejected, even if everybody agreed that there is no scientific basis for it. Should we ban Chinese fortune cookies on the ground that it is hard to see how they can give rise to accurate predictions?[122] In so far as astrology is for most people a bit of harmless fun, surely anybody could reasonably reject the proposal that it should be suppressed. I suppose that, if evidence emerged that a lot of people were taking disastrous decisions on the basis of astrological forecasts, there might be a case for some sort of regulation. But if I am right that public policy on drink and hard drugs is not mandated by justice, the same must be true of astrology.

Religious cults present more of a problem, but this is because of features associated with their being cults rather than on account of their cognitive content.[123] To the extent that cults (not only religious ones) subject followers to brainwashing techniques, deliberately encourage them to break with all their former associates and foster paranoid delusions about the government, they may be legitimately within the range of regulation. Since the parties in a Scanlonian original position are to be 'well-informed', it seems plausible that they would wish to be saved from the kind of entrapment and manipulation that some cults engage in. But if they were really well-informed would they wish to be saved from religion altogether, on the ground that all religious beliefs are unsupported by evidence? Richard Arneson makes

---

[120] See II.2 above.

[121] This conclusion is argued for in II.2.

[122] Caney, pp. 91–2. (In the film *My Dinner with André,* Wallace Shawn puts forward the example of Chinese fortune cookies as an illustration of an unsound basis for making decisions.)

[123] Ibid.

this suggestion, stating his belief 'that many religious doctrines [such as the idea of an immaterial soul that can survive death] are manifestly unreasonable'.[124] Grant for the sake of argument that this is right. What if anything follows? To address that question we are forced to ask about the place that religion plays in people's lives.

A practising member of a religious congregation will typically enjoy many benefits from participation including the affirmation of continuity across generations, membership in a community that cuts across other social divisions, more resonant *rites de passage* than secular rivals have (at any rate until now) come up with, and participation with others in a wide variety of social activities that (at the minimum) provide a regular retreat from quotidian existence. In addition, of course, religions normally offer some way of making sense of life: almost all, for example, incorporate a creation myth to explain why there is anything at all. Now suppose Arneson comes along and says that, in absence of any historical evidence for (say) the exploits of Hanuman, it is unreasonable for anybody to continue subscribing to the Hindu religion. I suggest that this contention could reasonably be rejected on the ground that it misses the point. At the same time, however, the lack of historical evidence for the exploits of Hanuman, the miracles of Jesus and so on is surely an excellent basis for my proposal that it is not unreasonable for anybody to refuse to accept the demands of any religion.

Diemut Bubeck repeats Caney's suggestion that it might be 'possible for people with different conceptions of the good ... to find further areas of agreement', in addition to the agreement on the evaluation of harm that I posit.[125] Again, however, I must emphasize that what I call the positive harm principle is not simply a shared evaluation of harm. Rather it constitutes an agreement in the original position on a plan of action – to make the prevention of harm a priority. The implication is that any society that does not make the prevention of harm a priority is to that extent unjust: as Bubeck correctly says, harm 'constrains the possible content of rules of justice'.[126] The question that has to be asked is not: might the members of some society agree on the collective pursuit of some conception of the good? They might well, and there is nothing to stop them from acting on this agreement, so long as they do not in the process contravene the (procedural and substantive) demands of justice. The question is, rather: is there any conception of the good that a society must pursue on pain of being unjust? Is there, in other words, any conception of the good whose pursuit has the same status as the prevention of harm?

[124] Arneson, p. 71.
[125] Bubeck, p. 170.
[126] Ibid.

The Scanlonian contractual framework entails that, for any conception of the good to have such a status, nobody could reasonably reject the proposal to give its collective pursuit priority. Are there any plausible candidates? If we were to postulate a homogeneous group of contractors with many values in common, we could trivially derive the conclusion that there are conceptions of the good whose promotion they *would* agree upon. But the requirement that nobody *could* reasonably reject a proposed rule is much stronger, and it is the one that is relevant here.[127] I remain unpersuaded that there are any positive (first-order) conceptions of the good that could pass the test. Let me add, though, that admitting a handful of them would not alter the main thrust of the theory of justice as impartiality, since the problem addressed by the theory – the problem of divergent conceptions of the good – would still exist for all remaining conceptions of the good.

2. Is Agreement on the Good Needed?

Bubeck's main argument against the priority of the right over the good is not the one I have been discussing. Rather, it is that, even if people have different conceptions of the good, this need not lead to conflict. To the extent that this is so, it may be said that adjudication between conceptions of the good is not essential for civil peace. The implication is that my 'Hobbesian' case for the priority of justice over the pursuit of the good fails.[128]

Bubeck is plainly attracted to anarchism, and it may be worth beginning by asking in what sense the theory of justice as impartiality is committed to the rejection of anarchism. If we understand anarchism in a political sense, as the claim that a specialized, centralized coercive institution (the state) is not necessary, there is nothing in the theory itself that entails its rejection. As I pointed out in an earlier reference to Bubeck's characterization of the theory as 'Hobbesian', I do not presuppose that justice requires coercive enforcement, as Hobbes (in effect) did.[129] I am as a matter of fact confident that the conditions under which anarchy is sustainable do not exist in contemporary large-scale societies, and that a just society will therefore have to depend on both formal and informal sanctions. But anarchists could perfectly happily take over the substance of the theory of justice as impartiality, and arrive at different conclusions about its implications.

Where I an unrepentantly 'Hobbesian' is in insisting that some rules and principles are required if conflicts between adherents of different conceptions of the good are to be avoided: the question of how such

---

[127] See Scanlon, p. 110.
[128] Bubeck, third section, pp. 165–70.
[129] See II.1 above.

rules and principles are to be implemented is secondary to this basic question of the need for them at all. If we take anarchy to be the denial that any such rules and principles are needed to avoid conflict between adherents of different conceptions of the good, it is indeed true that the whole of *Justice as Impartiality* is premised upon the rejection of this. Hobbes's idea that agreement on the just is the only route to peace, given disagreement about the good, seems to me entirely valid.

I have to say that I do not find any convincing argument from Bubeck against this. Even if we can find a few conceptions of the good whose pursuit would not lead to conflict, that would scarcely make a dent in the case for saying that no society can do without rules to adjudicate between conceptions of the good when their pursuit does lead to conflict. But I am not very strongly persuaded by Bubeck's own chosen examples of Buddhism and altruism. The history of Vietnam, Cambodia and Sri Lanka suggests that Buddhism is not in practice a guarantee of pacific behaviour, while altruism is far too vague a value to avoid conflict in its pursuit. If it means doing good to others, that leaves a lot of room for disagreements about what that good consists of. We might get round that by saying that the good of each person is to be understood as that person's conception of it (though that is a controversial interpretation); but even then there would still be no guidance from the bare idea of altruism when the choice is between benefiting one person and benefiting another.

Of course, if we imagine that each conception of the good comes complete with a specification of the limits to be observed in pursuing it, and if that specification is the same for all conceptions of the good, the problem is solved. But I would wish to say that this is simply to reintroduce justice as impartiality through the back door. Failing that, the problem of conflict remains unresolved, and I do not see that Bubeck gives us any good reason for doubting that. It is no use to cite, as she does, 'evidence' of 'peaceful coexistence' between 'different conceptions of the good, and "pursuers" of the good'.[130] For I am not, of course, saying that this is impossible. The whole point of my book is to say that it is possible – so long as everybody signs up to justice as impartiality. Thus, confronted with an example of peaceful coexistence, we have to ask what is its basis. Bubeck's own example is 'the two main religions in Germany, Protestant and Catholic, whose status is equal'.[131] I rest my case! This is precisely what the theory of justice as impartiality says should happen: 'equal protection' is a legal (and constitutional) provision for adjudicating between the potentially conflicting claims of the two denominations.

---

[130] Bubeck, p. 167.
[131] Ibid., p. 167, n. 35.

3. Why Fairness?

Diemut Bubeck tends to believe that the world is a more benign place
than I am inclined to think it is. In contrast, Russell Hardin regards
me as too soft-hearted. As his title suggests, he thinks that 'reasonable
agreement makes some sense as a political theory. It makes much less
sense as a moral theory.'[132] As a political theory, it can suggest the
terms for what Rawls describes as a *modus vivendi*, at any rate so long
as the rival forces are equal enough in strength to make moderation
pay. It seems to me that Hardin underestimates the limitations of this
way of underwriting the conclusions of justice as impartiality.[133] But I
am more interested here in the second claim he makes, which amounts
to a rejection of the whole rationale of justice as impartiality.

It is not at all clear to me whether Hardin's chief contention is that
the priority of the right over the good is logically incoherent or that it
is motivationally unlikely. In so far as he wishes to press the first
point, I am confident that he can be refuted. The second turns on the
kind of extremely high-level empirical claim that is in the nature of
the case open to interminable argument. I have already given my own
views on this in *Justice as Impartiality* and I shall summarize them
here simply to this extent: I do not see that the theory's validity presupposes that the desire to behave justly is a dominant motive in
everybody or even most people; it is enough if it has some efficacy, and
I believe that there is evidence to support that (pp. 114–15). Since
Hardin does not address what I say about the issue and appears to rely
on totally a priori psychologizing, I do not feel called upon to say any
more here.

As far as logical coherence is concerned, Hardin's argument (if it is
intended as one) is equally a priori but in this case rebuttable. It
is simply that 'what is "reasonable" to me, with my theory of the good,
is how much of that good I can get out of our political arrangements.'[134]
I entirely agree with his claim that, if I have a 'theory of the good', my
reason for pursuing it is not simply that, right or wrong, it is mine.
'I back that theory because I think it is compelling and correct, not
because it is merely mine.'[135] Indeed, I shall be using precisely that
thought to criticize the utilitarian way of treating diverse (first-order)
conceptions of the good.[136] But the contention that 'my theory of the
good should be trumped by a theory of mere fairness' does not rest on
its denial.[137] Rather, my point is that there are fair and unfair ways

---

[132] Hardin, p. 148.
[133] See III.2 above and *Justice as Impartiality*, pp. 37–9 and 163–4.
[134] Hardin, p. 149.
[135] Ibid.
[136] See IV.4 below.
[137] Hardin, p. 149.

of advancing one's conception of the good, and it is the job of a theory of justice to say which is which.

Suppose we accept Hardin's claim that 'compromise' is 'a pragmatic, not a moral matter'.[138] This means that the only cogent reason that I can be given for not pressing my conception of the good is that, given the actual constellation of forces, some compromise offers me the maximal expectation of success. Thus, if the alignment is currently favourable to my conception, I would be irrational not to go for it. As we know, some conceptions of the good hold that homosexuals should be jailed and apostates beheaded. Hardin could, of course, condemn the implementation of such ideas from within a competing conception of the good – and no doubt he would. But he is denying that there exist any normative resources that would enable him to appeal to the person with these beliefs not to act on them, given the power to.[139] This conclusion can derive only from an arbitrary limitation on the scope of morality. Hardin assumes that morality can have one subject: establishing what is good. Once we have decided on the answer to that question, there is nothing more to be said. Each person simply evaluates states of affairs according to the degree to which his conception of the good is instantiated in them.

Against this, we can set the elementary thought that we live in a world that is full of other people with different conceptions of the good, and that they should have a fair chance to pursue them even if we have the power to stop (some of) them. An adequate theory of justice should, I suggest, take that thought and give it specificity. That is what I claim to have done in *Justice as Impartiality*. If somebody is totally unmoved by the elementary thought that I have expressed, then of course the theory will not speak to him. But the theory can explain why it is justifiable to do whatever is necessary to restrain such people.

4. Neutrality and Utility

Justice as impartiality imposes a certain way of dealing with conflicting conceptions of the good. Within the limits imposed by justice, the outcome should be whatever results from people pursuing their

---

[138] Ibid.

[139] I am not persuaded by Gauthier's attempt (pp. 133–6) to show that his own theory can avoid running into the same objection. In *Morals by Agreement*, he devotes a long chapter (pp. 21–59) to arguing that the appropriate conception of utility for his theory is one that places no limits on the legitimate sources of utility. In his reply in this volume, he suggests that preferences based on 'moralistic' (or, presumably, religious) considerations can somehow be ruled out. But this flatly contradicts the position taken in *Morals by Agreement*, where he takes 'the Aztecs' preference for human sacrifice' as an unimpeachable element in their utility functions, given 'their belief in the hunger of the gods for human blood' (p. 29). If the Aztecs were rational, given their beliefs, to practise human sacrifice, why should not believers in the Old Testament be regarded as rational in persecuting homosexuals?

conceptions of the good within a neutral framework. To take an example much used in *Justice as Impartiality*, suppose the choice is between building a dam and preserving the only known habitat of a certain species of small perch, the snail darter.[140] Choosing either of these options must (implicitly if not explicitly) privilege some conceptions of the good over others, but neither option can reasonably be rejected in advance. All that can be stipulated is that whatever decision is reached must be executed justly (e.g. those whose property is taken to build the dam should be compensated), and that the decision must be reached fairly. What this means is that the decision-making process should not be rigged in favour of one side or the other. The forum within which the decision is taken – a referendum following a campaign, a legislative vote following hearings, a tribunal or enquiry whose recommendations go to the government, for example – should itself be neutral. But what goes into the decision can be (cannot but be) arguments based on different conceptions of the good.

This is, as notions of neutrality go, relatively weak. In a political context, it allows people to pursue their conceptions of the good, and accepts that a demand of neutrality cannot be imposed on the outcomes themselves. The basic reason for this is that there is no coherent alternative. Public policies inevitably reflect some judgement (or at any rate some decision) about the relative weight to be given to competing considerations. This means that they will normally reflect different conceptions of the good, or at the least different weights for the same conceptions of the good.

Arneson writes that 'a better interpretation of neutrality is that the policies enforced by a just state should always be justifiable in terms of neutral reasons, reasons that all citizens can share in so far as they are rational'.[141] I regard this as a wrecking amendment. Indeed, since Arneson repudiates the whole theory within which my notion of neutrality plays a role, I do not understand on what basis he presumes to say what would be a better version of it – unless, of course, it is taken to be a version that makes sure that the theory becomes unattractive even to its supporters. My reason, in any case, for treating Arneson's suggestion as a mischief-making one (whether by design or not) is that

---

[140] See *Justice as Impartiality*, pp. 145–59, *passim*. For a brief account of the Tellico dam affair, in which the snail darter played a leading role, see Bryan G. Norton, *Why Preserve Natural Variety?*, Princeton, NJ, 1987, pp. ix–x and 4–5. Environmentalists had opposed the dam even before the snail darter was discovered, so its prospective extinction was not the sole (or even the main) basis for their objection to it. The snail darter should be taken here to stand in for all the environmental values to be offset against the (alleged) advantages of 'hydroelectric power, a recreationally attractive lake, and flood abatement' (ibid., p. ix).

[141] Arneson, p. 67.

it calls for a kind of discrimination among reasons that cannot sensibly be operationalized.

Although Rawls toyed with the idea of 'public reason' in *Political Liberalism*, the only application of it in the book that seems to me to make any sense is the one that reduces to the idea of the ' burdens of reason', understood as what I call scepticism about conceptions of the good.[142] In so far as 'public reason' might be taken as corresponding to what Arneson prescribes, it is an unworkable idea. The notion of 'neutral reasons' is void of content, unless it is simply a way of referring to the procedural and substantive limits imposed by justice. Arneson's own gloss on the concept is that neutral reasons are 'reasons that all citizens can share in so far as they are rational'. This rules out either virtually nothing or virtually everything. I can share almost any reason with you in the sense that I can comprehend it and see how you might have arrived at it; but there is scarcely any reason that I must accept (at any rate as decisive in relation to competing reasons) on pain of irrationality.

As a consequence of the hypertrophication of the First Amendment in American legal and philosophical thinking, Arneson's notion of neutral reasons is quite commonly interpreted as entailing that nobody can legitimately support a public policy on the basis of reasons derived from religious beliefs. The attempt to implement this discrimination among reasons is what led to the unedifying spectacle of a number of eminent scholars arguing before the Supreme Court of the State of Colorado about the ancient Greek attitude to homosexuality, so as to establish whether a law prohibiting subordinate jurisdictions from introducing anti-discriminatory provisions could or could not be supported without invoking Christian beliefs.[143] From the standpoint of justice as impartiality it makes no difference what the answer to that question is, since anti-discriminatory legislation is required by justice. The potential victims of discrimination based on sexual orientation could reasonably say that it constitutes a denial of equal treatment, making them worse off than others in a way that they cannot reasonably be expected to accept. It makes no odds whether the bigots are religiously motivated or not: they get thrown out by justice as impartiality, whatever their reasons may be.

What makes Arneson's espousal of a filter for reasons especially peculiar is that his own idea about the right way to deal with conflicting conceptions of the good is to turn them all into preferences

[142] John Rawls, *Political Liberalism*, New York, 1993, lecture VI, 'The Idea of Public Reason', pp. 212–54.

[143] Romer *v* Evans, 116 S. Ct., 1620, *United States Supreme Court* (1996). For a discussion of this case see R. Dworkin, 'Sex, Death and the Courts', *New York Review of Books*, xliii, 13 (August 1996), 44–50.

and aggregate them so as to come up with a second-order utilitarian answer. 'Each person's aspirations are regarded as wants or desires, and the satisfaction of these wants is utility. The degree to which each person's wants are satisfied under proposed social rules is for the utilitarian the proper measure of each person's condition for the purpose of deciding whether the rules are just.'[144] Preferences and reasons are logically different kinds of entity. Even if we stipulate that, in order to count in the calculus, preferences have to be well-informed and well-considered, this still will not get us to the conclusion that public policies must be based on 'reasons that all citizens can share in so far as they are rational.'[145] Rather, public policies will be based on the relative strength of aggregate desire for the alternative options.

Paul Kelly defends precisely the same line as that advanced by Arneson, seeking to counterattack against the criticisms of it that I put forward in *Justice as Impartiality* (pp. 145–59).[146] In the remainder of this section, I shall explain why I do not think that Kelly has shown the superiority of the utilitarian approach to policy disagreement over that which I advocate. I wish to argue, indeed, that the examples produced by Kelly to illustrate the advantages of the utilitarian method actually show how problematic it is.

The problem which both the utilitarian criterion and my version of justice as impartiality address is as follows: given that different members of a certain society have different ideas about what should be done (e.g. whether to build a dam that will destroy the habitat of an endangered species of fish), what is the appropriate way of reaching a collective decision? My reply is that (within limits already set out) a theory of justice cannot be expected to do more than talk about procedures that are fair and that encourage the decision to be taken in a rational way.[147] This means, among other things, that people should not be able to get away with saying 'I want this outcome, and that's all there is to it'. They should have to explain why they think one outcome is better than the alternatives, and respond to criticisms of their claims. The relevant facts should be established as firmly as they can be, expert opinion should be given its due weight, and so on. It is no business of the theorist of justice to say where this process should come out in any particular case, but he will in general feel that things have not gone well if the actual process of public discourse has not itself had an effect on the outcome.[148]

---

[144] For this stipulation, see Richard Arneson, 'Neutrality and Utility', *Canadian Journal of Philosophy* 20 (1990), 215–40.

[145] Arneson, p. 67.

[146] Arneson is identified as a supporter of the approach on p. 140 of *Justice as Impartiality*.

[147] See II.3 above.

[148] See III.4 above.

Contrast this with the utilitarian way of looking at the same problem. Kelly makes it clear that the reduction of diverse notions to wants is to be regarded as a fair way of bringing them into relation with one another.[149] The ideal would be to form an accurate estimate of the amount that each person cares about the favoured outcome and then work out which alternative has the greatest aggregate demand behind it. Although Kelly suggests that voting might be treated as a practical approximation to the ideal, it is completely insensitive to intensity of preference. More sophisticated instruments such as cost-benefit analysis may well recommend themselves as capable of generating a closer approximation to the ideal.

I shall not pursue the question of implementation any further, however, because I want to suggest that this is the wrong kind of approach altogether. What in my view people choosing decision-making institutions should agree on is a process that enables (and indeed encourages) them to participate and interact as citizens, engaging in efforts at mutual persuasion in the hope of reaching a decision whose rationale everybody can appreciate even if not everybody supports it. This is totally absent from any approach that turns every belief that something is the right public policy into a want for that policy and then aggregates the wants, turning citizens into consumers. The crucial objection to the utilitarian proposal for dealing with conflicting values is that it privatizes what is (or should be) irreducibly public.

What about foetuses, non-human animals and future generations? What, indeed, about non-sentient and inanimate nature, which – according to the non-supernatural religion of a lot of people (including me) – deserves respect apart from any interests that human beings or other animals might have in its enjoyment or exploitation? There is no way of getting round the fact that the decisions about these matters will have to be taken by contemporary human beings, simply because there is nothing else in a position to take them. If trees are to 'have standing', it is people who have to decide that they shall and go to court on their behalf.[150] Similarly, if the interests of foetuses, non-human animals and future people are to be protected, it can come about only if contemporary people take the appropriate decisions. The only

---

[149] See esp. Kelly, p. 49.

[150] The reference here is to a famous article by Christopher Stone arguing that courts should be able to take account of the interests of trees (etc.) in their own right rather than as a by-product of the interests of human beings. See Christopher D. Stone, 'Should Trees have Standing? Towards Legal Rights For Natural Objects', *Southern California Law Review*, 45 (1972), 450–501.

question is how we should think about the right way to take such decisions.[151]

Kelly suggests that utilitarianism can incorporate the interests of foetuses, non-human animals and future people in a way that justice as impartiality cannot.[152] (He is understandably silent about non-sentient and inanimate nature.) But it seems to me that in saying this he is falling into the trap that he accused me of falling into: that of failing to distinguish utilitarianism as a theory of the good from utilitarianism as a theory of the right.[153] The utilitarianism that Kelly defends in his chapter is second-order utilitarianism. He is suggesting that, once people have formed their views about public policy (based on their own conceptions of the good), they should agree to have these treated as wants and aggregated with the wants of other people. It has to be emphasized that utilitarianism in the ordinary (first-order) sense is simply one conception of the good that people might have.

Second-order utilitarianism – the kind that competes with justice as impartiality as a way of dealing with conflicting values – will say that foetuses, non-human animals, future generations and, for that matter, inanimate nature will enter into the collective decision only to the extent that they play a role in the utility functions of the people whose utilities are to be aggregated to create it. Anthropocentric utilitarians, animal liberationists, Buddhists, Christians, secular ecocentrics and worshippers of Gaia will factor in some or all of these things in their different ways. But in the end the results will be reduced to individual wants for policies and will count only in that way. Thus, the survival of the snail darter will enter into the decision on building the dam to exactly the degree that the people whose views (in the guise of wants) are to be counted care about it. There is no way in which the fish will get a 'vote' in their own right.

Justice as impartiality, as a more complex theory than second-order utilitarianism, can make more discriminations, and it can offer a better account of the way in which we should think about these questions. As far as the interests of future generations are concerned, the premise of fundamental equality implies that the interests of people in the future should have no less weight than those of people in the present. I do not think that the contractual apparatus is useful in this context: it throws up more problems than it solves. Rather, my view is that we should take principles derived from the contractual situation and see how they apply. I cannot take the space to follow up this idea here. I will confine myself to saying that it has radical

---

[151] See Onora O'Neill, 'Environmental Values, Anthropocentrism and Speciesism', *Environmental Values,* 6 (1997), 127–41.

[152] Kelly, p. 58.

[153] See I.4 above.

implications for the way we live now if (as I am persuaded) that way of life is inconsistent with our leaving future generations with a fair set of opportunities.

Within the substantive limits set by the demands of justice, the theory of justice as impartiality shares with Kelly's second-order utilitarianism the idea that different views about the right answer, derived from diverse conceptions of the good, have to be somehow brought into enough of a relation to generate a collective decision. My point is simply that turning beliefs about the right answer into wants and aggregating them is an obnoxious way of going about this. Let us say that I want to save the whales or prevent the further destruction of the rainforest. Second-order utilitarianism says that my wanting it is, *pro tanto*, a reason for saving them. But it is simply false that gratifying me is a reason for saving them. (Gratifying somebody who wishes to destroy them would not, after all, be a reason for destroying them.) The reasons for saving them are the reasons there are for thinking they ought to be saved. Given a fair decision-making procedure (which there is not for such global issues) we can say: if enough people are convinced by those reasons, the whales and the rainforests will be saved; if not, not. But either way the point is that the gratification of wants does not come into the rationale of the collective decision.

V. SOME MORE MISTAKES ABOUT IMPARTIALITY

1. *Act- versus Rule-Utilitarianism Rides Again (in the Wrong Direction)*

Part III of *Justice as Impartiality* is entitled 'Some Mistakes about Impartiality'. It is now time to introduce a new mistake made by Richard Arneson, after which I shall take up an old mistake (originally made by Bernard Williams) which I had hoped had been laid to rest in *Justice as Impartiality* but which is exhumed by Susan Mendus. I shall then move on to the last chapter of the book and discuss some points arising from my discussion of contemporary feminist political theory.

So far I have had a lot to say about justice but not much about impartiality. I shall therefore begin by explaining the role of impartiality in the theory. There are two ways in which impartiality can play a part in our moral thinking. We may demand impartiality (of ourselves and others) in deciding what is the right course of action. The paradigm here is the impartiality that we expect of a judge: if you are entrusted with the job of awarding a prize for the best sponge cake, you should give it to the person who best merits the prize and not be swayed by irrelevant factors. You should not favour your friends or relations, or allow characteristics such as age, sex, religion or race to make a difference. This direct application of the idea of impartiality I call first-order impartiality. In contrast, second-order impartiality comes into play at a higher level: it is the virtue that we seek in rules and principles of justice. As Thomas Hill, Jr explains it:

All the impartiality thesis says is that, if and when one raises questions regarding fundamental moral standards, the court of appeal that one addresses is a court in which no particular individual, group, or country has *special* standing. Before that court, declaring 'I like it,' 'It serves my country,' and the like, is not decisive; principles must be defensible to anyone looking at the matter apart from his or her special attachments, from a larger, human perspective.[154]

Second-order impartiality is at the core of justice as impartiality, and the Scanlonian construction is one way (though not the only way) of representing it. But what is the relation between the two levels of impartiality? Commonsense morality takes the line that there are some contexts in which impartiality is demanded but that we are otherwise free to make use of the resources (personal and material) that we justly control in ways that violate impartiality. 'I like it' is an unexceptionable explanation for many actions that favour the interests of some people (including ourselves) in ways that cannot be related to any general ground of justification for discrimination such as need or merit. There are, of course, limits to this partiality that are set by the strictures of justice, but within these limits we have a right to act as we choose.

Similarly, to say 'It serves *my* country' is an acceptable move in some contexts. For example, at a special summit meeting for European leaders in May 1997, Tony Blair said 'Everybody here wants an agreement and so do I. But it must be one in Britain's interest.' This was treated by Helmut Kohl as demonstrating a 'constructive spirit', which makes sense in that it did no more than articulate the position of all the participants.[155] At the same time, there are, obviously, limits on what can be defended by saying 'It serves *my* country'. Within the context of European horse-trading, the Conservatives' strategy of blocking all business unless they secured some concession was seen as illegitimate, and other governments were willing to accept considerable costs to ensure that it did not succeed. 'Mr Blair won points yesterday from his fellow EU leaders by disavowing the threat of a fish quota veto at [the] Amsterdam [summit meeting] – something repeatedly threatened by John Major.'[156] But this should be seen not so much

---

[154] Thomas E. Hill, Jr, 'The Importance of Autonomy', in *Women and Moral Theory*, ed. Eva Kittay and Diane Meyers, Totowa, NJ, 1987, p. 132 (quoted in *Justice as Impartiality*, pp. 226–7).

[155] 'Blair Charms his Way to Treaty Deal', *The Guardian,* 24 May, p. 1.

[156] Ibid.

as a retreat as a recognition that any such threat would be counter-productive. Within this framework for haggling, the pursuit of national interest may be seen as consistent with the circumstances of impartiality.[157]

It is also worth observing that commonsense morality actually pre-scribes partiality in certain cases: thus, parents are ascribed special obligations to care for their own children. According to commonsense morality, there is a division of labour at work here: family members have responsibilities to one another that they do not have to others; organizations assign official duties to some people that they do not give to others; and citizens have obligations to one another (e.g. to contri-bute to taxes for common purposes) that they do not have to non-citizens. At the same time, of course, commonsense morality sets limits to the legitimate bounds of partiality: as I have already said, it would proscribe abusing one's position as a judge in a cake-baking compe-tition to favour members of one's family, for example.

The primary objective of Part III of *Justice as Impartiality* is to argue that justice as impartiality endorses commonsense morality's rejection of universal first-order impartiality as a demand of justice. I contend, in other words, that, in an appropriately constituted choosing situation, a rule prescribing universal first-order impartiality could reasonably be rejected (pp. 213–16). The secondary objective, which actually occupies more space, is to show (in Bubeck's words) that it is universal first-order impartiality 'that provides the easy target of critics of impartiality such as Williams or feminist critics'.[158] Thus, I point out in *Justice as Impartiality* the way in which crude versions of utilitarianism and Kantianism provide Bernard Williams with a good deal of cheap fun (pp. 217–33). Other crude versions, I go on to show (pp. 237–46), are constituted by Lawrence Kohlberg's two highest levels of moral thinking: a simple-minded application of utilitarian thinking (the fifth level) and a misappropriation of Rawls's theory of justice (the sixth level). To the extent that the feminist critique of impartiality may be said to have its origins in Carol Gilligan's critique of Kohlberg, I suggest in *Justice as Impartiality* that it may not be similarly decisive against a carefully developed version of second-order impartiality (pp. 236–7).

In the course of making this argument, I suggest that universal first-order impartiality is not a plausible implication of utilitarianism, of Kantian morality, or of Rawls's theory of justice. Thus, I argue that the pursuit of first-order impartiality, as advocated by William God-win, would actually frustrate the achievement of the utilitarian end

---

[157] See IV.4 above.
[158] Bubeck, p. 154 (citations suppressed).

(pp. 218–21). Again, I try to show that the maxims of action called for by commonsense morality are compatible with the Categorical Imperative (p. 230). And finally, I point out that Rawls's theory of justice is (like mine) a two-level theory that requires impartiality only at the point at which principles are to be chosen (pp. 213–16).

It will be observed that I have drawn the distinction between Godwinian utilitarianism and a form of utilitarianism that allows for departures from first-order impartiality without adverting to the distinction between act-utilitarianism and rule-utilitarianism. I believe I am correct in saying that the terms do not occur once in Part III of *Justice as Impartiality*. Despite this, Richard Arneson treats universal first-order impartiality and act-utilitarianism as if they were the same.[159] This is a mistake, because the two are addressed to different questions.[160]

Henry West has helpfully distinguished two approaches to ethics. One is 'the first person point of view', from which an agent is 'asking "What ought I to do?" with the behaviour of others given as if it were the circumstances of action'. The alternative is 'the social point of view "What morality ought there to be?"'[161] A theory of justice is concerned with the second question, and so is Godwinian utilitarianism. The act-versus rule-utilitarianism dispute is addressed to the first question: taking the behaviour of others as given, it asks how an individual agent should decide how to act.

What makes Godwin the archetypal exponent of universal first-order impartiality is not his idea that everybody should do the best thing open to him. What makes him distinctive is his idea that the best thing to do is behave with strict impartiality always and that this entails giving no weight to prior commitments or personal attachments. The question is whether the best way of achieving the utilitarian end is to do what Godwin says or whether it is to observe rules that assign settled rights to people. If it is the latter then that is what a utilitarian should do, and there is no room for a choice between following the rule and doing the best thing.

In the early editions of the *Logic*, Mill made the point with exemplary clarity, saying that there are 'cases in which, although any rule which can be formed is probably ... more or less imperfectly adapted to a portion of the cases which it comprises, there is still a necessity that some rule, of a nature simple enough to be easily

---

[159] Arneson, pp. 80–5.

[160] It is also, incidentally, a mistake because I discuss pseudo-Kantian forms of first-order impartiality as well as Godwin's utilitarian version.

[161] Henry R. West, 'Was J. S. Mill an Act- or Rule-Utilitarian?', paper given at the ISUS Conference in New Orleans, 1997, p. 16. West claims that Mill was primarily concerned with the second question.

understood and remembered, should not only be laid down for guidance, but universally observed, in order that the various persons concerned may know what they have to expect: the inconvenience of uncertainty on their part being a greater evil than that which may possibly arise, in a minority of cases, from the imperfect adaptation of the rule to those cases.' Mill perspicaciously added that 'the license of deviating from [these rules], if such ever be permitted, should be confined to definite classes of cases, and of a very peculiar and extreme nature'.[162] He thus anticipated by a century and a half Arneson's example of somebody in a life-and-death situation running a stop sign, and hundreds more examples of a similar kind in this barren literature.[163]

As Arneson puts it, 'if individual discretion is highly productive of good consequences, a society ruled by concern to maximize good consequences will make ample room for individual discretion'.[164] The puzzle is that he seems to think that he is saying something here that I am obliged to dissent from, whereas in fact I said much the same thing in *Justice as Impartiality*: 'Williams argues, in effect, that if people tried to follow the Godwinian prescription they would make themselves thoroughly miserable. But the implication of that is, obviously, that a society of Godwinians would score very poorly on the utilitarian criterion' (p. 221).

I attribute the difficulty Arneson has with my discussion of impartiality to his fondness for the first-person point of view. We have already seen an illustration of this in his suggestion that act-consequentialism is fine as a basis for making individual decisions because we can all plug into the formula any notion of good consequences that we like. My reply was that the chaotic result of everybody's behaving in that way shows exactly what is wrong with it.[165] So, here, he diverts my discussion of first-order impartiality into the well-worn channel of act- versus rule-utilitarianism by supposing that (utilitarian) first-order impartiality is an answer to the first-person question – an answer of the form 'Do the best thing in every situation'. On the strength of this, he supposes that it makes sense to say that universal first-order impartialism may or may not eliminate discretion, depending on whether or not allowing discretion will best further the utilitarian end.[166] In my terms, however, saying that 'act consequentialism can be upheld by a loose or a strict consequentialist

---

[162] John Stuart Mill, *A System of Logic Ratiocinative and Inductive*, pp. 1154–5 in the first (1843) and second (1846) editions, cited on p. 12 of West.

[163] Arneson, p. 80.

[164] Ibid., p. 81.

[165] See IV.1 above.

[166] Arneson, p. 82.

regime' is simply to say that act-consequentialism is compatible with either universal first-order impartiality or its denial.[167]

It is worth repeating that my main interest lies not in the implications of utilitarianism but in the implications of the kind of second-order impartiality that I advocate. The core of my argument is that universal first-order impartiality is not a theorem of second-order impartiality. My excursion into utilitarianism and pseudo-Kantian (or pseudo-Rawlsian) versions of universal first-order impartiality was designed to shed further light on the distinction between the two levels. Even if Godwin were right and the utilitarian end would best be achieved by a regime of universal first-order impartiality, that would not affect the case for saying that it would be shunned by Scanlonian contractors. However, the reasons for their rejecting it as a universal principle of conduct are also the reasons for its not in fact being a plausible version of utilitarianism.[168]

2. *The Magic in the Pronoun 'My'*

Two-level theories such as justice as impartiality are answers in the first instance to the question 'What morality ought there to be?' The answer to that question will, of course, have implications for individual conduct – otherwise there would be no point in asking the question in the first place. But the answer to the question 'What ought I to do?' will relate in some way to the deliverances of the higher-level theory. In particular, if the existing rules or norms governing an activity are such that they pass the higher-level test (e.g. could not reasonably be rejected in a Scanlonian original position), there is a straightforward answer to the question 'What ought I to do?' The answer is to do what is prescribed by the rule or norm. And where (as will commonly be the case) the rule or norm leaves open a range of permissible options, the answer is that – within these limits – the agent has discretion as to which option to choose. This is not to say that the choice made will necessarily be beyond criticism. It may reveal meanness, vindictiveness, pettiness, prejudice or all manner of personal defects. But two-level theories are in the business of giving answers about moral wrongness or injustice. So long as the choice made falls within the range acceptable at the higher level, it cannot be accused of being wrong or unjust.

The case in which the effective rule or norm in a society meets with approval at the higher level is (we may hope) a common one. Needless

---

[167] Ibid.

[168] The argument against first-order impartiality as a theorem of justice as impartiality is made in *Justice as Impartiality*, pp. 200–16; the connection with the reasons for thinking that Godwinian utilitarianism is an inferior version in comparison with Millian utilitarianism is drawn on p. 219.

to say, it is not the only one, but it is the simplest, and nothing more complicated is needed to provide a platform for the discussion of Susan Mendus's criticism of Part III of *Justice as Impartiality*.[169] She argues that I underestimate the power of Bernard Williams's attack on moral theories with a two-level structure. According to her, Williams is right to suggest that any such theory, by insisting that there is no sphere of life exempt from the demand that actions be justified, must compromise the quality of personal relationships and, indeed, subvert our very understanding of their significance in our lives.

I suspect that whether or not you resonate in sympathy with this kind of complaint about two-level moral systems will tend to reflect your temperament and overall outlook on life. In the (memorable) terms in which the conflict was presented in *1066 and All That*, the issue is whether you incline to be 'Right but Repulsive' with the Roundheads or 'Wrong but Wromantic' with the Cavaliers.[170] I shall do what I can to show that, however repulsive it can be made to appear in certain contexts, the two-level view is nevertheless right. This still leaves open the possibility of choosing to be wrong but romantic. I cannot undertake to do anything about that.

Mendus suggests that the underlying difference between Bernard Williams and myself is that I am interested only in a theory's getting the right answer, whereas Williams is interested in its leading moral agents to ask the right questions – or in some cases not to ask any questions at all.[171] I can see no basis for either half of this assertion. Taking up the second first, the question is about the content of Bernard Williams's essay, 'Persons, Character and Morality', which is the subject of our debate. Almost the whole of it is taken up with an argument to the effect that utilitarianism and Kantianism entail universal first-order impartiality and as a result are led to absurd prescriptions – for example that a man must toss a coin before deciding whether to rescue his wife or some stranger.[172] Only half way down the last page of the essay does Williams concede that 'moral principle can … [yield] the conclusion that … it is at least all right … to save one's wife'. The remainder of this last page is all that Williams has left in which to say what he nevertheless still thinks is wrong with the 'impartial system', after conceding the point that formed the basis of all the previous discussion. I would agree with Mendus if her proposition was taken to be that the rest of the essay is too perverse to be interesting. But it strikes me as very odd to say that what the essay

[169] Susan Mendus, 'Some Mistakes about Impartiality', pp. 177–82.
[170] W. C. Sellar and R. J. Yeatman, *1066 and All That*, London, 1949 [1930], p. 63.
[171] Mendus, p. 178.
[172] Bernard Williams, 'Persons, Character and Morality', pp. 1–19 in *Moral Luck: Philosophical Papers 1973–1980*, Cambridge, 1981.

is primarily about is a point that reads almost as an afterthought. (In fact, the structure of the essay suggests that it *was* an afterthought.)

To take up the first half of Mendus's charge, it is quite true that I am concerned about a theory's ability to generate the right answers, but I make no apology for that. What I strenuously deny is that I am not equally concerned with the way in which it reaches those answers. It is presumably her gratuitous assumption that I am not that leads to Mendus's elaborate puzzlement about my motives for attacking Williams despite his conceding at the end of his essay that two-level morality can get the right answer.[173] What I maintain is that the reasons offered by two-level morality *are* the right ones, and that Williams's attempt to dismiss two-level theories by ridiculing them depends on sleight of hand. I shall aim to substantiate this claim below.

As to what my actual views about the right answer are, I do not believe that Mendus's account of them gives an accurate description. According to her, my 'concluding flourish in the "famous fire cause" takes the form of a pronouncement that second-order impartiality will require that the Archbishop be saved, and second-order impartiality is right to do so'.[174] I can find no such flourish. I cannot even find anything without flourish that suggests the view Mendus imputes to me. What I do say, and I am happy to stand by it, is that if an impartialist theory of justice is to be taken seriously it must produce the conclusion that there are *some* circumstances in which people have to be prepared to sacrifice themselves and/or those to whom they are closest. The example that I offer in the book is drawn from the plot of Brian Moore's *Lies of Silence*.[175] You are abducted by terrorists and your family is held hostage. You are told that unless you plant a bomb in a department store, timed to go off when it is at its most crowded, they will be killed. I take the right answer to be that you should refuse (pp. 223–4).

What about the Archbishop? Contrary to what Mendus says, I do not conclude that you should rescue him in preference to your mother the chambermaid or your father the valet (depending upon which edition of *Political Justice* you read). Godwin himself admitted, as I mention in *Justice as Impartiality*, that it was hard to persuade people that the survival of Fénélon was as critical to the future of the human race as he had assumed (p. 223). This should not (as Mendus correctly observes) have been a problem for Godwin, since the smallest superiority of the Archbishop to the parent would still, within his system, generate the conclusion that the Archbishop's life should be

---

[173] Mendus, p. 179.
[174] Ibid.
[175] Brian Moore, *Lies of Silence*, London, 1990.

preferred. But it does make a difference for me, and I propose an alternative (illustrated by Bush and Quayle) in which failure to rescue the US President exposes the world to a ludicrously incompetent successor (p. 223). I should make it clear, however, that my conclusion (that you really ought to rescue the President) depends on the specifics of the case. If it were a matter of rescuing Bill Clinton, there would perhaps be something to be said for seeking out a stranger if there were no relatives to hand, on the ground that Al Gore could hardly do worse as a Democratic president and might do better.

Having cleared away some misconceptions about my position, I can now come to the main issue, which is Mendus's claim that I miss the point of Williams's attack on second-order impartiality. I reject this. Williams's objection, as I present it in *Justice as Impartiality*, is that two-level morality gives the rescuer 'one thought too many'. The thought that it's his wife should be enough: he does not need the additional thought that in cases such as this one it's all right to rescue one's wife. My complaint of sleight of hand is quite simple. The question was supposed to be one about the legitimacy of asking for justification. Williams has here changed it to one about what thoughts should ideally be running through the agent's head in some extraordinarily fraught situation. But as far as that goes 'It's my wife' will do fine. This does absolutely nothing to show that there is anything wrong with the idea, which Williams concedes can be reconciled with two-level morality, that in such cases it is all right to rescue one's wife (pp. 231–2).

The burden of Mendus's criticism of my treatment of Williams appears to be that I have missed 'the force of Williams's argument' to the effect that 'willingness to pose the justificatory question is, in part, an acceptance of [a] deformed model' of 'concepts such as love and friendship'.[176] I cannot, however, find any argument in the relevant half page of Williams's essay that is clearly distinguishable from the one about thoughts in the agent's head that I have already identified and dismissed as irrelevant to the issue of second-order justification.

What precisely is the 'justificatory question' that allegedly has such dire implications for personal relations? I have already emphasized that, where love and friendship are concerned, there is normally no call for partiality to be justified at the first-order level, and Mendus herself explicitly acknowledges that second-order impartiality endorses the free choice of friends.[177] That is to say, we do not have to justify our choice of friends by trying to show that it best conduces to some overall good state of affairs, or that our friends score higher in

[176] Mendus, p. 181.
[177] See V.1 above and, for the acknowledgement, Mendus, p. 181.

various tests of merit than other people with whom we might have become friends but did not. I am quite happy to accept that any notion of justification in terms such as those would run contrary to the nature of friendship, though I would prefer a less essentialist way of putting it.

The question of justification arises at the second-order level, where we ask how the practice of choosing friends freely is to be justified. And the answer is, basically, that it is justified for precisely the reasons adduced by Mendus, that is to say that the alternative of requiring impartiality at the first-order level would be destructive of an import- ant source of value to human beings in every society we know of or can imagine. On the particular form of two-level theory that I advance in *Justice as Impartiality*, we have to ask what social norms could not reasonably be rejected in a suitably constituted choosing situation. And it seems fairly clear that, if free choice of friends is as important as Mendus thinks, the norm to emerge will be one that permits it (see p. 201 for precisely this argument).

So far, then, I cannot find any disagreement between us, since I cannot find any arguments for the defectiveness of two-level morality in general or justice as impartiality in particular. In the penultimate paragraph of Mendus's discussion, we finally get a definite suggestion that the apparatus of second-order justification is itself destructive of the quality of personal relations. However, I do not think that the case is made out. Mendus picks up the example of rescuing the President in preference to some loved one, and simply endorses my remark that we must all hope never to find ourselves faced with such a choice. I do not, therefore, take her to be saying categorically that the two-level system produces the wrong answer in such a case, since she leaves it open that rescuing the President may be the right answer. Her claim is, rather, that 'the justificatory question, however it is answered in the disastrous case, jeopardizes the area of individual discretion and simultaneously threatens a quite general transformation in our understanding of relationships of friendship and of love'.[178]

How so? Mendus appears to regard it as self-evident, since she moves on after having delivered herself of this pronouncement. Her thought seems to be that individual discretion is threatened by the 'justificatory question' and that this has dire implications. But, as I have already said, the 'justificatory question' at the second-order level underwrites individual discretion, so it makes no sense to say that it threatens it. What is true is that the discretion rendered by the second-order apparatus is not absolute. But life is like that. The existence of limits does not mean that the discretion left within those

---

[178] Mendus, p. 182.

limits is any less authentic or valuable. Leaving aside psychopaths and the directors of privatized public utilities, everybody recognizes that there are limits to what we can legitimately do to advance our own interests or those of people to whom we are attached. We do not need a fancy two-level moral theory to tell us that.

If the existence of limits to individual discretion is a problem for the quality of personal relationships, it is a problem deeply embedded within the structure of commonsense morality. Justice as impartiality and its cognates offer a philosophical way of thinking about commonsense morality. But it seems absurd to blame that apparatus for undermining personal relations when all it does in this case is provide a rationalization of ordinary beliefs. Contrary to what Mendus claims, the problem (if there is a problem) lies in the 'right results', not in the way of arriving at them. Fortunately, there is no problem, and in *Justice as Impartiality* I identified the fallacy that underlies the belief that there is one:

> There is an idea around, perhaps more in unreflective popular thought than among philosophers (though Bernard Williams seems to me to trade on it) that you cannot really care for somebody unless your care is completely unconditional. This should be exposed for the sentimental tosh that it is. Johnson's exhortation to Boswell, in response to a piece of conventional sententiousness on the latter's part, remains valid: 'My dear friend, clear your mind of *cant*.' (p. 255)

If we want to know what Williams thinks is wrong with two-level theories, we can gain some enlightenment from his book *Ethics and the Limits of Philosophy* published a few years later than the essay that has been the focus of discussion so far.[179] Two-level theories, let us recall, are addressed to the question 'What morality ought there to be?' It is, in essence, that whole question itself that Williams now shows himself to regard as misconceived. He is not unremittingly opposed to any sort of reflective activity, though he professes not to believe that philosophy can contribute much to it.[180] But he apparently does not think that it makes any sense to ask for a justification of a way of life.

Williams's still more recent book, *Shame and Necessity*, reveals a curious nostalgia for the good old days of the Homeric heroes, to whom Christian or Kantian inhibitions deriving from a need to defend their conduct in terms acceptable to all those affected were completely alien.[181] We have even now, he claims in *Ethics and the Limits of Philosophy*, a legacy of 'thick moral concepts', which give us 'ethical

---

[179] Bernard Williams, *Ethics and the Limits of Philosophy*, Cambridge, 1985.
[180] Ibid., pp. 200–1.
[181] Bernard Williams, *Shame and Necessity*, Berkeley and Los Angeles, 1993.

knowledge ... and in the less reflective past there has been more'.[182]
But even granting all that (which I do not), it is too late now to tell
people to get on with living and stop asking awkward questions.[183] The
cat is not merely out of the bag but practically out of sight down the
street. In a society in which the rawest undergraduate arrives spout-
ing moral relativism, there is not much point in positing the existence
of a mass of common 'knowledge' – that is to say shared unreflective
convictions. This is about as helpful as the apocryphal economist's
solution to the lack of a tin-opener, 'Let us assume that we have a tin-
opener'.

Commonsense morality, as I have said, holds that parents have
special obligations to their children. If people are content to accept this
unreflectively, that is fine by me. But Williams is intolerably con-
descending to ordinary people in supposing that it is only some elite
that is ever going to ask questions about the justification of existing
practices.[184] It was not the conversation of Socrates but Athenian
contact with a variety of trading partners that led to questions about
the basis of their institutions. (Still, Socrates was guilty of destroying
'knowledge', in Williams's terms.[185] Would he have voted for the hem-
lock?) Similarly, it is notorious today in western countries that there
are other societies in which the biological parents have relatively little
responsibility for caring for their children. The question is what, if
anything, follows from this for our own child-rearing practices.

I think we have to be grown-up about this and stop pretending that
the existence of alternatives does not invite genuinely valid questions.
This means that we must (all of us – Government House is open to
everybody) be prepared to ask for a justification of our practices.[186] And
that drives us to two-level theorizing. If successful, this will typically
take the form of saying that ours are not the only justifiable practices,
but that they are nevertheless worth sticking with. Even if we can
imagine improvements, it may still be worth keeping the existing
practices, given the difficulty and disruption inherent in making a
transition. Thus, I would say that the (still incomplete) transformation
in the position of women in the past thirty years has been worth the
difficulty and disruption it has involved. But the extent of these should
not be underestimated.

As I understand him, Williams fears that this sort of reflection will
destroy our remaining 'knowledge'. But I do not believe that there

---

[182] Williams, *Ethics and the Limits of Philosophy*, p. 155.
[183] See ibid., p. 117.
[184] Ibid., pp. 106–11.
[185] As he says 'we reach the notably un-Socratic conclusion that, in ethics, *reflection
can destroy knowledge*', ibid., p. 148 (emphasis in original).
[186] For the notion of 'Government House utilitarianism', see ibid., pp. 108–10.

is any realistic alternative to it. We cannot return to unreflective traditionalism, so we must accept that our practices and institutions will be able to claim moral authority only to the extent that they can be justified in terms accessible to all. If Williams is right and that either cannot be done at all or cannot be done in a way accessible to anyone but an elite, I can see no alternative to a gradually spreading atrophy of the remaining moral norms.

3. Justice, Care and Privacy

In my discussion of contemporary feminist theory in Chapter 10 of *Justice as Impartiality*, I argued against the common assumption that there must be a conflict between an 'ethic of care' and an 'ethic of justice'. I suggested that, correctly understood (in terms of justice as impartiality), an ethic of justice needed to be supplemented by an ethic of care, and that they did not have to conflict because the ethic of care advised people how to use the discretion left open to them by the ethic of justice (pp. 249–51). I do not wish to maintain that all 'care theorists' (to employ Bubeck's term) will be satisfied with my proposal. In *Justice as Impartiality*, I illustrated this for the case of Nel Noddings.[187] More generally, I clearly cannot hope to accommodate those for whom care represents 'a genuinely new ethical perspective and/or epistemology from which to reconceive the moral realm, including justice.'[188] If they are right, I am wrong, and that is all there is to it. I can only reiterate my disagreement with Bubeck's suggestion that impartial justice is dispensable.[189]

One way of claiming that justice and care are compatible would be to assign them to 'separate social spheres, i.e. that justice applies to the public sphere and care to the private sphere.'[190] As Bubeck notes, I repudiate this idea. On one hand, I commend the line of thought pursued by Susan Moller Okin and others that seeks to extend theories of justice to family relationships (p. 246).[191] On the other hand, I argue that care has a public dimension (p. 256).[192] Mendus ingeniously suggests, however, that my endorsement of justice-oriented feminism threatens to undermine my claim that second-order impartiality is compatible with the rejection of universal first-order impartiality. She points out that the feminists whose views I endorse

---

[187] *Justice as Impartiality*, pp. 251–3, discussing Nel Noddings, *Caring: A Feminine Approach to Ethics and Moral Education*, Berkeley and Los Angeles, 1984.

[188] Bubeck, p. 163.

[189] See IV.2 above for a discussion of her argument.

[190] Bubeck, p. 162.

[191] See Susan Moller Okin, *Justice, Gender and the Family*, New York, 1989.

[192] I am puzzled that Bubeck (p. 162) claims not to be sure about my position on this, since the statement seems to me quite explicit.

are seized of the problems of domestic violence and marital rape, and concerned that traditional liberal theory, including Rawlsian theory, has nothing to say about the injustice of those practices. If they are right to be concerned about this, and if Barry agrees that they are right, then presumably the solution will be to bring those practices within the scope of a theory of justice as impartiality. But if that happens, what is to block the move to the kind of society which Barry fears – one in which very little is left to private judgement and almost everything is open to public scrutiny and censure?[193]

I do agree that they are right, but I do not see that there is really a problem of the kind suggested by Mendus. My answer to her question about the way in which to block the move is that we should apply the theory correctly. Her fear depends on what F. M. Cornford called the *Principle of the Dangerous Precedent*, which he defined as the principle 'that you should not now do an admittedly right action for fear you, or your equally timid successors, should not have the courage to do right in some future case, which *ex hypothesi*, is essentially different, but superficially resembles the present one.'[194] Why should the prohibition (both morally and legally) of domestic violence and marital rape have any necessary tendency to open the floodgates in the way suggested by Mendus? Presumably only if public intervention in cases where that is right somehow leads inexorably to public intervention in other cases where that is wrong. This seems to me an unwarranted degree of alarmism. To allay it we do not have to resort to speculation. We can appeal to experience. Domestic violence and marital rape are illegal, and morally condemned, in many places without this having had any discernible tendency to subject all domestic life to public scrutiny and censure.

Mendus, to be fair, goes on to concede that the alarmist scenario need not occur, yet she still diagnoses a 'strain'. But even this claim can be made plausible only on the assumption that I criticized in the previous section: the assumption that any limits to discretion somehow undermine the value of the remaining discretion. This seems to me no more reasonable in the present case than in those to which the same notion was applied earlier.[195] In a well-ordered society, individuals, families, firms, associations and states all enjoy an autonomy that is bounded by constraints imposed by the demands of justice. This is scarcely strenuous or esoteric. I should blush to claim any credit for such a trite idea. If I have contributed anything, it is to our ability to think coherently about where the bounds should be drawn.

---

[193] Mendus, p. 183.
[194] F. M. Cornford, *Microcosmographia Academica: Being a Guide for the Young Academic Politician*, London, 1964 [1908], p. 23.
[195] See V.2 above.

4. Conclusion

In this response, I have tried to maintain a coherent line of discussion, and this has inevitably meant that some of the contributions to the symposium receive more attention than others. To take account of all the interesting points raised would require much more space than I have already occupied, and I am sure that nobody (including me) would want this to be longer than it already is. I predict, however, that readers of *Principles of Justice* will be able to spot some further responses to questions raised in this book. For that stimulus to further thought, and for the challenges that I have attempted to meet here, I should like again to thank the contributors to this volume, and Paul Kelly for organizing it.

Index

EU Authorised Representative:

Easy Access System Europe Mustamäe tee 50, 10621 Tallinn, Estonia

gpsr.requests@easproject.com

Printed and bound by CPI Group (UK) Ltd, Croydon, CR0 4YY

22/04/2026

02095384-0001